Britain's Contested History

Britain's Contested History

Lessons for Patriots

Bernard Porter

BLOOMSBURY ACADEMIC
LONDON • NEW YORK • OXFORD • NEW DELHI • SYDNEY

BLOOMSBURY ACADEMIC
Bloomsbury Publishing Plc
50 Bedford Square, London, WC1B 3DP, UK
1385 Broadway, New York, NY 10018, USA
29 Earlsfort Terrace, Dublin 2, Ireland

BLOOMSBURY, BLOOMSBURY ACADEMIC and the Diana logo are
trademarks of Bloomsbury Publishing Plc

First published in Great Britain 2022

Cover design by Nicky Borowiec
Cover image © Ian Nolan/Getty

A catalogue record for this book is available from the British Library.

A catalog record for this book is available from the Library of Congress.

ISBN: HB: 978-1-3502-9638-1
       ePDF: 978-1-3502-9639-8
       eBook: 978-1-3502-9640-4

Typeset by RefineCatch Limited, Bungay, Suffolk

To find out more about our authors and books visit www.bloomsbury.com
and sign up for our newsletters.

CONTENTS

Preface vi

1 Britains 1

2 1800–1945 21

3 Empire 39

4 Politics 55

5 1945–2016 69

6 Culture 81

7 Europeans 89

8 Brexit 97

9 History 113

10 Patriotisms 127

Afterword 143

Notes 155
Further Reading 165
Index 167

PREFACE

First, and to clear up any misunderstandings that the subtitle of this book may have given rise to, I should make it clear that it will not be a 'patriotic' history in the conventional sense: glorifying Britain, that is, and papering over the country's deficiencies. 'Patriotism' of that kind does no-one any good, and can do great harm in the wrong hands. It also, quite obviously, falsifies any nation's history if it only paints the 'best' side of it, when everyone knows that all histories are a mix of 'good' and 'bad', and of disputed choices of what should be placed in either of these categories; or indeed in the 'neutral' – neither good nor bad – one.

Furthermore, in my view no 'patriotic' history can be truly patriotic if it doesn't address aspects of a country's present situation, arising from its past, which might need to be improved or corrected in order to make it *better*; which ought surely to be the objective of any true patriot. In Sweden, where I mainly live now, school children are taught about their nation's 'identity' in relation to its aspirations for the future, rather than based on its past history. (That's probably just as well, in view of Sweden's chequered history before modern times.) It may be thought surprising that the British appear not to have thought of that, but still seem wedded to their 'Island Story' as one of the bases for their attraction and loyalty towards the bit of the Earth they happen to inhabit. That's convenient for me, of course, as a professional historian, who wants to sell his books; but not if the versions of British history they read (or, more likely, view on TV) are less reliable than mine and my fellow professionals'.

So this won't be a celebratory history of Britain, with lots of flag-waving – an activity that used to be considered un-British, incidentally: too 'showy' – and with all the warts glossed over. Nor however will it be a hyper-critical version of the kind that might suit Britain's denigrators more. That is not because I can't find anything to criticize in Britain's past history – far from it; but partly because I don't want to condemn everything in it, or the nation as a whole, on the basis of these criticisms; and – more importantly – because all criticisms, especially from a later perspective, are likely to be subjective, and I should like to make this account as *objective* as I can. (That is despite my referencing personal experiences occasionally.) Yes, I am aware of the problems of this, both personal and philosophical – I'm fairly well versed in 'postmodernism' – and realize that my 'objectivity' may differ from others'; but I still believe that historians can get close to some truths, and in any event – and perhaps more importantly – can reveal obvious *un*truths, so long as they make allowances for their own biases, and don't make moral judgements on the basis of them. Indeed, rather than *judging*, my aim in this book will be to try to *explain*. One of its purposes will be to uncover some of the common misunderstandings that many people appear to have about Britain's history, and especially those that come in the form of *generalizations* about that history which take no account of its – to my mind fascinating – complexity.

*

From a more traditional patriot's point of view there must seem much to admire in Britain's past. For just a little country it has made quite a mark on the world. Conquering continents – all of them, except South America and Antarctica (poor old Captain Scott!); ruling perhaps a quarter of the world's people at one time; the winner of three world wars (the Napoleonic being the first); inventing manufacturing industry, liberalism and freedom; splitting the atom and discovering DNA; giving the world its *lingua franca*, together with football and – for those sophisticated (!) enough to appreciate it – cricket; spreading a great literature around the world, as well as, more latterly, popular music and period costume TV dramas: – all these are achievements for Britons to be proud of, surely? And all this from an island base of only 250,000 square kilometres, significantly smaller than modern Germany, France or even Sweden, stuck out on the edge of another continent, and with a pretty rotten climate on the whole. In view of all this, what country could be more deserving of national admiration and loyalty than Little Britain?

But of course there is another side. Yes, Britain can boast a proud history in many ways, although not necessarily all the ones listed above, which may be modified in the following narrative; but also a less-than-proud one in some others. In this respect it resembles every other country in the world, none of which could be said to have an entirely clean bill of historical health. In any case, the notion of 'pride' in this connection is problematic: with features that *you* might admire in a country being deplored by others – conquering continents, for example; and, perhaps more fundamentally, the idea of your being personally 'proud' of events and achievements that happened before your time being, quite simply, nonsensical. Besides, no-one surely is entitled to take 'pride' in the sheer accident of his or her birth. Only people who have *chosen* to live in Britain are strictly speaking entitled to that. That means immigrants. Many of Britain's present-day 'patriots', the more 'racist' ones, might feel uncomfortable with that.

This book's aim, therefore, is to give a very brief account of the history of Britain from around 1800 onward, in order to help 'patriots' and others, including critics of Britain, to come to proper terms with it. It will be organized thematically as well as chronologically, and treated both narratively and analytically; with not much detail – that can be gathered from countless other books, or even from Wikipedia – but lots of ideas. It should probably be regarded as an extended essay, or a series of them, rather than – for example – a 'textbook'. It certainly won't be comprehensive. I have tried to make it readable, for amateurs as well as experts in the field. It will avoid major generalizations (not minor ones), until near the end, when one will be offered, but only tentatively – and, it has to be said, fairly unoriginally. That is because of the aforementioned *complexity* of Britain's history over the past two hundred-odd years. The first chapter will outline some of the differences between Britons which contribute to this, and the country's various reputations both then and now. There is not and never has been a single 'Britain', towards which everyone can be either loyal, or critical. That is important to know.

Nor is there – to continue the theme of 'complexity' – a single type of 'liberalism', or 'imperialism', or 'progress', or 'conservatism', or 'socialism', or 'radicalism', or of any religious denomination, or – arising from this – of 'Britishness'; and so, it hardly needs to be said, of 'patriotism', which is so often seen in simplistic terms. 'If people are not proud to be British, or of our flag or Queen', as the Conservative MP Lia Nici tweeted in March 2021, 'they don't have to live in the UK. Perhaps they should move to another country they prefer.'[1] (I've actually done that, but for other more personal reasons too.) As it happens it was that statement of Lia Nici's that provoked me into writing this book; following on as it did from some equally simplistic and shallow utterances – and even actions: toppling statues, for example – coming from 'anti-racists' and 'anti-imperialists' of the Left. My quarrel with them was not directed at their anti-racism, which I share, but at their simplistic views of it, taken generally out of context; and of 'imperialism' – one of my specialisms – more generally. (I also didn't see why statues even of slave-traders, if suitably labelled, shouldn't be kept standing in order to make passers-by aware of this appalling episode in Britain's and Europe's – even Sweden's – history.)[2] Besides, *judging* people in the past is unprofitable, partly because it usually takes no account of the said context, which if you knew about it you might find at least partially excused them; and – more importantly – because it fuels the illusion, if the judgement is unfavourable, that they were to *blame* for what happened in history. I'll be coming back to this question of *agency* in the final chapters. Before then, however, I shall try to be non-judgemental; although to be honest that will be difficult in certain cases, especially as we approach the present day. History is ongoing, after all, and I'm a product of it as well as one of its chroniclers.

So this will be a 'warts and all' account; but with the warts never obscuring the patches of fairly healthy skin. Indeed, patriots may well find some objects of 'pride' in it still – if that's what they want – although not always the ones they might expect; and tempered, for accuracy's sake, with some of the darker sides of British history: atrocities that were committed abroad, for example, *under* Lia Nici's Flag, and *in the names of* successive Queens and Kings. But that will be up to them. It's not my object in this book to encourage readers to approve or disapprove of any events or trends in the story I'll be recounting, but only to lay some of the facts before them, as I see them, in order to get them to think about them, possibly in new and surprising ways, and then to come to their own conclusions. Those conclusions may not be simple; but it will be the process of thinking towards them which will be valuable, and should enhance readers' understanding of the said complexity of Britain's history over the past two centuries or so. In the end their views – their 'lessons from history' – may well turn out to be different from mine; but they will at least be more sophisticated than those of Lia Nici's 'patriots', or of the statue-spoilers of Bristol.

*

Britain's Contested History can be seen as a distillation of my nearly six decades of research into British history, specializing in certain aspects of that history: mainly British imperialism, foreign policy, the secret services, refugees, travel, and mid-Victorian architecture; about all of which I've published books and scholarly articles, as well as a longer and more conventional general survey of British history since 1850 (which rather bombed), and a couple of collections of essays. The second of these, *Britain Before Brexit* (Bloomsbury, 2021), bears on and elaborates several of the themes pursued here. I'll occasionally refer to those earlier works in chapter notes, if I feel that amplification is needed of what I write here. (My notes, incidentally, will be minimal, so as not to interrupt the flow; and bearing in mind that the sources of better-known facts and quotations can be easily 'Googled'.) But the present account is different from those earlier ones in many respects, as well as being briefer; not based on any new archival research, for example, only my old studies; and having been affected by recent and current events at this revolutionary time in Britain's – and the world's – affairs. The impact of those events on my interpretation of Britain's earlier history – for even writers on past times can't avoid being influenced by present times – will doubtless show through.

One way is an emphasis on the question of Britain's supposed 'exceptionalism', which might not have been necessary before 'Brexit', with its insistence on its *difference* from the European continent, arrived on the scene. During the debate over that it was the 'Leavers' (from the EU), who mostly appropriated both 'patriotism' and British history for their own cause, but without always understanding or even knowing much about the latter. You don't have to base your 'Brexitism' on a view of British history, of course – there are plenty of other good arguments for it – but if you want to, it may be worthwhile your reading this book first. I hope it might offer illumination to both sides: not simple answers to their questions, for history is rarely that straightforward; but some slightly more sophisticated ways of looking at them.

The book is being written in the unusual conditions imposed by another of the aforementioned revolutionary events: the coronavirus pandemic of

2020–21, which has forced me into a (pleasant) self-quarantine in the 'summerhouse' I share with my partner in the Stockholm Archipelago, with wi-fi to connect me to the internet, thankfully (how ever did the Vikings manage without it?), but no way of accessing libraries or even my own collection of books and notes back in England. (You can't find everything through Google.) In this connexion I must acknowledge the generous help given me by the staff of *Kungligabiblioteket* in Stockholm, despite their own working difficulties under 'lockdown'; by my Hull friends Robin and Sally; by the generous and perceptive, but anonymous, publisher's readers of the proposal and of the (almost) final text of this book; by Emily and Abigail, my excellent publishers at Bloomsbury; and by Mike, who took care of my English house while I was away. The virus, then, can be blamed for a few gaps in the referencing, which will be flagged up when I come to them.

On the other hand living 'abroad', as I have done for much of my professional life – not only in Sweden but in the USA and Australia too – has its upside. It will have given me a wider perspective on Britain's current condition and past history than I would have had as a 'little Briton', and which will, I hope, show up in the following pages. My university education may also have advantaged me in this respect by prioritizing foreign histories over British ones: which is normal, I think, in most British universities, unlike in many continental European and American ones, where I understand that national – that is, 'patriotic'? – histories generally dominate curricula. ('Why are you studying British history?' an American student of mine in Rochester, NY, told me a neighbour asked him. 'America has the best history in the world.') In fact I reckon I learned as much about Britain from studying his country's history and the Holy Roman Empire's, for context and comparison, than from the history I was taught of my own country. 'What does he know of England who only England knows?', wrote Kipling. He was of course referring to his beloved Empire; but it works for any kind of 'broad' historical study.

Quite apart from all that, my current situation on 'our' island, dodging the virus, is providing ideal conditions in other ways: especially the isolation and peace, for the business of writing for both of us. (She writes too.) To Kajsa must go my heartfelt thanks, therefore – and much more – for sharing our wilderness with me, to what I hope will be a good effect both healthwise and authorially. My readers will be the judges of that.

Bernard Porter
Svartsö, Sweden
4 August 2021

Between this book's completion and its delivery to the printers, events in Britain continued to evolve rapidly. To take account of these events, an 'Afterword' has been added at the end. Obviously it will still miss developments that occur while the book is in the press, and which might

possibly affect the arguments and conclusions offered in it. Will Boris
Johnson still be British prime minister, for example? That looked doubtful
in January 2022; but readers will know that for certain when the book
comes out.

January 2022

1

Britains

What comes to mind when we think of 'Britain', today, or in the past?[1] Of course there are various versions, reflecting our own viewpoints and prejudices, some of which others won't recognize; but many of them simply taking account of the multiplicity of 'peoples' and 'cultures' that make up 'Britain', and have done from the start. A 'patriot' ought to be clear which particular *patria* he or she is supporting, otherwise he or she can be misunderstood. A patriotic American, for example, might not take kindly to being associated with Donald Trump. Or – to take an example closer to home – a patriotic Briton to being tarred with the 'Brexit' brush. Of course there is enough tar in those brushes to make them not unfair partial characterizations of either people. But in both cases they *are* only partial, with other, sometimes contradictory, national identities also shining through.

Often this is obscured by the superficial *continuity* of certain institutions in British life, which can foster the impression that the country is more stable and conservative than it really ever was. Lia Nici's 'flag and Queen' are two of those institutions; with the 'flag' giving out very different messages according to who was waving it and when; and the Royal Family changing their meaning and significance over time almost chameleon-like, according to their historical environment too. The same applies to many – perhaps most – of the 'established' traditions of Britain, like its aristocracy, courts, Parliament, the Church of England, cricket, Public schools, and ancient universities, and even more recent ones, like trade unions; whose genuine and 'latent' functions (as the anthropologists call them, in order to distinguish them from 'manifest' or superficial ones), despite their formal timelessness – gowns, wigs, architectural surroundings, arcane customs – are likely to have changed radically from age to age. This is meant as a warning not only against the assumption of 'sameness' over time in British life and politics, but also against judging any modern British institution from its appearance, or even its name. The 'Conservative' party hasn't been 'conservative' since Thatcher's time, for example; and Labour is hardly any longer the party of the horny-handed men – or women – of toil. *Soi-disants* 'imperialists', as we shall see later, could come from the Left or the Right. We need to look behind the titles to see what they – and the aristocracy, and the

Royal Family, and Parliament, as well as 'imperialists' – were really up to, in different periods.

What a modern-day British patriot must recognize, therefore, is this simple fact: that Britain has always comprised many different sorts of people, with different ethnic roots (if we think these are important), different religions, different regional identities, different classes, different political views, different languages and dialects, different genders (of course), and even different nationalities; all of them changing and adapting – even their genders – from one decade to the next. This started off with 'ancient' Britain as a mish-mash of invading peoples, and has continued through to the present day. It could be said to be one of the things that makes the country interesting, and – possibly – worth its people's allegiance. There are also ways in which it can be said to have been terrifically to Britain's advantage: to have so many different *kinds* of people around. The town of Stratford-upon-Avon is naturally proud of its most famous son, William Shakespeare; but what would he have been if he had stayed in Warwickshire, with only people of his own kind around him for stimulus? So this initial chapter will devote some space to Britain's essential multi-culturalism at all times; before coming on to the *image* of the country, both abroad and at home. The 'proper' history – broadly narrative – will follow after that.

*

To begin with ethnicity. Every nation in the world – except perhaps Kenya, if what we used to be told about the origin of the human race is correct – began with immigrants, with Britain of course being no exception. In the latter's case the first migrations reached it before it had become an island, across what is called Doggerland, and now lies beneath the North Sea; but whose descendants may well not have survived the Ice Age that made Northern Europe almost impossible to survive in until 10,000 years ago, give or take a century or two. It was around then that Doggerland became inundated, meaning that new groups of migrants had to come by sea, which was not all that difficult in view of the facts that they had boats, and that the gap between the main British island and 'Continental' Europe was quite small. (On a clear day you can just see across it.) The sea has never been as great a barrier to travel for Britons as were, for example, the forests that covered most of Europe and Britain then. Thereafter a succession of European peoples sailed or rowed over to Britain, to settle, trade, convert, conquer or rape and pillage. (Some of them may have been brown-skinned, if recent DNA tests on 'Cheddar Man' are anything to go by.)[2] They included Celts, Picts, Saxons, Romans, Iberians, Danish 'Vikings' (reputed to be the rapists and pillagers), Normans (from France, but also Vikings originally), Jews from the mid-seventeenth century – they first came in the early middle ages, but weren't allowed to stay then, to put it mildly: the city of York massacred 150 of them in 1190 – Irish, French Protestant Huguenots around 1700; and thousands of assorted 'Continentals' – many of them political refugees – from the 1790s onwards. All these groups of incomers left marks, but not ones that generally speaking separated them from other Britons; apart from the Celts and the Picts, who still consider themselves to be distinct nationalities; the Irish, who faced discrimination; some Jews, who were happily integrated but maintained their own culture; and the Normans, who, as the historical basis of Britain's aristocracy, could be regarded as still 'lording it over' the common people, who as late as the nineteenth century used to refer to their servitude as a 'Norman Yoke'. Otherwise immigrants melted in, as they still by and large do; imperceptibly until 'heritage' online DNA-testing sites came along to tell us where we all 'come from'. (I turned out to be English and western European – a bit of a disappointment, actually; I was hoping to have some Viking.) So many of Britain's population who have made a real impact on the country are descended from recent (that is, post-Norman) immigrants as to make it tiring to even try to list them; but they include, of course, the late Duke of Edinburgh, a bunch of Milibands, most of the current (2021) English football team, Nigel Farage and Priti Patel. And some of them still, for example, support their countries of origin in sporting arenas, despite Norman Tebbit's (remember him?) notorious 'cricket test', which insisted that they had to cheer for England if they wanted to qualify as British. In truth that – the insistence – was very *un*-British, in a way. This is the original basis for the claim that Britain was always a 'multi-racial' or 'multi-cultural' country; if 'origins' have anything to do with it.

Historical ethnicity may lie behind the divisions between the four nations that formally make up the United Kingdom – although there are other acquired cultural factors behind those too; but not so much among *English* people, who have generally forgotten their 'racial' origins: with the exception, of course, of the Irish-English, and more recent and differently-coloured immigrants. The difficulty with the latter arose partly from the cultures – and especially religions – they brought with them and often persisted in; and partly from the hostility of white British racists: both of which had the effect of separating these new non-white 'Britons' from the 'natives'. Easily distinguished groups like these were also often targeted as scapegoats by those – usually people in positions of power – who wished to create distractions. The same was true of the poor, who could be said to comprise yet another 'Britain' – of victims, essentially. Whether or not these people – immigrants and the poor – were technically parts of the same nation as their oppressors, they probably shared more in common with the equivalent classes of people in foreign countries; which was one of the arguments behind calls for working-class *inter*national solidarity in the nineteenth century: 'workers of the world, unite!'

Internationalism of this kind was not confined to the proletariat. The uppermost classes of Britain generally felt more at home among foreign aristos, and even Indian rajahs and African tribal chiefs,[3] than with their own lower-class compatriots; which is why they hogged all the best jobs in the British diplomatic service, it being assumed that a British Lord – or at least a 'Sir' – would be able to converse more naturally with a *Graf* or a *comte* abroad. The Royal Family was even more international, with the monarchies of Europe comprising almost a nationality of their own superimposed upon the others: 'Don't forget, Bertie', as Queen Victoria wrote at the time of the Prusso-Danish war, when Bertie (later King Edward VII) looked like siding with the Danes, 'that *we are German*.'[4] In Britain 'class' mattered, though not perhaps quite so rigidly as in Continental Europe. After all, rich middle-class Brits could always effectively 'buy' their way into the aristocracy, although the stain of having done something useful in an earlier career might remain with them for life, or even for a couple of generations: 'his father ran a *shop*, you know', as was whispered about Edward Elgar after he had been (merely) knighted in 1904.[5] (Then there's the story about Lord Heseltine, a successful ex-publisher, but allegedly excoriated by Tory grandees because he had 'bought his own furniture': that is, instead of inheriting it.)

There can be no doubt that class was a powerful determinant of almost any Briton's 'identity' in the nineteenth and twentieth centuries, and even their self-identity, probably more so than their nationality. This could be regarded as one of the few 'continuities' of British history, although the conditions and functions of each of the classes may have subtly changed. Far fewer of the 'lower' classes are 'in service' now than they were in the nineteenth century, for example; which obviously affected the upper and middle classes – those they 'serviced' – too. Class differences were, and still are, bolstered by the kinds of education people received: at so-called 'Public' (in fact private and privileged), Grammar, Secondary Modern or Elementary schools, which trained them for their roles in society rather than as equal members of it. 'I know my place'. In Victorian Britain and some way beyond, this was regarded as the best way to cohere societies: by linking the classes with each other, the proletariat to work for the rich, who in return would look after them; rather than encouraging them to think the same way: towards their country, for example. One late Victorian imperialist suggested the following analogy: the working classes comprised the plinths supporting the statues of the great men who drove the nation forward.[6] You didn't require 'patriotism' in the former; just devotion to their duty to bear the weight of the classes above them. Besides, 'patriotism' was thought to be a dangerous and possibly combustible material in the early nineteenth century; more often associated with 'democracy' – *vide* the American Revolutionary 'patriots' – than with what we today would regard as the political 'Right'. Hence Dr Johnson's famous quip, calling patriotism 'the last refuge of the scoundrel', at a time (1775) when the American revolutionists were using it *against* the British Crown and Flag, rather than to shore them up, as today. It was only a hundred years later, under that great political conjurer Benjamin Disraeli, that it was magically transformed into a weapon wielded by the other side, to support conservative causes. (Or, in Disraeli's case, the very radical cause – for that time – of 'imperialism'.)

In the hands of the Right the call to 'patriotism' was often used to wean the workers away from other loyalties, especially those class ones, and to get them fired up to fight the nation's enemies. In both the twentieth century's World Wars this was clearly successful to an extent, with impressive degrees of 'volunteering' for the armed forces before military conscription needed to be imposed; but there must be doubts over whether national fervour was the main motivation for these men's 'joining up', or for their continuing to fight once the wars had started, as against the thrill of anticipated adventure early on, and then loyalty to their 'mates' who were fighting – and suffering – alongside them. If they did espy a greater 'cause' it was probably 'hearth and home', rather than King and country; and least of all the Empire. In the Second War it could have been anti-fascism.[7] That the ordinary fighting troops represented a very different 'Britain' from their officers' is indicated by the highly 'unpatriotic' industrial and political struggles that took place after the First World War, and the concessions that had to be made to them after the Second World War in order to prevent a reprise.

So 'class' often trumped 'nation'. But that was not the only dividing line between the different 'Britains'. Patriotism had other rival allegiances to compete against. *Regional* was one, with North–South differences and even mutual antagonisms in England, Scotland, Wales and (while it was still united under the British flag) Ireland being of significance, with – even today – Yorkshire people feeling very little affinity with southerners, or the native speakers of North Wales with Anglicized South Waleans, or Scottish Highlanders with Lowlanders, or – of course – the Protestants of Ulster with the Catholics of the rest of Ireland. In the last case that even erupted into civil war, more than once. Religion was the important measure of 'identity' there, of course; as it often was in England and Scotland too. There were anti-Catholic riots in London and the North of England in the 1860s. In mid-twentieth century Edinburgh Catholic girls were effectively excluded from nursing jobs in hospitals.[8] (In more Catholic Glasgow it was easier for them.) Edward Elgar, the pre-eminent 'British' composer of his time, felt that he wasn't really accepted as that because of his 'Roman' religion, and deeply Catholic music (*Gerontius*) – until his faith departed from him around the start of the First World War. Earlier in our period, Nonconformity could also set its adherents apart, with certain positions (and places at the ancient universities) being reserved to Anglicans, leaving Dissenters to fend for themselves. (These included Jews.) And if these Judaeo-Christian denominations were divisive, Islam was even more so, with Muslims facing serious discrimination in the later twentieth century; although here the picture was muddied by the fact that nearly all of them were also browner than the native population of Britain, bringing the factor of so-called 'race' into it; and were unfairly associated with the terrorist acts of the more 'extreme' of their co-religionists in Britain, as well as in most of the rest of the world. Of course this didn't prevent many – probably most – Northerners, Catholics, Methodists, Jews and Moslems from feeling loyal to the nation one of whose proudest boasts – if sometimes honoured more in the breach than in the observance – was of its 'toleration' of all classes, 'races' and beliefs: all except terrorism, of course. (And even notorious foreign terrorists were accepted into Britain at one time, as we shall see.) But it exemplifies how differently some sections of the population could conceive of their 'Britishness', and consequently how many 'Britains' there really were.

Other 'divides' included the urban–rural one; well illustrated by a speech Prime Minister John Major gave to a Conservative conference in 1993, in which he rhapsodized over an England of 'long shadows on county grounds, warm beer, invincible green suburbs, dog lovers and pools fillers and . . . old maids bicycling to Holy Communion through the morning mist';[9] representing one version of the 'true England' (not so much Scotland) which endured, especially in literature, for many years.[10] But it was of course a picture that the miners of County Durham, or the mill-workers of Manchester, could scarcely have recognized, and was much ridiculed as a result. The urban–rural divide was also reflected – roughly – in voting patterns, with Labour dominating the cities, and the Conservatives taking the 'shires'. That could also indicate a certain social backwardness in the country areas, in which the old 'feudal' culture had not yet given way to the capitalist (and then socialist) stage. That is, if one considers the idea of 'feudal' responsibility to people, rather than leaving them to the mercy of the market, to be 'backward'. But in any case, it clearly represents another deep division between different 'Britains'; which we shall see reflected in the politics of the country, too.

Gender may have been another divide; with women conceiving of 'Britishness' differently from men. Patriotism is usually presented in 'masculine' terms: soldiers and sailors, guns, flags, protecting the virtue of the little woman, and so on. In some cases men's loyalty to their gender could lead to misogyny, which could be considered another form of 'loyalty' entirely; as could some women's overriding regard for their own sex also. Normally however this did not mean that women were necessarily any less conventionally 'patriotic' than the men, although the suffragettes were accused of that, when they insisted on continuing their often quite violent campaign for the vote even after the outbreak of the First World War, so putting their sectional cause before the 'national' one. (The milder suffra*gists* suspended their protest.) Of course women weren't expected to *fight*, yet; but they served in different ways – munitions workers, drivers, occasionally secret agents – and otherwise kept their eyes on the 'home front' – typically their babies – while their menfolk 'joined up'; and with their vocal encouragement:

Oh! we don't want to lose you, But we think you ought to go
For your King and your Country both need you so;

We shall want you and miss you, but with all our might and main
We shall cheer you, thank you, kiss you, When you come back again.[11]

That was sung in music-halls in 1914, always by beautiful young women. They also – notoriously – used to pin white feathers, a mark of cowardice, on the lapels of men not in uniform. Whether any of this indicates a different *kind* of 'patriotism', and hence a distinct 'Britain', from the men's or the authorities' is doubtful. It seems rather to have complemented the latter, while still observing the strict gender roles of the time.

There *were* some women pacifists. One was sentenced to jail for trying to murder the prime minister, Lloyd George, by hammering a poisoned nail half-way through the sole of his golf-shoe. (So when he put it on and stepped down . . .) Alice Wheeldon did obviously represent a very different 'Britain' from Lloyd George's.[12] Her main anti-war activity lay in organizing an escape route to America for Army deserters, who otherwise could be shot. But that may have grown out of her socialism, rather than feminism; and there was no significant women's peace movement on the scale, for example, of Lysistrata's in the Aristophanes play. Indeed, the implication of that 1914 music-hall song is that women would withhold their affections from men who *wouldn't* fight, rather than the reverse. Alice's kind of woman was clearly not numerous enough to comprise a significant alternative 'nation' to the dominant one. One wonders what women's responses would have been if they had been asked to support wars which were clearly *aggressive*, as nearly all of Britain's were not *presented* as. Even its colonial wars were supposedly defensive. So Britain's world role was cast as 'protective'; which suited women too.

The last main category of Britons who might be considered to comprise a different nation was 'youth'. Conservatives certainly thought so, although they didn't put it like that. Young working-class boys, in particular, were suspected of lacking in 'patriotism', which was a major factor behind Baden-Powell's formation of his 'Boy Scout' organization in 1908. (There were others too; like the church-based 'Boys' Brigade', and the oddly-named Kibbo Kift Kindred; but the Scouts topped them all.) Baden-Powell had intended his creation to impart some industrial as well as national discipline into his lads, and so had his main eye on the problematic working classes; only for his platoons of marching and neatly – if rather ridiculously – uniformed young men, most of them middle class, to be hooted at by rapscallions along their routes. That may have been a sign that the hooters, and their parents, also belonged to another 'Britain', with different cultures and loyalties from the rest.[13] To come on to the present: this is not strictly comparable, but the age-profile of voters in the 2017 referendum on leaving the EU indicated that younger people voted very differently then from their elders: with 70 per cent of the under-25s voting to remain, as against 60 per cent of the over-65s who favoured the Brexit, or national-patriotic, side.[14] Young 'Remainers' clearly represent a very different

'Britain' from the 'Leavers', as became more and more apparent after Britain left the EU.

Different professions also held different positions on the question of 'patriotism', as they do today, with academics (the profession I know best) generally sceptical of appeals to simple 'patriotism' on what they regarded as intellectual grounds. Few academics or 'intellectuals', for example, supported 'Brexit' (although the movement was founded by one of them);[15] but there may have been material or snobbish considerations behind that. Britain was also *ideologically* riven, as we shall see later on. For whatever reason, there were clearly many different ways in which people could attach themselves to their country, or not. 'Flag and Queen' (or King) might have been adequate totems for some of them, sufficient to attract their loyalty to one version of Britain. But there were also other versions, many sorts of 'Britain' covered by the word; and so a variety of equally valid 'patriotisms'. This needs to be grasped before we can begin to understand the country's history.

And then, finally, there was Rudyard Kipling's famous rhetorical question: 'what do they know of England who only England know?'[16] He was referring of course to the British (or English) Empire; his point being that true patriotism depended on an awareness of and support for this great enterprise. The Empire was yet another of our 'Britains', and an important way of looking at the country; to which however we shall return in a later chapter, where we can hopefully sort out some of the confusions that often surround it in retrospect. Before then the remainder of this chapter will focus on *perceptions* of Britain in the nineteenth and twentieth centuries, both at home – its people's *self*-perceptions – and abroad.

*

Kipling's insistence that in order to understand Britain you needed to take account of its Empire was never lost on foreigners, and hasn't been today. Indeed Britain's historical reputation, certainly abroad and to some extent at home, is now dominated by the fact that it used to possess a world-wide empire; which has – sadly or thankfully – fallen from its grasp. According to former American Secretary of State Dean Acheson in 1962, that left Britain 'without a role' in the new, post-imperial world. Before then, however, it was *as* an imperial power that it was primarily regarded by others; not altogether accurately, as we shall see in a later chapter, but understandably in view of those great, red-bespattered world maps (Mercator's projection of course exaggerating the British bit on the top left), and the ways Britain and its people impacted on other countries. While it was throwing its weight about abroad, or seemed to be, it was difficult to see further than its fists. Obviously this was the case for its colonial subjects. Those other foreigners who tried to get beyond that superficial view, by visiting the country itself, came away with varying impressions. Of course these depended on where they came from, and where exactly they went.

There were however some common features. In the nineteenth century most of them related to Britain's situation as the leading industrial power of the time, and the effects that this seemed to be having on the nation's people. These included great riches and abject poverty, dirty northern cities, a certain kind of 'freedom', execrable food, and the virtual absence of art. The countryside was by and large neglected, as it wasn't all that different from the travellers' own. (All of us notice differences abroad, before the similarities.) Nineteenth-century refugees from political oppression in Europe welcomed the freedom Britain afforded them, but not the price it came at. The German socialist Joanna Kinkel, for example, was full of admiration for Britain's political liberties; 'but', as she wrote home in 1854, 'one must work terribly hard here.'[17] Others complained that in Britain poverty seemed to be regarded as a crime. 'Yes', wrote the English Chartist G. J. Harney, 'they have freedom. Freedom to starve beneath England's inclement skies.'[18] Another Leftist, the Frenchman Alexandre Ledru-Rollin, was so unimpressed that he wasted hardly any time at all after landing in Britain in 1848 to write a whole book entitled *De la Décadence d'Angleterre*. ('Decadence', especially with its late nineteenth-century Wildean associations, wasn't a word that Englishmen liked to apply to themselves.) But the second-most famous radical foreigner to live in Britain in Victorian times – famous in later years, that is – was the Manchester-based manufacturer Friedrich Engels, whose *Die Lage der arbeitenden Klasse in England* (1845), later translated as *The Condition of the Working Classes*, became the classic early study of 'capitalist exploitation' that bore fruit eventually in his and his even more famous foreign friend Karl Marx's *Das Kapital*. Of course, the political stances of all these critics will have affected both their viewpoints and their judgements. But the shock that they felt on venturing for the first time into the blackened industrial cities of the English North and Midlands, plus Glasgow, was pretty typical, even of non-Leftists.

That marked one side of Britain's economic image to the rest of the world. The other, and a more positive one, was the amazing *products* of those hellish places when displayed in – especially – the 'Great Exhibition of the Works of Industry of All Nations' held in Hyde Park, London, in 1851; where the 'all nations' part of the title couldn't obscure the fact that more than half the exhibits were made in Britain, and generally speaking put other countries' products to shame. Many of them found their way abroad, especially railway engines and machine tools, before other countries learned how to make them – often better – for themselves. These were what most early nineteenth-century Continental travellers came to Britain to wonder at.[19]

The main exceptions at the Great Exhibition – black holes in Britain's display – were works of art, where Britain was outshone by most other European countries, to the extent that its reputation in some circles was that it had no artistic culture at all. (We shall return to this.) European visitors to Britain in the nineteenth century didn't generally come to admire its paintings or music or great buildings. They did come to converse with its authors, who were much admired, literature being the one great exception to the 'British philistine' rule. Charles Dickens found it difficult to get rid of the Dane Hans Christian Anderson when he came as a house guest at Gads Hill in the summer of 1857; after which Dickens's daughter Katey remembered him as 'a bony bore, who stayed on and on'.[20] But then neither of them spoke each other's language. Apart from Dickens, Continental Europeans went for Shakespeare in a big way (Germans claimed he sounded better in German),[21] for Walter Scott, and for a clutch of Romantic poets, who inspired some of their greatest music, as well as their own writings.

So it was its industry that marked Britain out for foreigners, as much as – or even more than – its imperialism, which was after all a global enterprise in which most of the nations of Europe, and some beyond (the USA in particular), took part. Britain's Empire didn't mark it off from other countries, except by its size. (That too was misleading, as we shall see.) Those who *admired* it generally attributed it to Britain's lead in industry, commerce and capitalism (which was true), but also, in a couple of cases, to its educational system. In 1897 the French writer Edmond Demolins published a book entitled *À quoi tient la supériorité des Anglo-Saxons?* – the *supériorité* being evidenced by their Empire; to which his answer was – their Public schools. Forty years later a more famous European – an Austrian in this case – also credited the schools with Britain's imperial success: 'calculated' as they were 'to rear men of inflexible will and ruthless energy who regard intellectual problems as a waste of time but know human nature and how to dominate other men in the most unscrupulous fashion'.[22] That is a recommendation not often quoted in Public school advertising. Considering its source, that's not surprising. Adolf Hitler was not always the best judge of these things.

With Britain's having won the First World War, or at least been on the winning side, with its Empire staying almost intact (and even with a couple of 'colonies' added), its economy still pottering along, and the two new rising superpowers out of the game for one reason or another, its reputation seemed to be on the rise again; albeit not always favourably – not among the colonial subjects who felt oppressed by Britain, for example; and not at all realistically. We shall describe the difficulties the Empire was going through at this time in a later chapter. British governments were aware of these, and continually engaged in trying to manage them. But less so 'ordinary' people, both at home and abroad. For them those great world maps, with areas of British 'control' coloured bright red, still betokened the scope of its power, for good or for ill. Britain's reputation abroad between the Wars, and for a little time afterwards, was dominated by this image – a slightly misleading one, as it turned out – of being one of the 'Great' powers. Other stereotypes flowed from this, in many cases bolstered by the conduct of individual Britons: that they were 'proud', even 'arrogant', 'xenophobic', 'insular' in their opinions, if not in their actions, and prone to 'bullying'; but also strong, athletic (the Public schools, again), and trustworthy, within certain parameters. But there was no doubt that Britain was still one of the leading countries of the world; truly '*Great* Britain': although that name when it was coined was not supposed to indicate 'greatness' in the grandiose sense. (It was simply used to refer to the *four nations* that made up Britain; or otherwise to distinguish it from *Petit Bretagne*, in France.)

Other reputational stereotypes were less flattering. Britain was supposed to be the source of '*la vice anglaise*', meaning either sodomy or sado-masochism, according to your preference. (On the British side syphilis was known as the 'French disease'.) Its philistinism was so notorious it would have been hopeless to try to correct it, even if the charge had been unfair. (As it became, probably, in the twentieth century.) Britain's people were supposed to be cold and dull, which they may have been by comparison with the 'Latin' peoples of Europe: or was that just a stereotype on the other side? British food was still held up as being poor, but only more sybaritic countries, like France and Italy, made much of that. Britain's archetypal 'fish and chips' were widely mocked as proof of the nation's poor cuisine, although the mockers probably didn't know of the dish's origins in Portugal and the Netherlands (probably), and of the young Jewish boy who brought it over to London.[23] Britain was of course wet, but nice and green as a result.

The Second World War did it a lot of favours with Continental Europeans, especially, who admired Britain's brave stand at the beginning of it, the democratic principles it professed to be fighting for, and the fact that it wasn't *Germany*, whose stock plummeted during the War, for obvious reasons. 'Neutral' Sweden, which had always felt culturally closer to Germany before 1939, switched its allegiance and even its affections to Britain afterwards, encouraging all its citizens to learn the language, which they came to speak better than many native-born Britons afterwards. That also enabled them to appreciate and import large numbers of British films and TV series, to the benefit – one assumes – of the British Exchequer, especially those where the actors had to appear in 'period dress', or were seen solving murders in ideal (and unlikely) rural villages. (In exchange the Nordics gave Britain 'Scandi Noir'.) Most Europeans seemed to like British people, which was why they were so upset when 'Brexit' snapped the cord. The fact that Britain was in the EU had seemed to indicate that it had shed at least some of its 'arrogance'. On the other hand they were shocked by Britain's Press culture, to be discussed later in this book; saw Britain as 'backward' socially: in fact it could be seen as rather ahead of them in neo-Liberal terms; and were widely irritated by its provocative European diplomacy in the years before Brexit – Thatcher especially – which was seen to re-confirm the ex-imperial stereotype described above. (Or is this just Sweden? Other peoples may have been less tolerant.) Of course they attributed Brexit to imperial nostalgia.[24] They were only partly right in this.

As for the USA, reputedly Britain's 'special' ally for a hundred years, its attitudes to Britain ranged from the deep and empathetic knowledge of many of its leading intellectuals, especially historians, to the ignorance of (we can be sure) President Donald Trump; with a bucketful of myths, delusions and half-truths in between. One of the biggest of the half-truths may be Dean Acheson's, quoted already: that Britain had 'lost an empire and not yet found a role'; only a *half*-truth because it seemed to assume that Britain's only role before 1962 had been its imperial one. This was the voice of the diplomat speaking. But Britain was about far more.

*

So far as its citizens were concerned, they were not nearly so obsessed by their Empire as foreigners assumed they must be. (Strictly speaking, incidentally, they only became 'citizens' rather than 'subjects' in 1983. Not too much should be made of this. The change meant little in practice, being simply a rather tardy recognition of the reality. Or was it? Are the British people equal citizens even now?) Some old-fashioned Tories, called 'harrumphers' in one account,[25] hugely regretted the loss of their Empire after the Second World War, even forming a small but noisy 'League of Empire Loyalists' with the hope of preserving or reviving it; and continued identifying with the detritus of Empire – like white 'Rhodesia', and apartheid South Africa – when most of the rest had gone. Overall however, decolonization was greeted with – at most – apathy in Britain; certainly when compared with the domestic ructions that broke out over the Algerian issue in France. For Britain the evidence – or some of it; readers should be aware that this is disputed – suggests that the British people were generally 'absent-minded' over their Empire – the expression coined by the historian J. R. Seeley in 1883 – except at certain intervals when exciting events in the colonies grabbed their attention. The South African (or 'Boer') War of 1899–1902 was the main one of these, giving rise to outbursts of what was called 'jingoism' in some British cities, and in the popular Press: by then just beginning its long decline into the 'yellow' – another term that originated then – that characterizes it today. Unfortunately the 'jingoism' of the turn of the twentieth century came to be taken as typical of working-class 'imperialism' (or post-imperialism) at all times, although some evidence suggests that it was in reality more of a lower middle-class phenomenon, very infrequent (the last outbreak is supposed to have been at the time of the Falklands War), and not really associated with 'empire' per se. One indication that the 'harrumphers', at least, were not at all confident of the 'people's' attachment to the Flag is indicated by the lengths they took between the Wars to wean the workers away from their 'absent-mindedness'; with 'Empire Exhibitions', an 'Empire Day' (24 May), and a wealth of propaganda in films, boys' books, songs and even advertisements for just about anything one could think of, if the Union Jack or a British Tommy or a palm tree could somehow be brought into the picture.[26] There are of course two ways of looking at this propaganda: as indicating either the ubiquity of the imperial discourse; or the lack of it if imperialists believed it was necessary. There are books on this, arguing from both sides.[27]

What is not debatable is the fact that, so far as Britons' images of themselves were concerned, the Empire was not supposed to be their only distinguishing feature, or even the main one. In the nineteenth century if you asked a British man or woman what being British 'meant', he or she would almost certainly have mumbled something about 'freedom'; even those – a majority of them until after the First World War – who weren't allowed 'the Vote'. 'Freedom' meant two things: freedom as a nation – that is, not attached to or ruled by other countries or empires: 'Britons never never never shall be slaves', in the words of the old patriotic song about Britain's ruling 'the waves';[28] and secondly, freedom from government, even their own governments, in their individual lives. (So it didn't imply 'democracy'.) Most classes of society would have gone along with that.

What may be thought more extraordinary is that they – the middle and working classes, at any rate – also applied that to their *Empire*, insofar as they took any notice of the latter at all. This was because of the way it was sold to them, by all those imperial propagandists: as the idea of Britain's *liberating* colonial or soon-to-become-colonial subjects from – well, you could take your choice: barbarism, slavery and the slave trade, tribal wars, the Germans and Ottomans, false religions, or simply ignorance. Later the term 'Commonwealth' was chosen to replace 'Empire', in order to emphasize this more humanitarian side of the enterprise (supposedly), and at the same time to de-emphasize the element of 'conquest'. Indeed, the free, equal, multi-racial Commonwealth was sometimes presented as the very culmination of British imperialism, with Britain having governed the colonies originally 'rescued' from other tyrannies only in order to prepare them for self-government as independent nations. (We shall return to this in Chapter 3.) This turned the 'decolonization' of the 1950s and 1960s from being a mark of defeat and decline, as it was seen abroad and by the harrumphers at home, into the very opposite; with the Empire/Commonwealth presented as having all along been rather like a voluntary club or alliance that countries had asked to become members of: 'please can we join?'; rather than the final stage – or perhaps not so final, if we include financial imperialism – in the evolution of an institution that had originally been built on at least some degree of force. Hence colonial independence was always said to be 'granted' by Britain, rather than won *from* her. That may have been because, for Britons weaned on their mother's milk of 'freedom', the idea of theirs being an essentially aggressive, conquering power was difficult to digest. Of course this was misleading, even illusory, although there was some earlier history that could be used to justify the Commonwealthists' spin (we shall come back to this too); but the idea that they stood for 'freedom', both at home and in the wider world, was essential to most Britons' national self-image at the time. Otherwise how could they live with their Empire; or, in 1914 and 1939, criticize their new German enemy for its Continental imperialism?

This idea of British 'freedoms' was associated with – may indeed have grown out of – the 'liberalism' that was another essential ingredient in how Britons thought of themselves, from way back in time until almost the present day. The classic text of liberalism was of course written by an Englishman (John Stuart Mill's *On Liberty*), and Britain had a 'Liberal' Party sharing power for many years with a 'Conservative' one whose 'conservatism' embraced the conservation of many of Britain's new liberal institutions, and a Labour Party which claimed to be in its own way extending them. 'Liberal' was never the term of abuse in Britain that it became in Republican America. It covered not only liberal democracy, which indeed was fairly slow evolving in the nineteenth and early twentieth centuries; but also principles like toleration, the rule of law, and the 'emancipation', as it was called, of people excluded from full citizenship previously: slaves first, then Catholics, Jews, Nonconformists, and eventually women.

Even before they were 'emancipated', people were to be 'tolerated'; including foreigners desiring to come to Britain, whatever their characters. The Victorians were inordinately proud of the fact that foreign refugees, sometimes of the most fiery kind, were allowed into the country without the government's even having the *power* to exclude them, or to extradite them if they misbehaved fierily while they were there. 'Every civilized people on the face of the earth', *The Times* proclaimed in 1853, when European radicals fleeing from the failures of their 1848 revolutions started arriving in Britain, 'must be fully aware that this country is the asylum of nations, and that it will defend that asylum to the last source of its treasure, and the last drop of its blood. There is no point whatever on which we are prouder and more resolute.'[29] So there we have it: not the Empire, but their toleration of swarthy Continental anarchists with bombs. A little while after this a government was brought down because it was felt to be truckling to foreign 'despots' demanding the extradition of some of these ne'er-do-wells.[30] For most of the nineteenth century Britain remained totally open to all immigrants, from wherever they came. And they did come, in pretty large numbers – if they didn't mind having to 'work terribly hard'. Karl Marx, of course, was one of them; 'working terribly hard' in the British Museum Reading Room, and being part-subsidized by his manufacturer friend Engels.

Behind this toleration lay a deeper Liberal belief, which was – quite simply – that what we would call terrorism was usually the fault of the people being terrorized. This was Palmerston's excuse for not doing more to prohibit Continental socialists and anarchists from coming to Britain in the 1850s:[31] Britain's 'liberty' would soon disarm them. That was how far 'liberalism' was taken in nineteenth-century Britain, although not for long afterwards. It would, of course, be wrong to expect it now, in view of the very different historical conditions of the two widely-separated periods. History cannot be used to point specific lessons in this way. My point in recalling Britain's astonishingly liberal asylum and immigration policies here is not to imply that they could be repeated, but to alert present-day patriots to the fact that the 'history' they sometimes appeal to in order to buttress a view of Britain's present-day 'national identity' can be misleading. Some years ago a government minister justified a particular immigration measure on the grounds that Britain had always controlled its frontiers.[32] That was not so – except perhaps theoretically. (There has always been the Royal Prerogative.) What may be significant, however, is the fact that the British made such great play of this central feature of their 'national identity' in Victorian times, which they cannot do any more.

*

The British brand of 'liberalism' also took other forms. Britons were always worried about 'policing', for example, which was associated with more authoritarian states, like France, Austria and Russia. That is why mainland Britain was one of the last countries in Europe to institute an official police force (1829), and only in London initially, and distinctively uniformed. (Dublin got its Police department earlier. But then Ireland was always an exception to the liberal rule.) Hence the tall stove-pipe hats, designed to let honest – and dishonest – citizens know they were around; and not in 'plain clothes', which was felt to be illiberal and sneaky. One important desideratum was to avoid their being mistaken for *foreign* policemen, who were in ill favour just then. As one noble Lord told Parliament in 1811, after a particularly grisly series of murders in London's East End: 'They have an admirable police at Paris. But they pay for it dear enough. I had rather half-a-dozen people's throats be cut in Ratcliffe Highway every three or four years than be subject to domiciliary visits, spies, and all the rest of Fouché's contrivances.'[33] (Fouché was the much feared Parisian police chief.) Britain was better than that.

A plain-clothes 'detective' force (CID) *was* set up later, but it was very small, widely distrusted, and indeed had to be disbanded after just a few years when it was found to be corrupt. It was subsequently replaced, but the CID's officers generally had the reputation of being rather dull, as exemplified in Conan Doyle's depiction of Inspector Lestrade in the Sherlock Holmes novels. That was comforting to the middle classes, however, who seem to have feared their public servants' being too bright. Holmes himself – very bright, of course, even 'intellectual', almost too much so to be properly English, but obviously not an agent of the State – had to be accompanied by a bluff, salt-of-the-earth sidekick, John Watson, to be acceptable to readers. The working classes, of course, distrusted the police as instruments of State repression. And – beneath them – criminals often outsmarted them.

If the police were distrusted, 'secret services' were even more so, by all classes except those at the very top of the pyramid; and even they had to pretend to be horrified by the idea. Two aspects of secret service work that made it particularly 'un-British' were its political functions – only 'despotisms' had 'political police' forces; and the practice of secret 'surveillance'. That was the worst of 'Fouché's contrivances'. Even hiding behind a tree to observe an 'indecent offence' was beyond the pale, as one unfortunate police sergeant in 1852 found to his cost. (He was immediately demoted to constable.)[34] Spying abroad was more acceptable – Johnny Foreigner, after all, didn't play by the same rules – but only slightly so. Watching foreign politicos in Britain was also apparently OK; Karl Marx was still being tailed by a policeman months after his death and burial in Highgate Cemetery.[35] (Perhaps the police knew something we don't?) Even so the Liberal prime minister Gladstone absented himself from one of his own cabinet meetings so that he wouldn't have to hear about the work of his new 'Special Branch'.[36] All that changed, of course, at the beginning of the twentieth century, when Britain's official (but still secret) espionage agencies were set up.[37] But the prejudice against these 'foreign' practices still remained. This was another very real 'Victorian value' that is often forgotten, or more likely was never realized, by those who have wished in the recent past – Thatcher, for example, and possibly Boris Johnson – to restore the glory of those times.

One could go on. There was a prejudice against the military, too, in the nineteenth century: against its officer class, often the dull younger sons of aristos; its 'men' (ordinary troops), usually the detritus of working-class society; and in view of its frequent failures in the field, unless augmented by mercenaries and more powerful allies, and against poorly-armed 'natives', with 'glorious' defeats and retreats being celebrated more often than victories. The 'Charge of the Light Brigade' is the most notorious example, but there were others. (The Royal Navy on the other hand was regarded more highly, perhaps because it seemed more romantic; and in fact it did have a better fighting record.) Liberal Victorians felt particularly uneasy about having soldiers barracked in Britain, because of the way they could be deployed there against civic protesters. (The Peterloo 'massacre', 1819, was the great deterrent here.) It is important to be aware of this prejudice in Britain's history. It was never as 'militaristic' a society as France was in the nineteenth century, Germany under Nazism, or the USA today. That was another reason for national pride.

For it meant that Britain could concentrate on what Britain did best; which was, of course, *making* things, to sell peacefully (but protected by the Navy) around the world. That rested on another aspect of its 'liberalism', the one that has been elevated today into the ideology known as *neo*liberalism, which has taken the 'economic' element of the original theory and pushed it to the fore. The 'free market' worked best with minimal State involvement, which meant (in those days: not now) a minimal military and police. These were both considered 'unproductive' in economic terms. Indeed, strictly speaking they should be *unnecessary*, if the market were working as it should, to abolish poverty all round (and so diminish crime), and to make boundaries between nations – meaning travel and tariff barriers – redundant. Hence Britain's progressive abolition of its own customs charges in the early nineteenth century; its openness to immigrants from all countries; and its amazing industrial enterprise at home. These were central to Britain's self-image.

They also explained and excused the features of British society that were usually less admired abroad. The key to it all was 'utilitarianism', the concentration on products and practices that were materially 'useful'; which at this time excluded 'art', for example, and may explain Britain's relative artistic impoverishment then. Indeed, the charge of philistinism could even be considered a badge of honour. As the early Victorian travel writer Samuel Laing put it in 1842,

> The lisping amateur hopping about the saloons of the great, may prattle of taste, and refined feeling in music, sculpture, painting, as humanizing influences in society . . .; but the plain, undeniable, knock-me-down truth is, that the Glasgow manufacturer, whose printed cotton handkerchiefs the traveller Lander found adorning the woolly heads of negresses far in the interior of Africa, . . . has done more for civilization, has extended humanizing influences more widely, than all the painters, sculptors, architects, and musicians of our age put together.[38]

(There is a touch of Dickens's Gradgrind about that.)[39] Whether there is a general truth expressed here, that free market capitalism is intrinsically inimical to 'fancy' and to 'high art', is something that can be debated. But the likes of Laing – a pretty representative Victorian first-generation capitalist – certainly hoped so.

In its golden years – around the third quarter of the nineteenth century – the Victorian settlement managed to sustain, proudly, a society that boomed economically, with a few stumbles; and sustained an amazingly liberal culture in many areas. But it also possessed certain features that could *not* be matters of national pride or 'identity', and which in the end punctured the liberal dream. They included abject poverty and the criminalization of poverty, noted by our refugees; a cruel criminal code generally – it needed to be, in order to deter wrongdoers when there were so few policemen around; some unwanted repercussions of Britain's trade abroad (we shall come to 'imperialism' in a later chapter); the 'other island' reduced to starvation and provoked to rebellion by 'market' rules and British governments' disinterest, at best; a political soil in which a powerful alternative to 'the market' could be seeded and encouraged, planted by one of its refugees: not one of the fieriest, as it happened; and a degree of *social* oppression – against gays and 'fallen women', for example – balancing out the political 'freedoms' that Britons took such pride in, which made many of their own exiles on the Continent, in America and in the colonies feel significantly 'free-er' there than they had felt at home. Those were the downsides. But at least the 'lisping amateurs' were kept in their place.

*

It did not last, this widespread philistinism of the British. It began to lift at the very end of the nineteenth century; which one historian has taken to explain why their capitalism – the 'industrial spirit' – so declined from then on.[40] In the twentieth century Britons continued celebrating their industrial achievements, which were still considerable: cars, aeroplanes, ocean liners, the fastest steam-train ever built; until something put an end to that – the jury is still out on what that might have been – with manufacture being substantially superseded by banking and investment, or 'invisibles' as they were known, from the 1960s onward. But by then they had also built up a sizeable artistic portfolio; and an even bigger one of scientific discoveries and inventions, mostly stemming from their world-renowned universities. It was science that was mainly and proudly celebrated in the second 'Great Exhibition' of 1951, especially the 'Dome of Discovery', designed to bring a glow of patriotic warmth to the British people after the sufferings and privations of the Second World War. This elderly historian remembers that. It was great.

Thereafter Britain's self-image – which we are focussing on here, remember, not necessarily the reality – was dominated firstly by its share in the Allies' military victory over Nazi Germany: often the impression given was that Britain had won the War on its own; and secondly by the social 'progress' it felt the nation had made with its new 'Welfare State', and especially the National Health Service (NHS), which Aneurin Bevan, its architect, claimed marked 'a milestone in history – the most civilized step any country had ever taken.'[41] Here was another focus for national pride, more befitting, one would think, the new post-War and post-imperial age. Whether it survives much longer in the age also of late-stage capitalism (which we shall come on to in the final chapters) remains to be seen. It clearly didn't satisfy many Britons, including but not confined to the 'harrumphers', who hankered after something more obviously glorious to glory in. It also didn't hamper more traditional *liberal* patriots, who continued to appeal to all the old 'British' values of 'freedom', 'tolerance', 'stability', the 'rule of law', official 'probity' and 'moderation', as slogans at least, even after these had begun being chipped away from the 1970s onward. 'National identity', especially self-identity, can be based not only on history, but also on histories that have long passed.

Last of all we should take note of the strong tradition of *dissent* in British history, which was not of course made so much of by self-styled 'patriots' or by the definers of what made Britain 'British', at home or abroad, but which was certainly as characteristic of the country and its peoples as were any of those other elements of its 'identity'. 'Protest' and rebellion – often violent – have been characteristic features of British society since at least Roman times (*vide* Boudicca and Caractacus), and much admired ones for those who don't think obedience – or 'patriotism' – is all. Many of what later became established features of Britain's national character started off as protest movements: for democracy (for both sexes) in particular. Many of Britain's 'tolerances' – of slaves, Jews, Catholics, religious Nonconformists (or 'Dissenters'), trade unionists, homosexuals – began as anti-Establishment movements, before they too became 'established'. The downfall of the Empire was partly brought about by anti-imperialists and critics of empire (not always the same people) at home. British foreign policy provoked countless demonstrations against it over the two centuries covered in this book, culminating in the largest ever: the million or more who assembled in London on 15 February 2003 to protest the second Gulf War. (Not that it had any effect, except to besmirch for years afterwards the reputation of the British prime minister, Tony Blair, who had led Britain into it.) On an individual level there were countless acts of protest, like the almost daily ones of the Euro-behatted Steve Bray with his anti-Brexit display boards on College Green (outside Parliament) in 2019–21. At this level, indeed, protest could be seen as a distinctively British phenomenon, not far removed from the well-known English (or was it pan-British?) tradition of 'eccentricity'. And, it hardly needs to be added, if it was designed to make Britain 'better', an essentially 'patriotic' one. Hence it will be given its full due in this 'history for patriots'.

2

1800–1945

Britain entered the nineteenth century with a military and naval victory over the French, a pretty repressive Tory government, great social unrest, and an 'industrial revolution' in full flow. This last was crucial, in one way or another, to nearly everything that followed.

In truth, Britain didn't invent either industrialization or capitalism; but it was the first country to combine them effectively. The result was not only a soaring economy (with a few dips), but also a transformed society – half way, at any rate. It also began the transformation of the world. The material signs of the growth of British manufacture in the period 1750–1850 (roughly) were obvious, and still are, with their remnants mostly still with us, although with many now in ruins: huge new factories; country towns transformed into great cities – and villages into towns; railways; steamships; a vast expansion of foreign trade; and empire. The social effects included great movements of population from the remaining countryside and from Ireland to the manufacturing districts of England and Scotland; huge fortunes for the manufacturers and their backers; and jobs but also often dreadful working and living conditions for millions of the rest. Even by 1804, when William Blake penned his famous 'dark satanic mills' poem, ruminating on whether 'Jerusalem' was 'builded amongst' them,[1] much of northern England and central Scotland was unrecognisable from what it had been just fifty years previously. After 1804, and throughout the century, the change accelerated. For those who (quite rightly) prefer facts to poetry when it comes to measuring economies and societies in the past, here are some bald figures.

In 1800 the population of England and Wales was just over eight million. By 1850 it had doubled to 16,738,495. The city of Manchester grew from 17,000 to 250,000 between 1760 and 1850. In 1800, 21 per cent of the British population lived in cities – already a higher figure than anywhere else in the world; by 1850 this had risen to almost 40 per cent. By then Britain had become the source of two-thirds of the world's coal, and a half of the world's supply of cotton, textiles and iron goods. Its export trade – mostly in those last items – more than trebled over the same period. Railway mileage increased from nought in 1800 (the steam train hadn't been invented then), to 6,800 in 1851.[2] That should give an idea of the surging material progress that the country was making in the first half of the nineteenth century. But it's not the material facts we are mainly concerned with here; rather the industrial revolution's social and political repercussions.

It was this that determined most aspects of Britain's history for the next hundred years at least – economically of course; but also socially, politically and culturally. Socially it favoured the industrial middle classes most, together with the professions that serviced their needs. For the working classes it furnished new employment opportunities, and was supposed to bring greater prosperity 'trickling down' to them, but didn't, for a while at least. They remained poor, and when they came to fill the new jobs in the smoky industrial towns and cities, usually lived in worse conditions than they had done before, even in their rural hovels, which were at least open to the fresh air. Hence the social unrest. For the upper classes and aristocracy the industrial revolution could be seen to have edged them out of their dominant position in society, with the 'middles' getting richer than them, and their whole 'feudal' rationale – Lords 'looking after' their loyal peasants – undermined by the new 'market' ethic, or what Thomas Carlyle called the 'cash nexus', that was coming in.

If the politics of the day were to reflect this new situation on the ground, the Lords ought to have been displaced by the industrial middle classes at the top of the pyramid: that is, in government. That they weren't, entirely, with cabinets still dominated by the very upper classes until the end of the century, was the result of a very clever – albeit unspoken – arrangement between the two classes. In brief: the middle classes let the uppers stay on as their governors, so long as they governed in the middles' interests. It was a perfect solution for both 'sides'. Industrialists had no time for 'governing', as it didn't make a profit (or shouldn't do, unless power was exercised corruptly); whereas the upper classes had been bred for this role for centuries, and were educated for it in their 'Public' (in reality, of course, private and privileged) schools. All it needed was for the upper classes to accept free market rules, which they did by stages during the course of the first half of the century. The key moment is supposed to have been the repeal of the Corn Laws, which had previously protected the agricultural interest, by the Whigs (later 'Liberals') in 1846, with the support of some more 'enlightened' Tories. Middle-class domination was also increased by a series of Parliamentary Reform bills (1832, 1868, 1882) which rendered the House of Commons more predominately middle class by the end of the century, albeit still only representing men. The working classes agitated to be included throughout the century – the 'Chartist' movement of the 1830s and 1840s was their main effort – but with only marginal success. Throughout the nineteenth century, and well into the twentieth, it was the middle classes who determined how the country was run, with the aristos in government simply furnishing an illusion of continuity with the past. British politics was a 'hybrid' animal, with a middle-class torso, an aristocratic head, and – carrying the creature along – working-class legs.

The aristocracy, however, was not just there to serve the middle classes. There were some areas of government in which it played a more leading part, especially foreign policy, which was seen as a more suitable role for the upper classes, both because it was a 'higher' concern than the domestic affairs that the Commons mainly grubbed around in, and also because nearly all the foreign diplomats the country had to deal with were aristocrats themselves, which it was felt would help them to get along with one another in important negotiations. Their other importance, according to the American historian Martin Weiner, was in seducing some of the middle classes over to their side; those that is who had ideas above their station, and aspired to buy themselves – or educate their children – into what were considered to be the 'upper' reaches of society. The Public schools came in handy here, teaching non-useful subjects – especially the 'Classics' – to the sons of utilitarians. One result, according to Weiner, was that a section of the middle classes lost its interest in productive industry, investing instead in new country mansions and country sports to ape its role models, to the detriment of industry and entrepreneurialism in Britain from the second half of the nineteenth century on.[3] The evidence is visible all over, with great neo-Classical, neo-Gothic and neo-Tudor houses and even castles beautifying Britain's landscape (if you like 'neo' styles of architecture), albeit most of them now turned into hotels or private schools.

The possibility of rising into the topmost class, however, may have kept the middle classes going, and striving; just as the chance of climbing up out of the working class to the 'lower middles' – running a small shop perhaps, and owning their own houses – undoubtedly motivated many lower down the pecking order. Social mobility, for some, was a way of making people satisfied with their lots, and hence with the organization of society as it was then; rendering them less inclined to violent protest, and so minimizing any threat to the established order. That worked if you were ambitious, and so long as you felt there were no obstacles in your way. Those without social ambition were encouraged simply to accept the situations they were stuck in, as 'natural' or divinely ordained, perhaps; the latter expressed in the original third verse of the popular children's hymn 'All things bright and beautiful'.

> The rich man in his castle,
> The poor man at his gate,
> God made them, high and lowly,
> And ordered their estate.[4]

That should have given the rebellious ones pause for thought. (Obviously it didn't, for the Chartists; or, for that matter, the suffragettes of later years.) Besides, you needed different categories of people for a nation to function properly. Each – rulers, tradesmen, workers – locked into one another, with a working man's or woman's duty being to serve his or her betters; not necessarily to share the latter's nationalistic or any other beliefs. (Hence the 'plinth' analogy cited in the last chapter.) This was the 'lower' classes' 'patriotic' role. Class was central to almost everything British in the nineteenth century, and arguably remains fairly so today.

It wasn't the only thing to divide Britons from other Britons, as we saw in the previous chapter; but class had repercussions in almost every area of British life. It mainly determined where people lived, for example, with most large towns zoned (naturally) into different areas for the different classes, with separate middle class and 'poor' ghettoes, the former in the leafy suburbs, the latter 'inner-city'; except where socially-minded philanthropists, fearing the effects of class hostility, deliberately planned housing areas where people could mix.[5] The classes received different educations: 'elementary' for those at the bottom of the social ladder – reading, writing, simple arithmetic and the moralistic bits of the bible (for what use would literature be to a child destined to be a farm labourer or a servant?); 'grammar' schools for the middles, teaching literature, more advanced mathematics and perhaps a smattering of French; and the Greek and Latin classics – virtually those alone – in the prestigious Public schools. The ancient English universities were only there for the upper classes, usually for them to play around in; by contrast with those in Scotland, whose almost-as-ancient universities were more serious about work. In Oxford and Cambridge entry was confined to members of the Church of England; so during the course of the century a few other universities admitting non-Anglicans were founded in London and then in a couple of English cities. But university was a very minority vocation in any case.

Other ways in which the classes were strictly segregated from each other were legion. They had different jobs and professions, obviously, which were the most obvious delineators of class; very different cultural tastes, from opera 'down' to the music hall and from 'serious' literature to 'penny dreadfuls'; and played different sports: Association football and Rugby League for the working classes, Rugby Union for Public school boys, and cricket for both – but with 'gentlemen', amateurs, being separated from 'players', the professionals (usually bowlers), by being assigned different dressing rooms and even separate little gates through which to come on and off the field of play.[6]

So far as national politics were concerned, they became organized in fairly clearly delineated 'parties' during the first half of the nineteenth century, by the end of which period 'Whigs' – later Liberals – were confronting 'Tories', or Conservatives, across the aisle of the House of Commons in what must have seemed a permanent – almost natural – division of national opinion. As W. S. Gilbert's lyric put it in the (middle-class) operetta *Iolanthe* (1882): 'Every boy and every gal that's born into the world alive, Is either a little Liberal, or else a little Conservative' (to rhyme with 'alive'). Actually they weren't. Even in Gilbert's time socialism was rearing its head; explicitly in the Marxist Social Democratic Federation

(SDF), founded a year before the first performance of *Iolanthe* by H. M. Hyndman, a Cambridge graduate and former county cricketer. (So he will have gone through the Gentlemen's gate.) Socialism under other names long preceded the SDF in Britain, as did trade unionism, persecuted in one way or another for most of the century – *viz.* the 'Tolpuddle Martyrs', 1834 – and the Co-operative movement. In the 1890s the working classes, with a significant number of them now having 'the vote', managed to squeeze into the Commons under the aegis of a new 'Independent Labour Party', or else sponsored by local constituency Liberals. In 1900 the Labour Party proper was founded, initially as the 'Labour Representation Committee', and gained several Parliamentary seats in the 1900s. But it didn't ever represent all working-class voters, many of whom seemed content with the Liberals' softer form of market capitalism, or were seduced by the Conservative Benjamin Disraeli's appeal to their latent 'patriotism', especially with regard to foreign affairs. The latter has been a consistent and pretty reliable weapon in the Conservative party's armoury ever since.

None of this made much difference to British politics before 1900. These were dominated by the contest between the two major parties, over 'free trade' originally, until the Tories capitulated over that; then over the annual budget, of course; and various social and political reforms – widening the franchise; 'emancipating' non-conformists, Catholics and Jews: that is, extending the franchise and various other privileges to *them*; policing, with the first English police force being instituted in 1829, controversially, as police were associated then with foreign tyrannical regimes; liberalizing the penal code, so not so many executions; outlawing the British slave trade (1807) and then slavery itself, so far as the British colonies were concerned (1833); foreign, imperial and defence policy; the architecture of the Houses they were sitting in (the old Palace of Westminster had burned down in 1834); seemingly interminable squabbles over the Deceased Wife's Sister's Marriage Bill, to allow a man to wed his dead wife's sister, previously banned under canon law, which was only passed in 1907; and lastly – and most controversially and dangerously – Ireland. Some of these, including Ireland, remained debating points right through the following century. Two issues that came up in that century, but not in the nineteenth, were immigration, where there was plenty of it but no laws at all to limit it; and state welfare, which the free market principles of the day absolutely forbad, unless it was in the form of 'workhouses', for the genuinely indigent; or of course prisons.

For this was a *liberal* country before everything – even Tories were relatively liberal – and all the happier for it; or *should* have been. It all derived from 'free trade' ideology, and hence from the industrial revolution originally. Free trade in the earlier nineteenth century was not only a commercial policy, but also – supposedly – a socially progressive one. This was why working-class radicals supported it then. Domestically – though it is hard today to credit this – it was believed to conduce ultimately to social and economic justice, ironing out the gross inequalities that free traders claimed derived from the old privileged post-feudal institutions, which the market would take care of when it was allowed to function 'naturally'. By free traders the prospect was made out to be almost utopian, with everyone in the nation adequately provided for, and no-one *over*-provided; hence no poverty, no jealousy, no crime, no need for a police force, even; or of course for what today is called a 'welfare state'. John Stuart Mill, the great Victorian sage of 'liberalism', went so far as to write that if free market capitalism didn't in the end conduce to greater equality, he would abandon it and become a 'socialist'.[7] One must assume that if he were still alive today that's where he would be. Internationally the spread of free trade would also conduce to peace, with nations no longer having or wanting anything worth fighting over. Richard Cobden, the anti-Corn Law champion and negotiator of the first free trade treaty with France (1860), waxed quite lyrical over the prospect.

> I have been accused of looking too much to material interests. Nevertheless I can say that I have taken as large and great a view of the effects of this mighty principle as ever did any man who dreamt over it in his own study. I believe that the physical gain will be the smallest gain to humanity from the success of this principle. I look farther; I see in the Free-trade principle that which shall act on the moral world as the principle of gravitation in the universe,—drawing men together, thrusting aside the antagonism of race, and creed, and language, and uniting us in the bonds of eternal peace. I have looked even farther. I have speculated, and probably dreamt, in the dim future—ay, a thousand years hence—I have speculated on what the effect of the triumph of this principle may be. I believe that the effect will be to change the face of the world, so as to introduce a system of government entirely distinct from that which now prevails. I believe that the desire and the motive for large and mighty empires; for gigantic armies and great navies—for those materials which are used for the destruction of life and the desolation of the rewards of labour—will die away; I believe that such things will cease to be necessary, or to be used, when man becomes one family, and freely exchanges the fruits of his labour with his brother man. I believe that, if we could be allowed to reappear on this sublunary scene, we should see, at a far distant period, the governing system of this world revert to something like the municipal system; and I believe that the speculative philosopher of a thousand years hence will date the greatest revolution that ever happened in the world's history from the triumph of the principle which we have met here to advocate.[8]

It was nonsense, of course – or has turned out to be. (On the other hand we haven't passed Cobden's 'thousand year' point yet.) But it illustrates the optimism of these mid-nineteenth century years, the Victorians' belief in 'progress', which sustained nearly all of them, except perhaps hide-bound old reactionaries and the more perceptive of Radicals, through even difficult times. (And there were plenty of those.) If you believe things are going to get better – inevitably, even, for 'free trade' was regarded as a kind of 'natural law' – you're less likely to kick against the goads. A few periods in British history have had this. But not the one we're in today.

Ireland was the great exception to most of these generalizations, and indeed had been for many hundreds of years. A separate nation in most respects, with its own language and even religion (Roman Catholic, bucking the British Protestant trend), it had been warred against by England, particularly bloodily in the seventeenth century; colonized by English and Scots rather like North America was; and cajoled into a 'Union' with its larger neighbour in 1800, partly by means of bribery, with Ireland sending MPs to Westminster, but with preference in most things given to the Protestant minority over the Catholics. Irish rebellions were frequent (one happened just before our period begins, in 1798), and put down strictly. Ireland's greatest tragedy, however, was the 'Great Famine' (or 'Hunger') of 1845–52, after a potato blight, which more than decimated the population of the country, with about a million dying and another million emigrating to America; and Britain doing less than it might have done to ease the distress due partly to those same 'free market' or *laissez faire* principles that were supposed to make everyone happy. Thereafter Ireland was always one of Britain's major 'problems': or, rather, Britain one of Ireland's. Native nationalism there grew, taking many forms, including atrocities ('knee-capping' informers, for example), and, in the 1880s, the nationalists attacking mainland Britain with bombs. This had two effects on Parliamentary politics: firstly on the Liberals, who decided to appease the Irish with 'Home Rule' – that is, limited devolution – only to be stymied by the House of Lords and some rebel members of their own party, called Liberal Unionists; and secondly on the Conservative party, which took the Liberal Unionists under its wing, and later merged with them to give the party its full present-day title, which is the 'Conservative *and Unionist* Party'. Eventually – to jump ahead for the moment – Ireland achieved its independence in 1922, after a bitter civil war, but with its north-eastern province – 'Ulster', roughly – which contained a bare majority of Protestants, descendants of the English and Scottish settlers, hived off to cleave to its old master. Which – as everybody must know – didn't solve the 'Irish problem' for good.

The poor Irish didn't emigrate only to America. Many went to Canada and Australia, and so remained within the Empire, albeit some of them bearing grudges: and who could blame them? Others – perhaps most of them – simply crossed the Irish Sea to Scotland and England, where they remain as recognisable communities in cities like Glasgow and Liverpool to this day. In fact they comprised by far the major immigrant group in Britain as a whole before the 1950s, although they weren't classed as 'immigrants' early on because Ireland was formally part of the UK. Nonetheless they were met by the same kinds of prejudice and racist abuse that greeted West

Indian immigrants in the 1950s, and Polish workers in the Brexit age. There were occasional pitched battles between Irish and the native British in areas of high immigration, and an extraordinary one between Irish Catholics and Italian refugees, believed to be atheists, in London in 1862, apparently over the doctrine of Papal infallibility.[9] Irish people were also discriminated against socially in many ways; although clever ones like George Bernard Shaw and Oscar Wilde (both Protestants) were widely feted, at least until Oscar Wilde blotted his copybook with Lord Alfred Douglas in 1895. (It was worse because Douglas was a Lord. Gay liaisons with the lower classes were usually overlooked. 'Class', again.)

One of Britain's proudest boasts in the nineteenth century was of the country's willingness to take in foreigners of all types and nationalities, even what today we would call 'terrorists'; the theory being that terrorists were the products of tyrannous regimes, which Britain wasn't, so that their violent urges would be quickly emolliated in a 'free' country. Palmerston put it like this:

> A single spark will explode a powder magazine, and a blazing torch will burn out harmless on a turnpike road. If a country be in a state of suppressed internal discontent, a very slight indication may augment that discontent, and produce an explosion; but if the country be well governed, and the people be contented, then letters and proclamations from unhappy refugees will be as harmless as the torch upon the turnpike road.[10]

This is an early version of the reaction that was very occasionally expressed in British left-wing circles to the 9/11 (2001) Al-Qaeda attack on the Twin Towers in New York: that America (in that case) 'had it coming to her'.[11] Blame the victims. In Palmerston's case, these were the *illiberal* governments of the Continent. This fitted in with the 'happy' assumption of the time. The truth was, however, that 'tolerating' immigrants was not the same as 'welcoming' them, as many immigrants found to their cost. (Unless of course they could write amusing plays.)

Palmerston's view of the underlying stability of his country was supposed to be borne out by the recent experiences of the rest of the European continent, which had been wracked by revolutions in 1848, with only liberal Britain, together with ultra-authoritarian Russia, being spared. These were what had propelled most of Europe's refugees to Britain, in flight from the punitive measures taken against those uprisings, to join Karl Marx and Friedrich Engels who were already there. In 1851 Britain put up the 'Great Exhibition of the Works of Industry of All Nations' in the new prefabricated 'Crystal Palace' in Hyde Park, in order to show off the benefits of Britain's liberal policy; to the alarm of foreign rulers, who thought the government was asking for trouble by inviting all those foreigners in; including among them, surely, some bearded anarchists with bombs. In fact the police did pick up one plot, which however was not taken seriously. (It involved the Catholic Bishop of New York together with some European socialists – an odd alliance – sending in agents cunningly disguised as trees, in a park remember, blowing incendiary balls at promenading bigwigs through pipes.)[12] The exhibition was an enormous success; and after it people remarked how smiling and *safe* the Queen appeared when she opened it. You wouldn't have got that in Paris or Berlin.

This illustrates many of the key characteristics of an age that some present-day patriots would like Britain to return to. By one way of looking at it the 1850s could be said to mark the zenith of its relative prosperity and power, after which it went into a slow decline. That will surprise some people, for whom the great 'imperial' age that followed will appear more zenithy; but the fallacy of that will be explained (or argued) in a later chapter. In the 1850s and for a couple of decades afterwards Britain led the world in commercial enterprise, industrial production, and liberalism (of a sort). It can perhaps be regarded as the Victorians' 'golden age'.

No other country then could compete with them economically, although some were beginning to catch up; which meant that Britain had a vast area of *markets* to export to, almost uncontested. Its economy was growing. It felt so secure in its liberalism that it could make do with a minimal police force and no 'secret service', considered at the time to be 'un-British'; and admit thousands of the most revolutionary refugees in from Europe without anticipating any danger to itself. It went through a couple of serious wars: one in the Crimea against the Russians (1854–6), which the French allies won for Britain, with the suicidal 'Charge of the Light Brigade' being the British Army's only moment of glory; and the Indian Mutiny (1857–8), in which the East India Company's army saved the day, with the help of some appalling atrocities, like shooting mutineers from guns. After that Britain decided to take over the country directly, so adding another jewel to Victoria's imperial crown – almost literally, indeed, when the famous Koh-i-noor diamond, originally acquired by treaty (forced or otherwise) in 1849, was recut to show off its brilliance, and later set in one of the royal crowns. (It probably ought to be sent back now; but as three countries are claiming it, it's difficult to know to whom.) India, and the 'imperial' moniker she brought with her ('*Ind Imp*' on all the old coins), ought to mark Britain's zenith in terms of prestige, but it was always, even after the 'Mutiny', at least as much trouble as it was worth. No-one at the present day would want to take it over again, although in 1950 the Conservative politician Enoch Powell tried to persuade Churchill to do just that, only to be sent away with a flea in his ear.[13] In any case it obviously wouldn't be possible; or to reclaim any other of Britain's ex-colonies, for that matter. This shouldn't need saying. Clearly the situation of Britain today is so different from what it was in the 1850s, both absolutely and relative to the rest of the world, as to invalidate just about any solution for the present taken from its past. History may be used as a guide to the present, but not as a template.

After the 'golden years' came a period of trade depression; not quite as bad as other depressions in Britain's history – the 1840s, 1930s, 2010s – but enough to undermine faith in the ability of the free market to deliver the social benefits that John Stuart Mill had promised. The reactions of the two main parties were to swap places in some ways: the Liberals taking on support for state intervention, almost 'welfareism', in order to achieve real 'liberty' in equal conditions: from around 1900 it was called the 'New Liberalism', but mustn't be confused with modern 'neoliberalism', which is almost its opposite; and the Conservatives taking up the 'free market' positions the Liberals had vacated: some of them anyway, because the Conservative party always retained a number of old-fashioned 'feudal' paternalists, or what Margaret Thatcher came to call her 'Wets'. As a public performance – which was largely what Parliament was, even before television, with nearly all newspapers, even the 'popular' ones, publishing almost verbatim accounts of Commons debates – politics was dominated by *personalities*, with the Liberal W. E .Gladstone and the Tory leader Benjamin Disraeli jousting across the floor of the House. Each side, however, tried to outdo the other in offering 'social reforms' in order to win the support of the working classes, many of whom (men only, and with property) had been newly enfranchised in 1867. In Disraeli's case, as we have seen, he combined this with an appeal to what he detected as the nascent imperial patriotism of the 'lower' orders, although his governments did far less in fact to extend the British Empire than the supposedly 'anti-imperial' Gladstone's. Which suggests either that Gladstone was a hypocrite, which was a charge levelled at him at the time; or that he was carried along on a tide he could not control. We shall return to this. Another of Gladstone's undoubted achievements was his implementation in 1870 of an old Report – 'Northcote-Trevelyan' (1854) – reforming the British Civil Service, and establishing its guiding principles – neutrality, anonymity, permanency, non-corruptibility and public service – until at least the 2010s.

Disraeli died in 1881, but Gladstone carried on as Liberal leader into the 1890s, when he was in his eighties, with his last spell as prime minister running from 1892 to 1894. The twenty years after the so-called 'Great Depression' of the 1870s were dominated, at the level of 'high' politics, by Irish and imperial affairs, and by the strains that both these issues exerted on the major parties. The 'Home Rule' crisis of 1886, which was the occasion of the Liberal Unionists' split with their Gladstonian fellows, may have had as much to do with the Empire as with Ireland itself, with the Liberals tarred as 'Little Englanders' in spite of the colonial wars and expansion that had gone on under them. The Conservatives became the 'imperial' (as well as the Unionist) party in the state, although both the Liberals and even the nascent Labour party were also tarred with this brush. The Liberals in fact split – once again – over the major imperial event of the period, the South African or Anglo-Boer War (1899–1902), into at least three factions: 'Liberal Imperialists' (or 'Limps'), 'Pro-Boers', and those in between, who weren't given a snappy label. Labour generally kept out of it; instinctively anti-imperialist probably, but wary of the *apparent* jingoism of the working-class mob outside. In any case the Labour Party regarded its whole function at this time – the early 1900s – as being the narrow class one of defending and advancing working-class interests, which foreign wars seemed to have no immediate relevance to.[14] In the medium term this did neither the Liberals nor Labour much harm, with the Conservatives winning a 'Khaki' ('patriotic') election at the height of the war, but the Left (or Left-ish) getting its own back in 1906, with a Liberal landslide victory and Labour winning 29 seats – a 'gain' of 28. By that time most people were tiring of imperialism, especially after the pig's ear their Army had made of the South African War, and when it looked like pushing the price of imported food up as a result of a new Conservative scheme to abandon 'free trade' in favour of 'imperial preference'. (The object of that was to bind the Empire closer together.) They also liked the look of the quite major social reforms that the Liberals seemed likely to bring in, and did: including state pensions, unemployment insurance, and free school meals. Many historians trace the origins of Britain's 'welfare state' back to these. They marked a big shift from the days of *laissez faire*.

It was not enough, however, to dissuade tens of thousands of workers from striking in what was dubbed the 'Great Labour Unrest' of 1911–14; the most serious manifestation of working-class dissatisfaction with the status quo – or with their place in it – between Chartism and the 1926 General Strike. In fact this whole *fin-de-siècle* period, starting around 1890 and culminating in the 'Great' (or 'First World') War, was one of turbulence in so many areas as possibly to indicate a quite fundamental fragility beneath the surface of what, in retrospect after the horrors of the said War, was fondly but wrongly remembered as a glorious 'Edwardian summer'. The emergence of socialism in party political form – the Independent Labour Party (1892); followed by the Labour Representation Committee (1900), soon to become the Labour Party proper – were the most obvious signs of this; together with the breakout of feminism in the forms of two 'suffragist' organizations, one mild, the other quite violent; and radical developments in local government, especially in the 'progressive' new London County Council. Then there was the fear, almost amounting to panic, of German invasion, which provoked the formation of Britain's first modern espionage agency, later called MI6, around 1910, but secretly – spying was 'un-British', remember – which is why we can't put an exact date to it. In 1906 the first 'Aliens Act' for eighty years was passed, giving the authorities the power to refuse admission to the country of poor (only) immigrants. That was in response to an influx of east European Jews, fleeing from Russian persecution, over the past ten years, and nativist and even anti-Semitic demonstrations in London's East End (but mainly confined to there). At around the same time covert 'counter-subversion' was also extended to the domestic field, with the emergence of 'MI5' to keep a watch not only on German spies in Britain, but also on – for example – the suffragettes.[15] These marked further major divergences from the 'values' that had characterized the Victorian age, and may have indicated that those values were unsustainable over the long term, after all.

That would not be surprising, at a time when the whole basis of Britain's economy and therefore society and culture was being thrown into confusion by larger developments in the world outside: foreign industrial competition, especially German; rival empires, especially German potentially; the slow but inexorable growth of the financial sector, on its way to displacing manufacture as the staple of the economy (though not nearly there yet); and – a minor one this, perhaps, but important later – the increasing sophistication of an advertising industry, bringing an amorality into public life which of course had always been there, even under the godly Victorians, but was now thrust to the forefront. (H. G. Wells, the foremost chronicler of the sins of this age, including his own, published a novel – *Tono-Bungay* – about it in 1909.) The literature of the time reflected much of this; possibly most of all – albeit tangentially – the wave of 'Science Fiction' and futuristic novels that began to appear, (Wells's *War of the Worlds* wasn't the only one), most of them *dys-* rather than *u*-topian. Contemporary social and artistic movements reflected this uncertainty about the country's situation in a variety of what at the time appeared weird forms: vegetarianism; whole-foodism; pacifism; various forms of anarchism; Baden-Powell boy scouting; 'free love'; a 'Rational Dress Society' (women wearing trousers? Whatever next?!); homosexuality: not exactly a 'movement', but with its own discreet networks amongst the upper and artistic classes; various odd religious sects; poetry that didn't scan or rhyme; decadent and erotic art (Aubrey Beardsley): not all of these unique to the turn-of-the-century period, but particularly characteristic of it, and possibly – though who is to say, in particular with respect to 'art', which doesn't always 'reflect its times'? – symptomatic of a general national unease. At the very least they indicate that some people were speculating about how things *might* be, in the post-Victorian age.

Woven into all this were the implications and effects of British colonial expansion and rule; which were of course of great concern to some Edwardians, but in many different ways. We'll return to this in the next chapter.

*

Things were falling apart, therefore, even before the 'Great' War hit Britain in August 1914. In fact this alarmed much of the British political and military Establishment of the time, who were not at all confident, for example, that the striking working classes would rally to the flag 'patriotically' if it came to sending them to France to fight. Contingency plans were prepared for shooting rioters and looters on sight in British cities,[16] and it was always made plain that deserters would be shot, and 'conchies' (conscientious objectors) imprisoned, after compulsory military service came in early in

1916. Before then the volunteering was impressive, possibly out of 'patriotism' but more likely because it seemed exciting; because men could serve in regiments with their 'mates'; because it was a paid job, at least; but mainly because it was almost universally assumed that the war would be a short one – 'over by Christmas'. When it really got going, and turned out to be not nearly so much fun as anticipated, ordinary soldiers endured the appalling conditions in the trenches not so much out of patriotism but in order not to let their 'mates' and their loved ones down. Most of them despised their senior commanding officers and the politicians back home, who had landed them in this mess, at least as much as they hated the Germans. Class loyalty trumped national in this case.[17]

The end of the War saw a resumption of the industrial unrest that had plagued the pre-War period, culminating in the General Strike of 1926. It also saw big changes in Parliament, with (older) women winning the right to vote, plus more working-class men, to the benefit of the Labour Party, which actually formed a (minority and short-lived) government in 1924. Looking abroad, it also saw a Communist party taking over Russia, and very nearly in defeated Germany too. All this caused something close to panic in the British ruling class, one of the effects of which was to sustain the powers of the secret services long after the end of the War that had originally appeared to justify them. In 1920 the head of MI5 prepared a plan to hive off his department to a private agency that could continue its work of tracking Leftists, unanswerable to government, in the event that that government turned out to be a socialist one.[18] It's not known for sure whether that succeeded; but in any case there were plenty of clandestine and also overt anti-socialist organizations around. Some of these – or it may have been MI5 itself, in cahoots with the *Daily Mail* – will have been partly responsible for the Labour government's failure to secure re-election in 1924, when a forgery (the 'Zinoviev Letter') was printed in the *Mail* in the last days of the election campaign, implying that Labour was being manipulated from Moscow.[19] Some of these right-wing groups from the early 1920s were openly 'Fascist', designed on the Italian model: one of them, unusually, led by a woman; but with the assertively masculine Oswald Mosley's British Union of Fascists (BUF), founded in 1932, being the best known and most effective of them. The *Daily Mail* of the time supported the Fascists both in Britain and in Germany, which it has never been allowed to forget – in left-wing circles, anyway. Britain has always prided itself on resisting the Fascist siren, as contrary to 'Britishness'; but the *Mail*'s example shows that Britain might not have done so if it were not in the first place for Fascist Germany's becoming the national enemy in 1939; and secondly for the fact that British right-wing patriots had another flag – the imperial one – to rally round.

The rise of the Labour Party came at the expense of the Liberals, who had been leaning in Labour's direction for some time now, as we have seen – espousing their new and less fundamentalist view of 'liberty' – and some of whom in the interwar period slipped over to Labour quite easily. But that still left the Liberals the second-largest party in Parliament, although they were never able to form a government after 1922 (and that one was in coalition). So the Tories dominated British politics until the Second World War, through the next 'Great Depression' of the 1930s, triggered by a Wall Street 'crash', to which they responded with what later became known as 'austerity', causing widespread distress and hunger; as austerity invariably does. In 1931 they persuaded the Liberal Party and some Labour MPs, including their leader Ramsay MacDonald, to form a coalition or 'National' government to see the crisis through; for which MacDonald was widely excoriated as a 'traitor' by the Labour MPs he left behind, and is still regarded as such in the Labour Party today. His 'betrayal', however, pales beside Winston Churchill's, who switched parties twice: from Conservative to Liberal in 1904, and back again in 1924. 'Anyone can rat,' he is reported to have told his private secretary, 'but it takes a certain amount of ingenuity to re-rat.'[20] That left him in a good position to help his party navigate the next crisis of the interwar period, which was, of course, the coming of the Second War itself.

Politicians then were divided over whether to 'appease' Hitler or not. Many Conservatives welcomed his stand against Russian communism, and may have shared some of his other prejudices. (Even Churchill at one point appeared to enthuse over the discipline and patriotism of the *Hitler Jugend*.)[21] Mosley, the leader of the BUF, had once been a Labour MP, until he lost patience with the whole Parliamentary system's inability to 'get things done'. (*Im*patience is a common Fascist trait.) Labour contained a few principled pacifists, but were otherwise solidly anti-Nazi, and were the ones who mainly projected the warrior Churchill into the premiership after the Conservative policy of appeasement had failed. It should be pointed out in fairness to Neville Chamberlain – one of history's great villains after his notorious Munich trip – that he used the time gained by the latter to set in motion re-armament for the trial to come. If Britain had stood firm in 1938, the country would almost certainly have been defeated. Thereafter, however, and right through the War, it was the working classes who were most steadfast in their support of it, according to official government surveys, and the uppers who appeared most flaky.[22] This needs saying, in view of the common misapprehension that because Churchill was a Tory, Labour must have been on the other side. The Second World War, from Britain's point of view, was a *People*'s war, not to be credited (or debited) to any particular party. This was reflected too in the make-up of Churchill's war cabinet, which included a couple of Labour MPs, including his deputy Clement Attlee; who incidentally had had a far better First World War record than Churchill – he saw more action, and worked his way *up* to Major – though he made less of a song and dance about it.

Some modern 'patriots' appear to believe that under Churchill Britain 'won' the Second World War; which of course it didn't, in any real sense. If one is seeking to distribute medals to collective entities like 'nations' in this conflict, Britain assuredly deserves some: for 'standing alone' against Germany in the very early months, for example: a genuinely heroic national act; for the 'Battle of Britain', fighting Goering's airborne invasion of its south coast in the summer and autumn of 1940; for its people's resilience during the 'Blitzkrieg' of London and other cities in 1940–1 and thereafter; for the ingenuity and hard work of the men and women at Bletchley Park who managed to break the German codes – for example of crucial messages to U-Boat commanders; for the individual bravery in appalling conditions of most of its soldiers, sailors and airmen, justly both celebrated and regretted on 'Remembrance Days' (11 November) subsequently; and, for all I know (I'm no military expert), for one or two land victories in Europe and North Africa. The code-breaker Alan Turing, hounded to death after the war on account of his homosexuality, is rightly remembered today – even being pictured on a UK banknote – for *his* contribution. But these accomplishments – however admirable, even heroic – didn't win the War for Britain. The British Empire helped, with brave battalions recruited from Canada, Australia, New Zealand and India (South Africa wasn't quite so keen), and volunteers from most of the countries the Germans had occupied. (More than a hundred Battle of Britain airmen – conventionally pictured as rosy-cheeked young Public school boys – were in fact Poles.) But the major contributions to the allies' victory came from the USSR and the USA, when they eventually joined in (in June and December 1941 respectively, both after they were invaded themselves); and by far the greatest sacrifice – more than 20 million dead – was made by the Soviets.

Still, Britain came out on the winning side, and Churchill as the hero of the hour: not because of any particular contribution he had made to military strategy – contemporaries agreed that most of his ideas in this field were impractical – or because of his previous history as an MP and a minister, which was patchy, to put the best construction on it: it's the particular form of his 'imperialism' that has attracted the most criticism of him in these post-imperial times; but because of his foresight of the Nazi threat in the 1930s; his steadfastness despite regular bouts of depression; his very 'image', if you like, as the personification of the 'British bulldog'; and his inspiring speeches to rally the people (if they needed to be rallied) during the War. 'I was not the lion', he said after it was all over – that was the people; 'but it fell to me to give the lion's roar'.[23] That seems fair, and possibly enough to outweigh his considerable deficiencies; most of which were common among the upper classes of his time. (Don't be misled by the other title that was sometimes bestowed on him, as the 'Great Commoner'. He was born in a palace, for goodness' sake.) It was enough, in any case, to elevate Churchill in the British historical Pantheon as *the* great patriotic hero; around whom the political Right, especially, could rally round for decades after his death in 1965, and after a State funeral such as no other British politician had been afforded since the Duke of Wellington in 1852. And Wellington was easily the better soldier of the two.

*

We shall come on to the post-War period in a later chapter, after we've dealt with imperialism, whose neglect may be felt to be surprising in the foregoing narrative, but which requires a separate chapter to dispose of the confusions that have surrounded it ever since the British Empire's 'decline and fall'. But 1945 is a convenient point to pause in any case, and to try to sum up what Britain had become by then.

The country had gone through two total wars and a major trade depression since 1914, not to mention (yet) the dozens of colonial wars that had clearly – though this wasn't so clear to Churchill – weakened it considerably. The broader context of this was a global struggle between two politico-economic systems, capitalism and communism, or by another way of looking at them democracy of a kind and socialism of a kind, or – by a third way of looking – the USSR and the USA; which was to dominate international politics, and also to an extent Britain's domestic politics, until at least the 1980s. This period (from 1914) followed a century of relative peace and security for Britain, although not in the colonies or Ireland, and not for those whose social situations – usually at the 'bottom' – left them far from secure. Despite this the nineteenth century in particular was a period of clear if irregular 'progress', by the ways 'progress' was measured at that time: growing prosperity overall, industry and trade increasing exponentially, liberal freedoms extended, 'democracy' advancing, the people's health improving, and the bounds of knowledge expanding. This was at a time when Britain's nearest neighbours mostly lagged behind economically, and some of them didn't even have settled national boundaries yet, giving rise to wars and even revolutions that Britain could easily keep out of. The wider world was free for Britain to explore and plunder. So the nineteenth century could be said to be a 'lucky' time for Britain as a nation, although the luck was already starting to pall when the twentieth century came on.

What if the First World War had never happened? (It was a pretty pointless war in any case.) One result might have been that Britain continued the decline that a number of perceptive contemporary observers were already strongly predicting in the early 1900s – it was one of the reasons for their wanting to beef up the Empire, in order to reverse or slow the trend – so that Britain's slide from the top of the mountain would be obvious to its people too. But that didn't happen. For a number of reasons – chief among them the fact that the USA and the USSR, the two emerging 'superpowers', receded into their shells for different reasons after the War was over – Britain was placed in the *false* position of still being seen, and seeing itself, as a 'great power' on the back of its (and America's) victorious War. That seemed to be confirmed by the result of the Second World War, after which Britain was given part of Germany to look after until it was democratized, and a place at all the diplomatic 'tables' that would work out how Europe (and the world) would be organized afterwards. These included a permanent seat on the new United Nations' Security Council, which, if the other Councillors had known it, future world developments would hardly entitle it to.

The result was an inflated sense among many Britons of their own importance, which made its *de*flation in the post-war years particularly hard to bear. This was one of the results of its having won – well, helped to win – the Second World War. The illusion may have been strengthened by the fact that it still had a worldwide Empire – or most of it. That wasn't to last.

3

Empire

Britain's relationship with its world-wide empire has always been complicated, as have its colonial subjects' relationships with Britain.[1] This is another reason why we shouldn't generalize too much about British 'imperialism', and what it signified. In particular, we shouldn't lump it together indiscriminately with other historical 'imperialisms'. Some in nineteenth-century Britain did tend to do this: the Public school 'Old Boys', for example, who had been brought up on the 'Classics', and took pride in the echoes of the *imperium Romanum* they thought they detected in their own 'Greater Britain'. Others however emphasized the differences they claimed lay between the two, with the British being an empire of 'freedom', either actually (Australia, Canada); or potentially: when the natives had been 'civilized'. That – however strange and even hypocritical it seemed to foreigners, and even to some Britons – helped to reconcile 'liberal' Britons to what otherwise would appear a highly illiberal enterprise.

Indeed, both ways of regarding it are misleading; the result of employing the word 'imperialism' too generally, and usually – on the Left – too pejoratively; without taking notice of the complex of activities that came under its name, and which should be individually debited, or credited, with its outcomes, rather than 'imperialism' per se.

*

Here is how it came about. Britain's Empire went back a long way – some claimed to mediaeval times (Ireland, Wales, Calais); but in its modern form it had its roots in Britain's 'industrial revolution'. As Britain's manufacturing boomed as a result of this, so did exports overseas. This wasn't inevitable. Most countries in history have simply produced what they needed for their own populations, and exchanged their little surpluses for imports of things that could not be made or grown at home. But Britain's commerce was much bigger than that. It manufactured products *for* export, which probably could have been consumed by its own people if they had had the means; but which they didn't, because most of them were too poor. That was the late Victorian and Edwardian economist John Atkinson Hobson's explanation for the British imperial expansion of his day: manufacturers – and those who invested in their businesses – needed world-wide markets for surpluses which were only surplus because their economic system impoverished the people who otherwise might have been their customers at home.[2] The solution was to redistribute wealth. If the working classes were paid enough, they would consume the stuff – or most of it – that presently was being sold abroad.

That, according to Hobson, explained Britain's excess foreign trade. It is obviously a simplistic solution (Hobson's version was more nuanced), and also, of course, a rather socialistic one for those capitalist times. As well as this, it doesn't cover some of the much less reputable trades British merchants were engaged in: slaves from Africa, for example, although that came to an end at the beginning of our period; and the trade in opium between India (where it was grown) and China, which still went on, and gave rise to a couple of wars: the British insisting on supplying the drug to the poor Chinese against Chinese government objections, in the interests of 'free trade' – and of course of the traders themselves. Nor does it explain why even the fairer sorts of trade should sometimes morph into *imperialism*: seizing the countries you traded with, or wished to, rather than leaving them to decide for themselves whether they wanted your goods or markets. (In China's case that resulted in the acquisition, on a long lease, of the hinterland of Hong Kong.) A common reason given for that was that many of those countries were unable to provide the basic conditions for a free and fair trade between them and Britain, either because they were politically unstable, or what Britons called 'primitive'; or in some cases were threatened by another country – a neighbour, or one of Britain's European rivals – which might not be as open to the idea of a 'free and fair trade' as Britain was. Some of the 'instability' was caused by wicked or just clumsy British merchants rubbing native peoples up the wrong way, provoking reprisals that then the merchants felt it was their government's duty to avenge. The latter was usually chary of intervening in this way: that is, with armed force – hence the term 'reluctant imperialism' sometimes applied to this stage in the imperial process; but if the men in whose interests the intervention took place were British subjects – as not all of them were – Britain as a country had to take some of the responsibility, whether it be seen as to its credit or to its blame. The same applied when the intervention became more intensive: setting up plantations, for example, or digging mines, using native labour. (Not slave labour any more, after its formal abolition in 1833; but often pretty close.) At that stage Britain felt it *had* to take over their countries, if their potential was to be fully exploited; to the natives' advantage it was always claimed, but more obviously to Britain's and its capitalists'. This isn't to excuse these imperialists, of course; only to explain.

After the first commercial incursions into these people's countries had been made (or sometimes a little earlier), other men and women with different motives came in to complicate things. They included explorers, adventurers, missionaries and anti-slavers: men like the Welshman Henry

Morton Stanley, who saw it as his duty to put a stop to the cruel Arab slave-trading that still persisted across Africa after 1833, capturing the Africans who were then marched to the west coast to be shipped abroad. In the course of that, as well as 'finding' the missionary-explorer David Livingstone – his most famous exploit, although Livingstone wasn't exactly lost: *he* knew where he was – Stanley helped secure much of central Africa for the British crown; as well as – deeply unfortunately – for King Leopold II of the Belgians. (He turned out to be the most villainous imperialist of the lot.) That – annexation – was where the Public school-educated upper and upper-middle classes came in. Their Classical texts had taught them all about 'ruling', the Public school ethos prepared them for it morally, and the sport and cold baths fitted their bodies for it; so out they went to 'look after' and hopefully 'civilize' the poor benighted 'primitives' who were sheltering under the Great White Queen's motherly wing. They were never very many, incidentally; fewer in total over the whole of the Empire (disregarding the natives trained up to assist them), than are required to run a medium-sized English municipality today.[3] So they were always fairly vulnerable; which forced them to 'get along' with their subjects as best they could, militating against their developing any 'race prejudice', aside from a degree of condescension towards their 'inferiors'. But they had that in Britain vis-à-vis the workers too. Some of them became so enamoured of their new environments, especially in India, as to lead them to stay on there after retirement, and even after the Empire had gone. Many of them felt the 'old country' had gone to pot then in any case. All that socialism, for a start; and the fact that they were usually reviled as imperialists – their services not acknowledged, let alone admired – back 'home'.

It is difficult to generalize about the motivations of the people who went out to win and rule Britain's Empire in the nineteenth and twentieth centuries, and probably wrong to try. They comprised Scots, Welsh and Irish as well as English, with Scotland if anything contributing more to Britain's imperial 'push' than any other Home nationality. (Don't believe Scots who try to portray themselves as imperial 'subjects' or 'victims' of the English, historically.) One historian, Ronald Hyam, attributes it – tongue in cheek, probably – to the desire for sex, more freely available to frustrated European males in the less stuffy colonies; otherwise known as the 'surplus sex urges' theory of imperialism (to rival Hobson's 'surplus capital'). Much of this would be classed, rightly, as sexual exploitation today. But in any case, their *motives* were not necessarily the underlying reasons for this major but not unique phenomenon in modern history – most other European countries with coastlines shared in it, after all, in France's case in a substantial way – which makes any value judgements about imperialism in *terms* of 'motives' unreliable. It also undermines the position of those 'patriots' who look back at the 'Titans Who Forged Britain' – to quote the subtitle of a recent and widely panned book on *The Victorians* by Jacob Rees-Mogg – 'this clichéd, lazy history often reads like it was written by a baboon', was how the *Daily*

Telegraph reviewed it[4] – when actually they were themselves very largely forged by the situation in which Britain found itself in the nineteenth century. Not only Rees-Mogg, but other observers and students, often present the British Empire as a 'project', achieved by (usually heroic) individuals, or 'imperial*ists*'. In fact impersonal forces, both domestic and international, especially the 'natural' growth of 'capitalism', may have been of greater underlying importance; casting doubt on the 'great men' view of history, which still seems to be common popularly, and especially on the Right; but also on the propensity of critics to load the *blame* on individuals – like on the pretty unpleasant Cecil Rhodes – when things go 'wrong'. This is quite apart from the usual defence made of them, and a plausible one: that their opinions and activities should only be 'judged' in the context of their times and – in the case of Churchill, for example, whose name is often brought up in this regard – their upbringings. (The Head of Churchill's Public school, a great imperial zealot, had a lot to answer for.)[5] The Empire is especially suited to this kind of interpretation in terms of personalities, peopled as it was by so many men – and a few women – who at the time seemed 'larger than life'. That of course is ideal for focussing novels, feature films and TV dramas on. Impersonal forces and even 'contexts' are far harder to dramatize.

*

For Britain the Empire became a thing of some pride, but not generally speaking until well after the middle of the nineteenth century. Before then its people were too imbued with the idea that theirs was a liberal country, leading the world to a stage where, as we saw the Free Trader Richard Cobden put it in 1846, wars and empires would fade to nothing, and mankind would become 'one family', each member of it exchanging goods with the others peacefully.[6] Shortly after that Cobden was instrumental in negotiating Britain's first free trade treaty with France; which might now be seen as a very early small step towards the creation of the free trade area later known as the European Union. He was wrong, of course; free trade didn't augur an idyllic world of brotherly love – even between Britain and France. But his ideas still resonated long after his death in 1865, informing a discourse in Britain that was always a significant rival to what is supposed to have been the dominant 'imperialist' one. We shall come on to this later.

The Empire is often presented as a single great entity, all coloured in the same shade of red (with a few exceptions, like the 'Anglo-Egyptian Sudan', and some pinker bits in the middle of India), but in fact it comprised at least two distinct types of 'colony': one 'dependent' and directly ruled, the other self-governing – so far as its settlers were concerned. Few people back in Britain were equally enamoured of both sorts. The governing classes liked the 'ruled' parts, and rather looked down on colonies like Australia and Canada where mainly lower-class Britons emigrated in order to be 'free': free-er than they had been, generally, back in the mother country, and nearly always more prosperous. Many Britons, incidentally, migrated to and can even be said to have 'colonized', parts of the European Continent. They are usually ignored in accounts of British emigration, because they can't really be characterized as 'imperialists'. But they may shed some light on the other emigrants' situations and motives.[7] And beyond all this – though often before it in time – was what has come to be called Britain's 'informal' empire, of trade and investment, carried on in such a way as to give it a dominating influence over its ostensibly free customers, and other advantages. This is also called 'the imperialism of free trade', and of course exists to the present day, under the name of 'soft power'. The USA is supposed to have been its main practitioner over the last century, but may be being superseded by China today.

So far as the *echt* 'settlement' Empire was concerned even convicts, shipped to south-eastern Australia against their wills (obviously), could flourish mightily after their sentences came to an end, and were often granted parcels of land to make a living on. Recent research has suggested that these weren't always 'low' criminals in any case, but political offenders: either ostensibly, or because stealing could be seen as a kind of 'political' crime – against ill-gotten property.[8] (This has encouraged long-settled Australians to begin to take pride in their convict origins. Fifty years ago they mostly claimed to be descended from warders. If that were true, someone worked out, there must have been twenty warders guarding each convict.) Much later (transportation ended in 1850), a great deal of effort was put into encouraging emigration to the 'settlement' colonies, to ease overcrowding and poverty back in Britain; and for some people in order to solidify an 'Empire' that Britons could take pride in. The settlers themselves – apart from the rebellious Irish – also generally remained proud of their British origins and connections; choosing to teach themselves British history rather than their own colonial or regional histories (again: don't believe Australians who tell you this was forced on them by an oppressive imperial regime); and adopting the new 'Empire Day' holiday (24 May) long before the stay-at-home Brits. Of course – and it may be demeaning to them to treat these people only as a footnote – none of this applied to the native populations of these colonies: the original Australians ('Aborigines'), New Zealanders ('Maoris') and Canadians ('Indians'); most of whom were treated atrociously – by the European settlers, not their metropolitan government. The Maoris, highly skilled in warfare, probably came off best. The European populations of these colonies however were virtually 'free' throughout the nineteenth century; and became more formally free in the twentieth. By that time they were coming to be called 'Dominions', in order to distinguish them from the Empire's lower, 'Dependent' level.

*

'Lower' it might have been, measured in terms of this 'freedom'; but one directly-ruled colony was accorded immeasurably more status than any of the others, and has come to represent the spectacular side of 'British imperialism' for most people today. India, in fact, wasn't even technically a 'colony', but rather an 'Empire' in its own right. It was ruled from Britain, true; but from the offices of a commercial trading company at the beginning of our period, and from an 'India Office' quite separate from the 'Colonial' one after the great 'Indian Mutiny' – as it was called in Britain, to make it sound somehow less than a 'war of independence', which in many ways it was – of 1857–8. The two Offices hardly ever exchanged personnel, and the India Office had a *cachet* very much of its own. It even had its own 'Public' school to service it: Haileybury in Hertfordshire, full name 'Haileybury and Imperial Service College', founded in 1807 by the Company that ran the Indian empire before the British government took over the formal reins. Haileybury even had tutors shipped in from the subcontinent to teach its pupils the local languages, which the Colonial Office never bothered with. Clement Attlee, the Labour prime minister, was an Old Haileyburian, which might be thought to suggest a link between socialism and the paternalism of the past. It also had a short-lived daughter school, called 'Westward Ho!' (with the exclamation mark) in Devon, which was cheaper and distinguished from other Public schools by beating boys on their backs rather than their buttocks.[9] The Anglo-Indian Rudyard Kipling – storyteller, inspirational poet and later Nobel Prizewinner – went there.

Indian civil servants were reputed to be brighter than 'Colonial' ones. In the twentieth century applicants to join the Colonial service were rejected if they were thought to be too clever. (One was turned down when it was found that he had completed the *Times* crossword in the waiting room.)[10] 'Character' was what was needed in imperial prefects; and probity. That was important, and stood against Colonial governors' ever seeking to *profit* from their posts in Africa or wherever, aside of course from their generous salaries, early retirement on good pensions, and long 'furloughs' in order to help them recover from their often demanding duties in the tropical heat. Most of them would have felt rightly insulted if they had been lumped together with the *exploiters* of their colonies – the capitalists, planters, mine-owners, settlers – as a single category of 'imperialists'. They were, after all, Public school-educated (usually 'minor' Public schools. Not Eton). Much of their time in fact was spent trying to protect their 'subjects' from the harm done by these people, and by their racist attitudes; not necessarily more 'racist' than their own, but more dismissive and dangerous than the prefects' often paternalistic – but still wounding – sort. One of the reasons for this was to prevent native rebellions, which could be costly in view of the rulers' small numbers (again), and the reluctance of the Home government to back them up. Another, however, was the genuine respect for native societies and institutions that many of them developed 'in the field', and which annoyed the exploiting imperialists greatly.

It is important to realize – it often is not – that British imperial rulers were not generally all that keen on forcing their 'Western ways' on subject peoples;

especially after the shock of the 1857 Indian 'Mutiny', and with the exception of the Christian missionaries whose proselytizing efforts were often blamed for that event. In west Africa the same considerations fed into what became a distinctively British model of colonial government in the twentieth century, called 'Indirect Rule', or 'Rule the Native on Native Lines', accompanied by an economic model of 'Peasant Proprietorship': natives owning their land and cultivating *it* along their own lines, albeit with technical help from the Colonial government. This was supposed to make British colonial rule less onerous; and also to an extent less 'racist', or at least racist only in a paternalistic way. British capitalist 'developers' hated this too. One moved his palm-oil industry out of a British colony into a neighbouring one in order to avoid these restrictions on his enterprise.[11] But of course colonial subjects could pick up Western ways regardless. Later, African nationalists objected to 'Indirect Rule', seeing it as a way of keeping the natives 'down'. Which was of course one of the motives; but not the only one, and not an especially 'capitalist' one.

Imperial rule became most problematical when both these sorts of 'colony' were combined. Majority native colonies with substantial minorities of European settlers caused British governments more trouble than any others outside India, and can probably be regarded as the least 'successful' examples of British colonial rule; and hence the least deserving – if any can be regarded as at all deserving – of retrospective patriotic 'pride'. South Africa, Rhodesia (Zimbabwe) and Kenya are the leading examples of colonies that went very wrong indeed; together with three colonies (one strictly a 'Mandated Territory') where ethnic rivalries that didn't involve Britons made governing them very difficult indeed. All these colonies, Cyprus, Malaya and Palestine, together with India, were in the end 'partitioned'. In Palestine's case it was in a way that pleased virtually no-one, with the Jewish immigrants – the equivalents of 'white settlers' elsewhere – wanting more of a country which they claimed God (no less) had 'promised' them, and which they felt they required in order to protect them after the recent horrors of anti-Semitism in Europe; and on the other side the Arabs, who had taken the land over since God had left the Jews to their own devices, demanding their country back, or at least their own independent nation alongside the new state of 'Israel'. That last conflict, of course, is with us still.

This is not the place to go into the details of these colonial conflicts, distressing and appalling as they usually were. They included wars, racism, bad faith, betrayals, atrocities on all sides (but including of course by the British), extra-judicial hangings, bombings, 'shooting men from guns' (in the Indian Mutiny), avoidable famines (India again), rape and pillage worthy of the Vikings, forcing prisoners to eat their own genitals and pushing hot eggs into women's vaginas (both in Kenya),[12] hut- and farm-burning, strafing Iraqi villagers from planes, the notorious South African 'concentration camps' (but not at all the same as the Nazis': these were designed to *protect*

Boer women and children from the warfare that their men were engaged in, although they didn't do that very well: disease in the camps was rife) . . . and probably much more. These atrocities are more familiar to us now than they used to be, with some of them only now becoming publicly revealed. (For years the records of the African ones were squirrelled away in Hanslope Park, an adjunct of the British Public Record Office which historians were not meant to know about. It was only a Court of Law, answering to cases brought by ex-victims, that got it opened up.)[13] It is these horrors that have given British imperialism such a poor reputation today; clearly justifiably, even if atrocity cannot be shown to have been essential to the original 'project'.

In this connexion, indeed, it is worth emphasizing that not all these atrocities, and other 'bad' results of empire, *were* the results of an original malevolence on the 'imperialist side'. In other words, you didn't have to be a Fascist to be an imperialist. (Churchill wasn't.) In Kenya, yes, and the southern African settler colonies; but otherwise it is important to recognize that bad results could stem from the best – even the most humanitarian – of intentions, with interference in alien societies and polities often causing harm regardless of their motives. The British and Americans learned this in Iraq and Afghanistan in the early twenty-first century, disastrously for those two countries and their peoples, and painfully and indeed fatally for many of their own brave troops. Of course the motives in both of these cases were mixed; but one doesn't need to attribute 'evil' ones to Bush, Blair and their successors in order to condemn their *judgement* in invading these countries. Even the best of intentions can turn out badly. It is also important to be aware of how these places were *before* the imperialists took over. In many of them the people's lives were pretty rotten, even under their own rulers, and at the mercy of – for example – Arab and Moslem (not European and Christian) slave traders. That said, however, it is difficult to ignore at least the Europeans' cultural arrogance, however well-meant, that contributed to many – not all – of these and other post-imperial disasters.

Indeed, when the British state got into these kinds of situation, it was usually as policemen (not police-women, yet) rather than as colonialists or imperialists, and certainly not as exploiters, although many of the situations they had to 'police' had been created by the imperialists and exploiters in the first place. Some of them were not the faults of 'colonialism' at all; or not of *British* colonialism especially. It could be Moslem or Hindu in India (*possibly* exacerbated by British 'divide and rule' methods), or Chinese in Malaya, or Turkish or Greek in Cyprus, or Jewish in Palestine. 'Policing' presented Britain with different and often quite intractable problems. Palestine was a major example: wracked with terrorism on both sides of the divide, and panned as Britain has been on each of those sides for its 'favouritism' towards the other. Britain may have been held back by naïveté: unable to see why these peoples couldn't live together peaceably; Britain had different 'tribes' of its own, after all, who didn't go around slaughtering one another.

(This was before the Northern Irish 'Troubles'. And Ireland was an exception – an exceptional ex-colony, indeed – in many ways.) Nonetheless, if we feel we need to pass judgement, Britain (or past British governments) should not be exonerated from guilt for *allowing* most of these horrors; so long, that is, as we recognize that the Empire's worst atrocities do not necessarily paint a complete picture of it. The only message the above account has tried to convey is to point out the complexity of the whole scene, making generalization here – as in many other cases – grossly misleading. Just as there wasn't a single 'Britain' (Chapter 1), so neither was there a single and indissoluble 'British Empire', but many of them; acquired at different times, in different ways, and with different problems. 1950s Kenya was not 1950s Nigeria, or even 1920s Kenya; and obviously not Australia, at any point in the latter's history.

*

The other important thing to note about the Empire, especially in view of the historical myths that surround it, is how essentially *weak* it always was. Here all those red-stained world maps may have contributed to the myth; together with the examples of former empires, the Roman especially; and possibly the word 'empire' itself. That comes from a Latin word meaning 'command, control or dominion'; which gives a misleading picture of what in reality was a rather loose and in places highly vulnerable collection of countries bound together formally, but not as tightly and powerfully as *soi-disants* 'imperialists' would have liked. It is supposed to have made Britain *the* 'Great Power' of the nineteenth and early twentieth centuries, on a level with the indisputably Great Powers that succeeded it – the USA, the USSR, and now China (incidentally British imperialists had predicted China's rise as early as the turn of the twentieth century) – but that hid an awful lot of flaws in its design. That was probably because it *wasn't* 'designed' in any meaningful sense, but just grew, 'like Topsy'. The flaws included a small and generally inefficient land army, by comparison with France, Russia and Germany/Prussia, except when it came to fighting Africans armed only with assegais, or in India, whose Army was separate and its native soldiery particularly proud and effective. (Even with its help, Britain nearly always lost against the Afghans.) This meant that Britain was one of the weakest of the *European* powers. Hence its avoidance of Continental wars between 1815 and 1914, relying as it did on diplomacy to keep itself from being attacked. After 1914 the deficiencies of its Army were shown up time and time again (*vide* Gallipoli and Singapore),[14] with only the help of the dominions and the intervention of the USA in 1917 and of the USA and the USSR in 1941 saving it from probable defeat. Britain's weakness in this and in other ways also explains – if it doesn't excuse – its failure to control its imperialists on the ground. Economically too the country was falling behind Germany, especially, from the early 1900s onward. In many ways it was something of a miracle that it survived half of the twentieth century with its

Empire more or less intact; indeed, slightly augmented after 1918, with the League of Nations 'mandated' territories it gained. That was mainly due to the USA's and the USSR's withdrawal from the scene, for different reasons, leaving no-one to challenge Britain seriously.

Apart, that is, from 'the natives'. They started getting very restless indeed in certain parts of the Empire in the interwar period, notably India, Ireland and Egypt, leading to forced concessions of independence or near-independence for all three. The 'dominions' were also released from the very loose and mainly theoretical control that London had been supposed to exert over them, by the 'Statute of Westminster', passed in 1931. (In these latter cases the true 'natives', their indigenous peoples, were largely ignored.) Palestine – one of the imperial 'gains' Britain was supposed to have made from the first War – was even more troublesome, and in the event turned out to be no gain at all. ('Troublesome', of course, is putting it mildly.) Indeed, this could be said of the entire Empire after 1918, and indeed – incipiently – for some years before. In this historian's view, the real 'decline and fall' of the British Empire began with the British Army's pathetic performance against the tiny amateur army of rebellious 'Boers' (Dutch-origin immigrants) in South Africa in 1899–1902; a war that it was supposed to have won, but at the expense of conceding almost everything the Boers had demanded, including their right to be racist in relation to their African natives. Not that the British in South Africa objected too loudly to that.

*

Britain has usually been good at making the best of bad jobs. It's part of its reputation (in France, for example) for 'perfidy'. Seeing how the wind was blowing, its more liberal imperialists reverted to an idea that had often been touted in the previous century, quite genuinely, of turning their 'Empire' into a broad society or confederation of free and independent nations: rather like the League of Nations was projected at that time, or the United States of America, or the German *Zollverein*, or the later European Union. The name for this that emerged between the Wars was the 'British Commonwealth', or 'Commonwealth of Nations', or later simply '*The* Commonwealth'; with its original membership comprising the existing 'white' Dominions, but with India now added, and with the prospect of all the directly-ruled 'dependencies' joining up later – as most of them did – when they were 'granted' their independence. However we assess the present Commonwealth's role in the world, it could be regarded as a noble ideal, nobler in one way than the European Common Market, in that it was more multi-'racial'; and there can be scarcely any doubt that it eased the pain of 'losing' the Empire for many Britons, convinced as they were that a 'commonwealth' of some kind had been the goal of the 'imperial project' all along.

In fact there is some evidence for that. The early Victorian historian, poet and Secretary to the Indian Board of Control Thomas Babington Macaulay, for example, claimed in 1835 that the day India achieved independence would be 'the proudest day in English history'.[15] The fly in that ointment is his insistence that the Indians would have to become thoroughly Anglicized before they merited that – reading Shakespeare, for example, before the Hindu epics – which indicates 'cultural imperialism' on a large scale; but it at least it wasn't a race-based prejudice; which might be said to be something in its favour? (Or not.) It also tied in with the old liberal idea of British imperialism's being an educative and humanitarian venture rather than simply a matter of conquering, exploiting and enslaving, which might be regarded as foolish and delusional, but was not wicked. (True 'conservatives' are much sounder in this regard: 'leave them alone'.) Traces of this 'liberal imperialism' persisted even into the post-(formal) imperial age, especially in the excuses given – and possibly believed – by the Americans and Tony Blair for their military interventions overseas.

None of this is intended to defend or excuse the British Empire; which in any case was too *natural* a phenomenon to require a defence. All countries, as little Finland's President Paasikivi admitted to a visiting German diplomat in 1940, would seek colonies and empire if they were big and strong enough.[16] Britain was that, of course, relative to the places it needed to trade with, influence and control. Most nations of the world have expanded, or been the results of expansion. (Otherwise – if the ethnologists are right – we would still all be huddled together in the Rift Valley of Kenya today.) Growth is a fundamental law of every kind of nature; and of the capitalism that could be seen as the real and original offender when it comes to most British 'imperialist' crimes: 'expand or die'. With this in mind, it might be the strong nations which have elected to stay within their original borders that need to be explained.

Today 'imperialism' is still happening right across the world, albeit usually in what historians call 'informal' guises rather than the blatant conquests of the past. The spread of McDonald's fast food outlets is often cited as an example of American 'soft empire'; as well as foreign investment, wherever it originates, including from Britain, but dominated today, of course, by China's. It may be stretching the word somewhat to call this 'imperialism', and it certainly shouldn't lead us to infer an exact equivalence between it and conquering people by the sword. It is on these grounds, however, that no 'liberated' nation – ex-colonies from British rule, or Britain itself from 'Brussels' – can ever claim to be truly 'independent', in the *inter*dependent or 'Global' world that was given a great boost in the nineteenth century, impersonally, by the expansion of British trade and the resultant British Empire. The latter was in most ways an accident of history, more so than retrospective 'patriots' like to acknowledge; and a more complex phenomenon than many of them assume. 'We used to rule half the world', yell the Brexiters. No, 'we' didn't. Not really.

*

There were loud-mouthed patriots like that in the late nineteenth and early twentieth century too, especially at the time of the South African (or 'Boer')

War of 1899–1902; but it is arguable that they were no more clued up on the Empire and imperialism, than the Brexiters were on Europe. The notorious 'Jingo' riots of May 1900 were limited in size – though they made a lot of noise in the narrow streets of the City of London – and were at least as likely to be made up of lower-middle class as of working class young men. (Reports agreed that they were predominantly male.) There are many possible reasons for people to riot, especially joyfully (the 1900 demonstrations were to celebrate the 'relief' of the besieged town of Mafeking);[17] and simple fun and a partisan press geeing folk up are often two of them. In this case the riots also clearly indicated relief that 'their side' was at last coming back into the game, after several months of embarrassing military setbacks for the British Army against what until then had been portrayed as a bunch of barely-trained peasants. If the 'people' had been genuine 'imperialists', they – or the ones who had the vote – would have backed the noted imperialists in Parliament more than they did; but in fact it was the Liberals who won the next election, in 1906, and by a landslide, despite being divided over the issue of 'imperialism'. (Readers should be aware, however, that there are historians who argue the other way – that the working classes of the time were mostly 'Jingoes', just as they were xenophobes in 2016. It is impossible to settle this issue finally on the basis of the available evidence alone.)

So far as the British upper and middle classes were concerned, the evidence for imperial sentiment is firmer – simply because they were better able to register their views. In fact some of the forms that imperial ideology took in the late nineteenth and early twentieth centuries are probably the closest Britain has ever come to taking on the ideas and characteristics of what today is sometimes called 'proto-' or 'neo-Fascism': an exaggerated patriotism that puts the 'nation' before any other consideration, focuses on 'masculine' power and the military, rejects the idea of class division and so 'socialism' (unless it can be drawn in to supporting authoritarian ends), offers easy answers to the people's gripes, emphasizes 'race' as the basis of identity and loyalty, is hostile to incomers and 'Others', idolizes the 'flag', decries 'intellectuals', uses violence, follows a charismatic 'Leader', marches aggressively, and shouts a lot. It is arguable that this sort of thing is deliberately cultivated by conservative and reactionary governments – maybe some others too – as a way of distracting people from other problems they may have; getting them to wrap 'the Flag' around them to fall in behind an otherwise oppressive or incompetent ruling class. This is seen in other countries too, as a common feature of near- and fully-blown 'fascisms'.

There was some of this sort of thing, expressed as ideology, in *fin-de-siècle* Britain; quite a lot of 'racial' theorizing, for example, by so-called 'ethnologists' and political writers, many of them calling themselves 'Social Darwinists', and some of them quite 'intellectual'. Indeed, one Englishman, Houston Stewart Chamberlain, is credited with having furnished the basis of Nazi philosophy, no less, in a book published in 1899, *The Foundations of The Nineteenth Century*, on the basis of which he has been dubbed 'Hitler's John the Baptist'; but he had become a German by that time – he married a daughter of Richard Wagner: how more German can you get? – and wrote the book in German originally.[18] It is interesting in this context, incidentally (or perhaps not so incidentally), to note how many other leading imperial propagandists had German, Anglo-Indian or Anglo-Irish pedigrees; and how few of them therefore could be characterized as 'true Brits', if that means anything.[19] Certainly most of them seemed to have been kept quarantined from the 'liberal' strain in the British national character, which might help explain their illiberal views. Other 'theorists' of imperialism included Benjamin Kidd and Karl Pearson[20] – both moderately celebrated writers in their time. And then of course there were the more popular authors Kipling (the Anglo-Indian), GA Henty (for boys) and Bessie Marchant (for girls), and a few others. Scots may have been more 'imperialistic' than the English. (A share in the Empire's profits is supposed have been one motive for their joining the UK in 1707.) More in practice than in theory (practice being of course more important to down-to-earth Britons), imperialism was closely associated with militaristic movements like the Baden Powell Boy Scouts, calls for compulsory military service and shooting practice for young men, Public school 'Officer Training Corps' – 'officer' because no Public school boy would think of going into the Army as a mere squaddie; and anti-suffragism: for what woman MP would vote in Parliament to send her sons away to risk being killed in a colonial war? It has also been linked by modern historians with monarchism, although it is difficult to see a solid connection here. The Flag: yes. That was generally a Right-wing thing, then as now. Indeed, planting the Union Jack in foreign soil was generally regarded as a sign – if not proof – of imperial possession.[21]

*

Imperialists did shout more, of course, especially in that short moment a few months into the Boer War; but noise doesn't necessarily equate with dominance. Genuine imperial sentiment may have been a rarer commodity in Britain than people – including contemporaries, who could have been deafened by the shouting – have tended to assume. It largely depends on how you define it. Wars like the South African one, which provoked all that 'jingoism' at home, were first and foremost contests, in which you needed to take sides, which would generally be your 'tribe', and cheer them on. Doing so did not necessarily mean that you supported 'imperialism' as a policy of expansion and foreign rule, or even knew much about it. The evidence suggests that the Empire was not celebrated very much or taught in schools, even the 'Public' ones, until the interwar period, when the Empire was flagging in any case; which may have been why imperial propaganda increased: in order to counter the naysayers and apathetes.[22] Naysayers there were a-plenty, with J. A. Hobson, mentioned before,[23] only the most prominent among them.[24] Anti-imperialism, or more often *criticism* of the British Empire – because if you were 100 per cent 'anti' it meant you didn't care about what happened to your colonial subjects when they merely fell into the hands of other predators, or into the maw of unfettered global capitalism – was just as significant an ideology in Britain throughout the twentieth century; rooted as it was in the old and enduring Liberal – Cobdenite – ideology, infused with nonconformist religious morality (some of it), and now buttressed by socialist anti-capitalism. Scrape away the new imperialist stucco on the building, and the rather more fundamental public discourse of Victorian Britain – the liberal one – would be seen shining through. Hence the extraordinary efforts made by the imperial propagandists between the Wars to 'make Britain great again'.

In fact 'anti-imperialism' could even be said to be a British *invention*, which imperialism, of course, was not. Strictly speaking anti-imperialism, or empire-criticism, ought to be defined as opposition to *all* empires, and not just the one that is binding and oppressing you at the moment; in other words, as anti-imperialism *in principle*. That of course disqualifies the American patriots, who were only against the *British* Empire, and not at all averse to doing a great deal of 'imperializing' on their own accounts once they had thrown off its chains.[25] British supporters of American independence, of which there were many, could be said to have had a better claim to the 'anti' title, as it was their own nation's empire they were criticizing. So could the many Britons who journeyed to India in the later nineteenth and early twentieth centuries to support the nationalist cause there, out of loyalty to what they insisted was a truer British 'patriotism'.[26] There may have been earlier examples of principled anti-imperialism: perhaps some French politicians, or someone in Classical times. If not, however, it is something – perhaps a very small thing – that should be put on to the other side of the scale, when weighing up Britain's imperial 'guilt'; together of course with the leading part it played in abolishing slavery, including its own citizens' slave-trading, in the early 1800s – albeit with only the slave owners being compensated. (Years ago that was almost the only aspect of Britain's colonial history that was taught in schools, ignoring its slave-bloodied guilt in the first place; which emphasis was clearly wrong, but we should give some credit to the anti-slavers too.) This *anti*-imperial tradition might also even function – if this is what you're looking for – as an alternative focus of patriotic 'pride'.

Nonetheless British anti-imperialism (or criticism of empire) didn't succeed in bringing an end to the British Empire. It might be said to have accelerated events in the Congo, misleadingly named the 'Congo Free State', when a movement that originated in Britain – the Congo Reform Association – was largely responsible for ending the appalling rule there of King Leopold II of the Belgians; perhaps the worst example of colonial capitalist exploitation from this period – although others ran it close. The Congo was not exactly 'liberated' by this, however, but simply gifted over to the Belgian state to rule. Both there and in Britain's colonies ultimate 'decolonization' was achieved by the colonial subjects themselves, in the context of an inexorably declining Britain (and Europe) in any case. But before that, metropolitan 'anti-imperialism' and imperial criticism had an undoubted impact on the way the dependent colonies of the British Empire were run, together – again – with the structural weakness of Britain's colonial administration: so few men to rule it, for a start. If liberal-minded Britons were to tolerate having an empire, it would have to be ruled 'liberally', which was generally the stated intention of its rulers, even if in some notorious cases that was cruelly betrayed. When it was – Omdurman in 1898, Amritsar in 1919, Ireland and Iraq in the 1920s, Kenya in the 1950s, Rhodesia in the 1960s (although that was mainly on the heads of the white Rhodesians), Suez in 1956, India and South Africa at various times ... (forgive me if I've missed out your favourite atrocity) – it nearly always provoked protest at home, so long as it was reported there; occasionally in ways that caused some harm, or at least considerable embarrassment, to governments. Rather like the USA's enduring racism, it also affected the reputation that Britain wanted to give out to the world, as a liberal and/or democratic nation. (Liberalism and democracy, incidentally, are not the same thing. You can be one without the other. Britain was arguably more liberal without being democratic in the nineteenth century, and is arguably more democratic without being particularly liberal today.)

In the twentieth century anti-imperialism mainly became a socialist cause, but not always, with the earliest socialists being either apathetic towards the Empire – it was thought to have nothing to do with them, after all – or, in a few notable cases, quite keen on aspects of it: in particular the more 'progressive' and democratic colonies of Australia and New Zealand. Some of them may also have found it difficult to contain their pride in the sight of all those red-daubed world maps, and in the more successful exploits – where there were any – of their red-clad soldier-comrades overseas. But the fundamental socialist critique of capitalism was always bound to break through when the latter was shown to be exploiting and oppressing indigenous peoples under the protection of the Union flag, as Hobson and a handful of others (not all of them socialists) were beginning to claim from the 1890s onwards, making it difficult for a socialist to defend imperialism: except perhaps on Marx's ground, that it was at least helping to raise people up from *feudalism*. (Socialism couldn't take off before that stage had passed.)[27]

All that is why 'imperialism' had to be given a separate chapter in this book. It is often treated as if it were peculiar to the British; an or even *the* essential part of their historical national identity; a source of *power* to them in the nineteenth century; more *deliberate* than it may have been in reality; and more *generally* 'atrocious' than it was. (That's neither to deny nor to excuse the wicked – if I can be allowed just one moral judgement – individual atrocities.) The reason why British imperialism is so highlighted today, apart from those old red-bespattered world maps – which were always misleading, and which incidentally only started appearing in the 1900s – probably derives from the quite understandable Anglophobia of exasperated Continental Europeans wanting to demean 'Brexit' as fundamentally reactionary, fed as it is by the 'we used to rule half the world' chants of present-day 'Jingoes', who themselves have been presented with images of the old British Empire – in films, TV series, Johnson's and Rees-Mogg's utterances and (God forbid) their school history lessons – which can only have encouraged this inflated view of the whole enterprise. The Empire was a crucial part of Britain's historical identity, certainly; but a complex one; not one that distinguishes it from many other nations; and standing on a level with other equally or even more important British traditions, which include liberalism and *anti*-imperialism as two of the main ones. We should not allow an obsession with 'empire' to crowd these out.

In any case the British empire didn't last for long: a mere moment by comparison with, for example, all those years that England was under the sway of its distinguished Roman predecessor; or with many of the other 'great' world empires that history has thrown up, 'naturally'. Does this read like 'excusing' it? It isn't intended to; but merely to beat it down to size. We shall come on to the empire's sudden demise later, when we reach the period after 1945.

4

Politics

The unusual domestic stability that Britain had enjoyed in the nineteenth and twentieth centuries, despite two World Wars and give or take a riot or three, was generally attributed to its political system, and that system's gradual evolution over the years from a sort of feudalism in 1800 still, run by a monarch, a cabinet chosen from the 'ruling class', a House of Lords and a gerrymandered 'Commons' – 'rotten boroughs' and the rest; into something fairly 'democratic', if not ideally so. In school History books this is usually marked out in terms of the succession of 'Reform Acts' passed over the course of the nineteenth century and the beginning of the twentieth, extending the popular franchise so that eventually it even included women, egad! – which made everyone feel they had a say in how they were ruled. Occasionally governments had to be prodded with popular protests – the 'Chartists' of the 1830s and 1840s and the Suffragettes of the 1900s were the two main pro-democracy movements of this period, both using shows of violence to some extent – but in those school books the extension of the franchise was usually presented – rather like colonial independence – as a 'gift' from enlightened governments. It is this that fed the 'Whig' or progressive theory of British history which dominated for so long, and helped to discipline the populace. It was comforting to feel that, however bad things might be just now for you and your country, at least they were 'on the up'. You could leave off protesting, and hope.

Once represented in Parliament, however, you still needed to learn the rules of the game. And politics in Britain was played *as* a game right through this period, with ideologies and policies only slightly more important than the strategies and tactics used to promote them, or to hold them back. These were more complicated in Britain's case than in many countries'. For a start there was its 'division of powers' to cope with, its three branches of government: the Executive, the Legislature and the Judiciary. In themselves these were not particularly distinct from other countries' systems, but they were complicated in Britain's case by the participation in the Legislature of a 'House' consisting of survivals from the old feudal aristocracy, later leavened with some modern additions, new 'creations' and 'Life peers', and with only what were called 'delaying' powers when it came to actual legislation. The Lords were also not allowed to debate Budgets. The Executive consisted of the Prime Minister and his or her Cabinet, charged with preparing legislation for Parliament to approve, and assisted by the state bureaucracy, or Civil Service, which had traditions of its own. The judiciary could rule on the strict legitimacy of any measures thus taken. These were intended to prevent hastily thought-out government legislation, and rule by what all respectable Victorians feared as 'the mob'. (Today it is called 'populism'.) That was all well and good so far as it went; but it could be cumbersome, to the frustration of politicians who yearned for more 'efficiency' in government. We shall meet some of these later. For those however who preferred proper scrutiny to efficiency – that was the justification for the complexity – this was not the main problem with the British system.

That lay in the way that Members of the House of Commons (the 'Lower House') were chosen to represent 'the people'. In common with only a few other countries (the USA was one), Britain did it with a system called 'First Past the Post' (FPTP): 600-odd separate elections taking place all over the country, returning 600-odd Members, who then determined who should form their government. The great advantage of that was to give every UK citizen a personal link with the government: a local 'MP' who represented him or her, and could be called upon to intercede with the authorities on his or her behalf. The disadvantages were that it often produced governments that were not representative of the population as a whole, with very few administrations after 1945, for example, being supported by even 50 per cent of the popular vote; and secondly, that it made it virtually impossible for *new* parties, representing perhaps new popular trends, interest groups or ideologies in society, to break through. Theoretically a party could win 49 per cent of the votes in every constituency, and still have no MPs. That of course was an unlikely scenario; but there *were* elections in which significant 'third parties' were left out in the cold. In recent years the 'Greens' have always suffered from this mathematical anomaly; as UKIP – the United Kingdom Independence Party – did quite grotesquely in 2015, where it won only one Commons seat on the basis of nearly four million votes. That had consequences, as we shall see. The problem may have been exacerbated by the physical arrangement – the architecture – of both Houses of Parliament, with 'government' and 'opposition' MPs ranged on benches *against* each other rather than in a semi-circle, as in most other legislatures; so emphasizing the *adversarial* nature of British politics, which was often unruly as a result. There are ways of solving these problems – reconciling the 'constituency' system with a more 'proportional' one, and so enabling compromise;[1] but with the major parties doing so well – alternately – by the old system, the widespread myth that 'coalitions' are ineffective and unstable, the failure of the 'reformers' to settle on a particular alternative, and the general apathy of people on this issue – partly because the FPTP 'game' is such fun to play and watch – all feeble efforts to this end came to nought.

Earlier in our period this mattered less, partly because until 1919 only a minority of British subjects had the vote in any case. Government was accepted as being carried on by others on their behalf, with an occasional input from *some* of the 'people'. It was also widely accepted because of people's trust in the *probity* of their representatives and rulers, underscored by religion, and by the old-fashioned virtues taught in the 'Public' schools. (It was this that could be said to justify places like Eton then. Less so today.) Of course there were exceptions, giving rise to 'scandals'; but – and this was the point, really – they were regarded *as* 'scandals' and not just accepted as the way politics was done. If the rules were broken, the miscreants were expected to resign; as the Defence Minister John Profumo famously did after lying to the House of Commons about an extramarital 'affair' in 1963. An illustration of this 'honour code' from another area entirely is the fact that when Public schoolboys played football early on, they saw no need for referees – would be insulted, indeed, if it were hinted that they were needed – because they would always own up to their own fouls. (Referees only came in when the working classes took to the game.)[2] The same reason lay behind the surprising circumstance that for a long time there were no laws against government employees selling state secrets to foreign powers, until with the increase in public business governments ran out of trustworthy Public schoolboys to employ.[3] It was not until then (1889) that the first 'Official Secrets Act' was brought in.

In Parliament, Members were all technically 'Honourable', and not allowed even to accuse other Members of 'lying, being drunk or misrepresenting their words'.

> Words to which objection has been taken by the Speaker over the years include blackguard, coward, git, guttersnipe, hooligan, rat, swine, stoolpigeon and traitor. The Speaker will direct an MP who has used unparliamentary language to withdraw it. Refusal to withdraw a comment might lead to an MP being disciplined.[4]

There were, of course, ways of getting around this. Winston Churchill once did it by replacing the word 'lie' with the phrase 'terminological inexactitude'; and the socialist MP Denis Skinner more cleverly (albeit only reputedly), when he was asked to withdraw his claim that 'half the members on the Tory benches are crooks', by substituting it with 'half the members on the Tory benches are *not* crooks'.[5] Later (in 2021) a Scottish MP avoided the Speaker's sanction by *asking* the prime minister whether he was a liar or not.[6] In July 2021 a Labour MP, Dawn Butler, called Prime Minister Boris Johnson out as a 'liar', and was suspended from the House (briefly) as her punishment, but with the result that her statement reached far more ears than it would have done otherwise.[7] This was all part of the 'game', which even rank outsiders like Skinner (an ex-miner) had to learn. But it gave a patina of respectability and honesty to the procedures of British government.

The Civil Service, which did the government's work for it, also had strict rules; laid down originally in the 'Northcote-Trevelyan Report' of 1854, and later codified in the form of the seven 'Nolan Principles': selflessness, integrity, objectivity, accountability, openness, honesty and leadership. These were designed – as we have seen – to ensure its independence and non-corruptibility. Civil Servants, usually recruited (again) from the Public schools and the older universities, were prohibited from taking overtly political roles or displaying partisan allegiances, or working with 'lobbies' – pressure groups for particular interests. They nonetheless were said to have a group ethic or functional mentality that inclined them towards conservatism (with a small 'c'); and – when it came to 'Brexit' – gave them an allegedly undemocratic partiality towards the EU. (The leading Brexiter Nigel Farage wanted the Europhiles in Whitehall – 'fascists', he called them – rooted out.)[8] In order to neutralize what was seen as the unhelpful impartiality of the Civil Service, Ministers from Harold Wilson's time onwards began appointing their own 'Special Advisers' ('Spads') on the government payroll, who were allowed to be partisan in their Ministers' interests, and whose numbers increased exponentially, to around a hundred under Boris Johnson. That rather undermined the morale of the traditional Civil Service, several members of which resigned after coming into conflict with their Ministers' Spads.

That describes the engine of government, on a UK level. Localities – counties, cities, town, rural districts, villages – also had their legislatures and bureaucracies; and the nations of Scotland, Wales and the part of Ireland that was British, had their own administrations (set up in the 1990s), exerting whatever powers were 'devolved' to them. In the case of Scotland that was quite a lot, but did not include – something that was to cause trouble later on – the regulation of foreign trade.

*

All this could be said to have softened the weight of government on the backs of the people it governed. But it didn't necessarily make it truly 'democratic'. Of course, none of the reforms that were implemented in the nineteenth century was intended to, with 'democracy' never being a stated objective of most in the Liberal Party, who feared it almost as much as the Conservatives; the word 'democrat' then, indeed, carrying about the same resonances as the word 'communist' later on. Despite their efforts to stem it, however, 'democracy' in the sense of broadening the voting franchise progressed by stages until it included nearly everyone (apart from peers, who had their own 'House' of Parliament; criminals; and the certified insane); giving people the impression that the whole nation was, in a real sense, ruling itself.

As it was, of course, formally. But there were limits. Firstly, there were the difficulties associated with Britain's voting *system*: the 'First Past the Post' way of selecting governments, for example, described already; and – also arising from FPTP – the problem of unequal constituencies. These were meant to be subject periodically to independent 'boundary reviews' to level them up roughly; but could nonetheless be 'gerrymandered' by sitting governments to give them the advantage. Citizens could be disfranchised in other ways: by living abroad for too long, for instance; although one could say that they merited this if they didn't intend to return to live under Parliament's laws. But these could all be said to be technical problems, easily corrected – even FPTP. Secondly however, and quite apart from FPTP, there was the fact that, with all these complications, the whole system was vulnerable to 'corruption', of various kinds – 'buying' parliamentary votes, for example – instances of which bubbled up from the murky lower reaches of politics at various times; to the extent that it *could* be said that 'corruption' was one of the major factors determining the way Britain was ruled – the political 'game' that was played – throughout our period. (We shall return to this.) And finally, there was a third difficulty, less easily solved than the others; which may take us to the very heart of British 'democracy'.

This question came down to whether the electorate was making *informed* choices. Intellectuals and academics would like those to be made on the basis of the information before them – the rival political programmes and ideologies they were offered; but of course we have to be aware that we are all – even 'intellectuals' – influenced also by the 'personalities', or personalities as they are presented to us, of the rival candidates. This may be a function of the need that people feel for 'leaders' they can identify with, rather than for political programmes. In any case, around the turn of the nineteenth century, and then from the 1850s onwards, both local and national politicians were certainly aware of the importance of their personal appeal – what today we would call their 'image' – in the public domain.

This was conveyed not only in reports of their speeches, which in the nineteenth century could be read at length (sometimes very great length) in newspapers, even working-class ones; but also by the caricatures that were sold from printers' shops in the early 1800s, and then appeared in weekly satirical journals like *Punch*, from 1841, and its less well-known rival *Judy*, which ran from 1867 to 1907; and finally in a dozen media from the beginning of the twentieth century. These were not particularly flattering – Lord John Russell for example was portrayed as very tiny, and Disraeli with stereotypically 'Jewish' features, although that didn't seem to do him any electoral harm; and later the political cartoonist 'Vicky' (Victor Weisz) turned the very old-fashioned Harold Macmillan into a very unlikely 'Supermac': one step on the way to the savage 'Spitting Image' puppets of politicians shown on television in the 1980s. The *Guardian*'s Steve Bell (portraying David Cameron in a condom and Boris Johnson as a bottom) continued this tradition. This may have been one of the factors explaining the decline in people's regard for nearly all politicians from that time onwards; although the sectional interest of the Press in demeaning them, and their own tendency to demean themselves – 'cash for questions', illegal lobbying, expenses scandals, lurid 'affairs' – must also have played a role. This was a shame, because many politicians were honourable men and women; or, as Dennis Skinner had suggested, 'not crooks'.

Among more honourable and consequently admired political leaders, Gladstone and Disraeli stand out, together with Russell and Peel; and after them Joseph Chamberlain, David Lloyd-George, Winston Churchill, Clement Attlee, Aneurin Bevan, Harold Wilson, Harold Macmillan, Margaret Thatcher and (for a time) Tony Blair. (Others might make a different selection.) The 'leader principle' – in German *Führerprinzip* – can of course be dangerous, so it may be fortunate that none of these figures sought to over-exploit their appeal; which would anyway have seemed 'un-British' of them: as it did in the case of Oswald Mosley, leader of the BUF in the 1930s, and the only one to strut around Germanically. And not all of them can be said to have made actual *differences* to the political drama that was ongoing, to compare with others in the wings: quiet reformers, activists, leaders of 'movements', protesters, MI5 'spooks', rich people, conspirators, J. M. Keynes, Lord Beveridge, God, the Devil, even the Royal Family (but unlikely, that), and dead people (Churchill was wheeled out by both sides during the Brexit debate);[9] and beneath these the underlying impersonal forces that may have been responsible for most things, and which we shall come on to at the end of this book.

As well as 'personality', voters were influenced by 'images'; and it was these that could be most easily manipulated to affect elections (and referenda), especially in the twentieth century. 'Propaganda', usually directed *against* opponents, could involve downright lies, like the 'Zinoviev Letter' affair, already mentioned, of 1924. But it was usually more subtle than this. Based on the techniques developed by the commercial advertising industry in the later nineteenth century – H. G. Wells' aforementioned novel *Tono-Bungay* (1909) is the classic fictional account ('Tono-Bungay' was a medicine which was marketed as a cure-all but was in fact a fraud) – it was eagerly seized on by politicians and their agents to help 'sell' their candidates and policies to voters. Most of this was honest and harmless, as commercial advertising usually is; and the notorious example of Josef Goebbels in Nazi Germany generally kept British political propagandists' noses fairly clean in this regard. In view of what was to come in the new century, however, we should keep our eye on this new agency. Indeed, any history of modern Britain that makes no mention of the 'Persuaders', and their evolving techniques, can ever be complete. They could explain a lot.

*

A more important factor in British politics, however, may have been the power of the Press, often called the 'Fourth Estate' (after Crown, Lords and Commons). Newspapers were always problematical, usually for governments, like those of the Conservative Stanley Baldwin between the Wars; whose famous attack on them in March 1931 set the tone for many of the complaints against them in subsequent years, and popularized a famous phrase: the 'harlot' one, although it wasn't his originally. (He took it from his cousin Rudyard Kipling.)

> The newspapers attacking me are not newspapers in the ordinary sense. They are engines of propaganda for the constantly changing policies, desires, personal vices, personal likes and dislikes of the two men. What are their methods? Their methods are direct falsehoods, misrepresentation, half-truths, the alteration of the speaker's meaning by publishing a sentence apart from the context ... What the proprietorship of these papers is aiming at is power, and *power without responsibility – the prerogative of the harlot throughout the ages.*[10]

This could be regarded as a kind of 'corruption', too. The 'two men' singled out by Baldwin were Lords Beaverbrook and Rothermere, who owned the mass circulation *Daily Express* and *Daily Mail* respectively.

But the 'Yellow' or 'Tabloid' Press went back further than Baldwin. It first appeared in Britain (reputedly modelled on the American 'Hearst Press') at the time of the British–South African (or 'Boer') war of 1899–1902. It was one of the factors behind the notorious popular or popul*ist* 'jingoism' of that time, stoked by newspapers with sensational and often 'fake' accounts of Boer 'atrocities', designed to thrill and anger their readers. The historian H. John Field has shown how the *Daily Mail*'s leading war correspondent, G. W. Steevens, appears to have deliberately misreported events, probably to please his imperialist proprietor.[11] But the root of it may not have lain in anyone's political prejudices, but in the newspaper industry's take-over by large-scale financial capitalism in the later 1890s, making newspaper publishing a *business* for capitalists, rather than a vehicle for public-spirited (if sometimes wrong-headed) journalists. That will have been understood by Baldwin, who was – unusually – born into a 'business' family himself; which had however sent him to a posh Public school.

Slogans posted in newspaper offices from the early twentieth century onward enjoined journalists to remember that they were 'writing for the meanest intelligences', and to 'use only words that a nine-year-old would understand', which will not have encouraged sophisticated reporting. The staples of their journalism then were sensation, sport and scandal, which were supposed – as in later times – to be what their readers craved for most. As a result political events were sensational*ized* as much as possible; in wartime, for example, by exaggerating the heroism of British combatants and the depravity of their enemies. This went under the name of 'patriotism'. Most of the popular newspapers' proprietors were rabid imperialists (Rothermere and the Canadian Beaverbrook especially), which may explain the jingoistic lines they took in their papers – unless they were merely responding, or thought they were, to popular opinion. One commentator regarded Rothermere as 'only a tradesman speculating in the reaction';

which if true may confirm this, but also establishes the mercenary motive behind most of the yellow press's consistent Right-wing stance.[12] This is a feature that may be peculiar to Britain, which used to pride itself on its 'free press'; and probably explains why its proprietors took such umbrage when anyone suggested its being regulated by an outside body. That might indeed have been injurious to 'freedom of speech' and the rest of the great liberal principles, had the Press had been genuinely 'free' in most respects. By many standards, however, it was not. In 2020 Britain was ranked only 35th in a table comparing 'press freedoms' in different parts of the world. (The four Scandinavian countries and the Netherlands came out on top.)[13] This was because British press proprietors conceived of 'freedom' only in narrow market terms, defining it as the liberty to buy and sell items of 'property', which is what the newspapers represented to them. That of course fitted in with the political climate of the time, when – in Britain and much of the world – Capital was clearly King.

When a form of democracy was eventually brought to Britain in 1867 – enfranchising more working-class voters, if they were men – Prime Minister Benjamin Disraeli, nervous as most of his Conservative followers were of entrusting the fate of the country to ignoramuses, accompanied that reform with an extension of state education to those same workers; with the famous argument that 'we must educate our masters': that is, make the new electorate knowledgeable and intelligent enough to come to informed decisions on matters of national import. This was his way of guarding against 'mob rule'. Whether he succeeded in the long term, enough to counteract the influence of mobbish propaganda, especially of the popular or tabloid or 'yellow' press, is a matter for debate.

Indeed, the role of the press became particularly controversial in the early years of the twenty-first century, when – as it happened – a journalist actually became prime minister. That was unprecedented; although Palmerston and one or two other Victorian statesmen had done a bit of journalism in their times. Journalists had long pontificated about politics, apparently authoritatively, without of course ever having to 'do' it, or being held responsible for the impact of anything they wrote. In July 2019 the nation would see whether one particular journalist's deeds were as good as his words. That will await a later chapter.

*

Then, of course, there was ideology. What impact ideas and ideology had on 'events' in nineteenth- and twentieth-century Britain – a country usually resistant to 'intellectual' things – is questionable; but there were plenty of them around. Britain buzzed with ideas, theories, schemes, plans, philosophies and sheer eccentricities; usually of a practical kind, or claiming to be. This was especially true of the years around the turn of the twentieth century, possibly because people believed that a new century demanded them. That was the great birthing period of British science fiction, for example – H. G.

Wells didn't stand alone; and of new movements, social, political and artistic, which consciously and deliberately sought to put the stuffy Victorian age behind them. But the Victorians weren't so stuffy, either: less so than the *fin-de-siècle* radicals generally painted them. They buzzed too. This in fact was one of the main characteristics of Britain at this time and probably others: its ideological complexity, even muddle; which is another reason why any generalization about Britain's 'dominant discourse' or 'national identity' must be doubted – unless it be along these lines.

One exception could be made for what was probably the most important 'idea' coming from Britain in the nineteenth century, the 'Theory of Evolution'; because it impacted on so many other ideas too. For a start it is supposed to have challenged the Christian faith of many Victorians, although it is difficult to see why, unless they insisted that to be a Christian you had to take on board all that obvious mythology in *Genesis*. Christianity is surely more sensible than that. Secondly, Evolution affected – or infected – politics, in the guise of so-called 'Social Darwinism', developed from Charles Darwin's theory of the 'survival of the fittest' – although he never himself applied this to human society – to justify capitalism, social and 'racial' hierarchies, cut-throat competition between individuals and nations, and imperialism. Maybe that is why liberal Christians were wary of it. Unless you derived your morality *from* it, it was not a very 'moral' set of ideas.

Despite Darwin, Christianity remained the dominant religious ideology in the nineteenth and much of the twentieth centuries, in its several Protestant forms in England, Scotland and Wales, and in its Catholic version in Ireland and a couple of western British cities. Its influence is difficult to measure, because people could so easily adapt it to what suited them, picking and choosing verses of the Gospels to fit, and even making bits up, like the ban on homosexuality.[14] Religion may have been less genuinely influential than *utilized*, in order to divide peoples, in British India, for example (although Hindus and Moslems didn't need much encouragement to separate them); and to strengthen their identities as rival tribes. Ireland was, in this sense, the most tribal part of Britain, with the horrendous 'Troubles' in the north of the country from the 1960s onward a vivid illustration of the power of religion, in certain hands, to generate hate. The increased presence of Islam in British society in the later twentieth century appears to have corroborated this.

Christianity, or the British and Gospel-based versions of it, was however influential in keeping most of the Empire's ruling classes honest, and its missionaries generally charitable but dogmatic. Some settlers and capitalist exploiters may also have been touched by it, but not so many. Nineteenth-century Liberalism had a strong Christian component, especially Nonconformist; as did the turn-of-the-century Labour movement, which – in terms of the old exam question – may have 'owed more to Methodism than to Marx. – Discuss'. This was not – it hardly needs to be said – the sort of 'Christianity' which is identified today with the Republican Party in

America. In Britain the established Church of England *was* associated with Toryism – the suffragette Agnes Maude Royden called it 'The Conservative Party at Prayer'[15] – mainly because of the status its bishops held in the national hierarchy, including the Upper House of Parliament (26 of them, called 'Lords Spiritual'). But what spiritual sanction they felt they had for their Conservative views is not clear; and in any case some latterly were quite Leftish, upsetting the 'Lords Temporal' no end. The Church of England also ran many of Britain's schools throughout the nineteenth century, and some into the twenty-first. (This is quite apart from the mostly solidly Anglican 'Public' schools.) Generally they tried to inculcate not only religion but also obedience and a respect for the established order in their pupils; the 'Nonconformist' schools slightly less so. And religion is felt to have been a powerful motive behind the abolition of colonial slavery, various Acts of 'toleration', prison reform, and other humanitarian measures passed in Victoria's reign.

Secular ideas were also widespread, however, although only influential scatteredly. At the start of the nineteenth century the 'Romantic' movement (Keats, Shelley, Wordsworth, Mary Shelley, Sir Walter Scott) caught the imaginations of many artistic and literary-minded Britons; but at the same time as 'utilitarianism' (Bentham) was endeavouring to stifle their impractical musings from the other side. Both of these mainly affected the middle classes. The aristocracy was too busy chasing foxes to have time for all this, and the proletariat too bowed down by work. (*Of course* there were notable exceptions to both these gross simplifications. They are meant to be *characteristic* of the two classes, not *typical*.) The same is true of the more marginal and esoteric ideas that arose in the 1890s and early 1900s; not only 'Sci-Fi', but also, for example, the 'Rational Dress Society', encouraging women to wear trousers and men to wear skirts (Scottish men already did, of course); the 'Legitimation League', seeking to remove the stigma of bastardy from illegitimate children but also championing 'free love', for which it had the Police set on it; various forms of 'Anarchism', associated in the public eye with bomb-throwers, but generally more pacific than that; what was called the 'Oscar Wilde tendency', although that never developed into a formal 'movement' until much later; vegetarianism and the crusade for healthy food, like Thomas Allinson's wholemeal 'Bread with Nowt Taken Out'; the National Trust and the Royal Commission on Historical Monuments; a practical Women's movement (just beginning then to be called 'feminism'); and various socialist groups, including the Labour Representation Committee (later the Labour Party), founded on the dot of 1900. That of course soon ceased being 'esoteric'; as did a few of the others, later on. It was at this time, too, that Association Football became a mass spectator sport, to the discomfort of many Conservative patriots, who felt it was distracting the workers from more nationally-useful forms of leisure-time activity, like rifle practice and marching up and down. *Circa* 1900 has been highlighted here not because it was necessarily a more exciting time ideologically than the rest of the period covered in this book (although it may have been); but because it comes half-way through, and should give an idea of the varied tapestry of thought that Britain was capable of boasting at any time.

So far as politics were concerned, Conservatives of course were bent on 'conserving' (traditionally, but not always – Thatcher was anything but a 'conserver'); the Whigs and Liberals were more interested in 'freeing' society in various ways; Labour concentrated at the beginning on improving conditions for the 'workers', usually by quasi-socialistic means; and the 'Right' – a disparate succession of small and usually short-lived parties – aimed to radically change society by means ranging from extreme free-marketism (anarchism in effect), to authoritarianism, narrow nationalism and hyper-imperialism: not all of them of course rowing in the same boat. But it was more complicated than that. Party lines, in particular, could muddy the boundaries between all these ways of thought. Conservatives could come very close to 'socialism' by supporting social welfare measures imposed, patronizingly, from 'above'. The *noblesse oblige* inculcated in Clement Attlee at his 'imperial' Public school (Haileybury) probably contributed to his radicalism at least as much as any more overt 'socialist' teaching did. 'Free market' liberals or Conservatives could be pretty authoritarian if that was seen to be the best way to impose economic 'liberalism' on folk. And any MP could become 'corrupted'. As well as this, the ideological inspiration for all these parties and sects came from a number of sources, some domestic, others foreign. It is in fact interesting to observe how many of the important political and social developments of British society over the past two hundred years find their pretty close equivalents in roughly contemporary European nations, although sometimes in different guises. This indicates either that Britain was influencing them; or that Britain got a lot of its ideas *from* them; or, thirdly, that there was something happening underneath that moved them all in similar ways. We shall return to this in a later chapter. At any rate, it shows how 'international' these aspects of Britain's national existence and development were.

The dominant economic ideology during most of these years, albeit in Britain first, was the 'free market' one, which in the second half of the nineteenth century was most closely associated with the Liberal party, but was also – reluctantly – embraced by the Tories; and early on in the twentieth century modified to take account of the fact that 'free competition' between individuals could only work fairly if their starting conditions were roughly comparable. This 'New Liberal' turn brought them close to the already fairly egalitarian Labour Party, with whose leading thinkers they swapped ideas, laying the foundations of the 'Welfare State'; plotted by a Liberal but inaugurated by Labour after 1945. John Maynard Keynes, whose immensely influential ideas were designed to save capitalism from collapse, was basically a 'Liberal' in this 'New' (not of course 'neo') sense. Ideological barriers were fluid then. Which is why, again, we should never fixate too

much on Party labels when studying nineteenth-, twentieth- and – for that
matter – twenty-first-century politics. Keynes vacillated; as did Joseph
Chamberlain, moving from Radical-Liberal to Unionist; Oswald Mosley
(socialist to Fascist); and Winston Churchill, who moved both ways.

Liberal economics, in both its forms (and even possibly the 'neo' one),
owed much of its appeal to its intrinsic utopianism. We find this in Richard
Cobden, quoted in the last chapter but one. Some Victorian thinkers
genuinely believed that (a) capitalism was a route to financial and social
equality (yes, you read that right);[16] and (b) the world would be at peace if
every nation were won over to the free market. That meant that they
wouldn't need to waste money on warships and soldiers. (That's Cobden,
again.) At home, the market would eliminate the need for police forces and
prisons, as nearly everyone would be too satisfied and happy to want to
steal or cheat or murder. Not many people, probably, were confident enough
to live by the implications of this (not locking their front doors, for example);
but it was a pretty thought for some far-off future. It was almost religious
– a vision of an earthly heaven – and one of the reasons behind the stubborn
optimism of so many middle-class Victorians, whatever troubles any of
them might be going through at the time.

*

Authoritarianism was another 'ideology' (if it can always be dignified with that
title) that was floating around in the air of nineteenth- and twentieth-century
Britain, and some way into the twenty-first. The idea that the common people
need to be controlled or disciplined was a basic assumption behind the left-
over feudalism with which our period begins, side-by-side with the 'paternalism'.
It was also, of course, intrinsic to the way the Empire was ruled. Otherwise
what you got was 'mob rule' – or 'populism', as it is generally called today – to
the detriment of the whole of society; for who could be confident that the
lower classes knew what was best even for themselves? Naturally it was better
if it could be done without the weals and scars of the authority showing up too
much; which was the downside of the 'Peterloo Massacre' of 1819, when a
popular demonstration for democracy was put down by cavalry, but at the cost
of eighteen demonstrators being hacked to death, which was the aspect of it
that lingered afterwards in the public mind. In later years Police were trained
in 'crowd control' (not always to much better effect); but before Britain had a
proper Police force the only way to deter mobs, and criminals, was thought to
be to have a vicious penal code. It wasn't called 'authoritarianism'; but that
was the unstated 'ideology' behind it.

The Victorians, however, were clever. Around the middle of the nineteenth
century they reformed their prison system, diminished the number of crimes
for which offenders could be hanged, and instituted certain social reforms
which they hoped would keep the 'people' happy. These were not, it should be
emphasized, merely cynical ploys, but arose from genuine liberal and in many
cases religious feelings. But they had the effect of making people feel – most

people, not just those who had the 'vote' – that they lived in a 'free' country; indeed, probably the free-est in the world. That's how Britain was portrayed, in public propaganda, including school History books, with their 'Whig interpretation': that is, British history being seen in terms of social and political 'progress'. After 1850, when the economy began picking up after a difficult start to the century, to everyone's benefit *potentially*, it became the main reason why Britain calmed down socially, and the prime source of British patriotic pride. Not, mark, the Empire, or not immediately; except that this kind of liberal self-congratulation started having imperial repercussions later on. Empire, whatever its real and original motives, became justified on the grounds that it was bringing 'freedom' to others. Which morphed into the ideology of 'Liberal Imperialism', and in that form became associated with 'imperialism' proper, of a genuinely 'authoritarian' kind.

*

The really dominant 'ideology' of the British people in all these years, however – and here we *can* generalize, because it took very vague and disparate forms – may have been the *anti*-ideology of apathy, indifference and ignorance; coupled in some more positive cases with overt anti-intellectualism, which can be seen as an 'ideology' of a sort. It may well be that very few people felt themselves to be affected by 'politics' at all, except the 'gaming' aspect of it; and more by – for example – their 'tribal' instincts and prejudices. Or is this too patronizing? (It should of course apply to 'intellectuals' too.) That in turn could have encouraged – or at least permitted – the sleaze and corruption which *may* have underlain British politics and society throughout this period, in various forms – bribery, lobbying, the press (again), entry to the ancient universities, and so on – despite Boris Johnson's insistence, in November 2021, that they never had.[17] The possibility has to be at least *considered*, that corruption was as deep a tradition in British life as any of the ones that Britons were prouder of. But in any case, how much and how effective any of this was in past years is impossible to say, just as it is difficult to be sure how widely and deeply 'imperialism' pervaded then. In more recent times the degree of ignorance and apathy in Britain now has been revealed, shockingly, to 'thinking' and perhaps naïve people by the new medium of the internet, by means of which anyone can display his or her ignorance simply by 'commenting' on 'posts'; and 'corruption' likewise. Even the 'liberal discourse' may always have been powerless against all this. For certain political operators, however, not so much affected by 'discourses', it offered promising opportunities. We shall come to this further on.

5

1945–2016

After the Second World War politics in Britain settled into a fairly regular routine, with Conservative and Labour governments alternating every five or ten years, and occasionally a minority party getting a toe in, and indeed a whole leg so far as Scotland was concerned; but with all parties broadly accepting the political settlement that seemed to have been tacitly agreed between them once the fighting was over. That will have minimized the need for the naughtier sorts of propaganda, like 'Zinoviev'; although Churchill – the hero of the War but the loser in the General Election that followed it – could be said to have offended when he claimed that Labour in power would bring in a 'Gestapo'. He may have thought that the people would elect him regardless, out of gratitude; but they didn't. Even returning soldiers voted Labour, on the basis of their *peacetime* memories of the Conservatives, and maybe radicalized by the political education they were given in their camps. No generation has probably been better educated politically than this one. So in the end Clement Attlee's Labour Party won the election in July 1945 by a landslide.

Labour's first go at real power – its pre-war governments had both been minority ones – produced perhaps the most radical administration of our whole period, certainly before Thatcher, in the sense of changing a lot. Of course it turned out to be not at all the authoritarian socialist dystopia that Churchill had imagined. Indeed, Labour had never turned its back on liberalism, or even the 'market', entirely; partly because it had seen what was going on in fully 'socialist' states like Soviet Russia.[1] Before and during the War it had developed an alternative semi-utopian vision, which was of a halfway economic position between Communism and *its* Utopia, and what it conceived of as the devil-take-the-hindmost capitalism of the United States; an approach that was sometimes dubbed the 'Third Way' (although that moniker has been applied to other policies too, including 'New Labour's' in the 1990s), and which sought to rub down the sharp edges of the capitalist system through the agency of the government. The practical expression of this was Britain's new 'Welfare State', providing essential social services free to its needy citizens (and to the less needy, through the principle known as 'universalism'), including education, healthcare and cheap housing. Labour also took a number of vital industries into public ownership, in what were called 'the commanding heights of the economy', including gas, electricity, coal and the railways.

This approach can be said to have had both a national and a European genesis and character, with the reforms of the late 1940s and 1950s clearly growing out of the very British 'New Liberal' tradition of the 1900s onwards, and the new 'National Health Service' being a particular object of patriotic pride for years afterwards; but with the rest of Labour's welfare reforms being very much in line with what was going on on the Continent too. Indeed, the nearest equivalent to them was probably contemporary Sweden's 'Social Democracy' – Sweden had been lucky (or unlucky) enough to have had a Social Democratic government since 1933 – which for many British socialists became (to adapt a favourite American expression, referring to something else entirely) their 'Shining City on the Hill'. For a few years in the 1950s, 1960s and 1970s, indeed, Britain and Sweden seemed to be marching together along this consensual path; until Margaret Thatcher – with a very different idea of what the 'patriotic' way for Britain was – blocked that road in the 1980s, and Britain's and Scandinavia's forms of 'progress' began to diverge.

Britain's 'socialism' however, while it lasted, gradually drew it away ideologically from its friends and allies across the Atlantic, which, after flirting with a kind of 'socialism' themselves for a while – the 'New Deal' – reverted to the kind of 'freedom' they associated with capitalism alone. It also alienated some of Britain's own Right-wing politicians, who broadly shared the American way of looking at things, and believed that what they saw as the stagnation of the British economy in these post-war years – although it wasn't all *that* stagnant compared with the years after the Right-wing politicians took over (Britain had still made cars and aeroplanes then, for example) – could be mended with a large dose of 'free enterprise'. (It was called that rather than 'capitalism', which was no longer a respectable word in these social-democratic times.) Before the late 1970s, however, these naysayers were relegated to the margins of British political life, ridiculed even, and so not taken as seriously as it subsequently turned out they deserved.

They emerged blinking into the light for a short time under Prime Minister Edward Heath (1970–4), who seemed to be one of them until he reneged, under pressure from the militant trade unions, who were suspected to be under Soviet direction at this time. The Right-wingers never forgot or forgave that; or, for some of them, Heath's taking Britain into the European 'Common Market'; although the public's acceptance of that was confirmed by a whopping majority (67 per cent to 33 per cent) in a referendum held on it in June 1975. That 'betrayal' had to wait for a while to be corrected; but in the meantime the Right found a new champion for its 'free market' ideas in Margaret Thatcher, who became prime minister in 1979, after a period of industrial turmoil dubbed the 'Winter of Discontent'; and won the Right's support – and even worship – by facing down a great miners' strike that threatened to do for her what those same miners had done for Heath. If Britain could be said to have had a 'revolutionary year' (before 2016), then it must be 1979; or a 'counter-revolutionary' year, if you count 1945 as marking the real revolution, which 1979 then cancelled out. It was a massive reversal of what had been widely assumed to be a steady course of liberal or social-democratic 'progress' for Britain since the 1900s, and it surprised many people at the time; as right-wing revolutions usually do. But the unions now having been brought to heel (and the Argentinians too, incidentally, in the short Falklands War of 1982, which did her reputation no end of good), Thatcher could concentrate on her main historical task: which was, in her words, 'to destroy socialism, because I felt it was at odds with the character of the people.' In this she succeeded, in her own estimation at least. 'We were the first country in the world to roll back the frontiers of socialism, then roll forward the frontiers of freedom. We reclaimed our heritage . . . I turned round the whole philosophy of government. We restored the strength and reputation of Britain.'[2] The practical side of this was mass 'privatization': turning nationally-owned companies (even water) into private concerns, which was supposed to make them more competitive and therefore 'efficient'; and even changed the public discourse of the time, with 'passengers' now called 'customers', 'Personnel' becoming 'Human Resources' departments, and voters described as 'stakeholders' in the new GB plc. These were followed by the customer-owned Trustee Savings Bank's being floated onto the market (it was bought up by Lloyds a few years later); and 'Council' (social) housing being sold off cheaply to its tenants, in the hope of turning them into small-time capitalists too. Under Thatcher's successor 'British Rail' was sold off, to little obvious public benefit, or even savings for the State. (The rail companies – some of them owned, ironically, by nationalized foreign railways – were still heavily subsidized. And a number of them collapsed.) Next in line was generally predicted to be the NHS: the 'socialist' institution which was probably closest to the heart of the British people and their image of themselves. That would make the Revolution – or the Great Reaction – complete.

All this was done in the name of 'patriotism', although it was – obviously – a very partial view of patriotism, involving just one of the several 'Britains' described in the first chapter of this book. In fact it was probably more of a 'class' than a 'national' reading, of only one of the characteristics that had fed into Britain's identity in the past. But it became the dominant economic one under Thatcher, and also under her successors, Labour as well as Conservative; until the crises of the early twenty-first century made some people think again: either Leftwards, or more to the authoritarian Right. We shall come on to this in the next chapter but two, on 'Brexit': which can be seen as one of Thatcher's unintended legacies.

Her main achievement, however, was to preside over the restoration of the older sort of Liberal free marketism to Britain, aware as she was that it *was* a 'restoration', by her use of the term 'Victorian Values' to describe it. (That came fairly late; earlier she had called them 'middle-class values', which may be more accurate.[3] Thatcher was nothing if not a class warrior.) Her kind of 'liberalism', which she shared with other world leaders like Ronald Reagan in America and Augusto Pinochet in Chile (so it wasn't a peculiarly 'British' trait), dominated British politics for the thirty or forty years after she came to power, even under the long-serving Labour prime minister Tony Blair; and spread fairly widely in the world. In Thatcher's case, however, it was coupled with nationalism, which would have puzzled the original free trade prophets; and with a measure of authoritarianism, especially restrictions on the freedom of trade unions to use industrial 'strikes' as a weapon, which would have distressed them even more. But it was a natural corollary of Thatcher's highly individualistic conception of 'freedom' – 'there is no such thing as society', as she once famously proclaimed[4] – which of course ruled out 'collective' action of any kind. Her basic philosophy was dubbed 'a free economy in a strong state'. That seemed a contradiction to those whose 'liberalism' had always been political as well as economic. It's the key to that 'neo-' prefix.

Before Thatcher, however, the Labour governments of 1964–70 and 1974–9, under Harold Wilson and then briefly James Callaghan (Heath came in between), continued along the path of *social* liberalism that Attlee had mapped out, with a number of important reforms which Wilson's Home Secretary Roy Jenkins is usually credited with. They included the abolition of the death penalty, decriminalization of homosexuality, abolition of the Lord Chamberlain's powers of theatre censorship, liberalization of the licensing and betting laws, liberalization of the divorce laws, and the legalization of abortion: perhaps the most impressive clutch of 'progressive' reforms (if the betting one can be regarded as 'progressive') introduced in short order, and the one with the most liberating effect on 'ordinary people', in the whole of Britain's history. All of them were borne along by the current of the so-called 'swinging' 1960s: a period of cultural liberalization and even licence, greatly influenced by American artists, and expressed especially in its popular music (Bob Dylan, Joan Baez, Woodie and Arlo Guthrie, Pete Seeger, Joni Mitchell, Aretha Franklin, Jimmy Hendrix, John Lennon...), and tied in with the anti-Vietnam War, anti-nuclear, anti-racist, anti-apartheid and pro-recreational drugs movements in Britain and the USA. All of which, of course, didn't endear it to the so-called 'moral' British Right, or even to the political middle, and may have helped provoke the reaction that brought Thatcher to power in 1979. 'Culture' can be a powerful weapon in the hands of the reactionary Right.

In the meantime Wilson himself – a far better and more effective prime minister than was generally acknowledged subsequently – resigned in 1976, probably because of incipient Alzheimer's, although there were 'conspiracy theories' floating around that he was the victim of an MI5 plot to tar him as a traitor. If there were a plot it wouldn't be surprising, in view of the contemporary Right-wing tendencies of the security services, and their ridiculous belief that Wilson was a Soviet 'mole'; and indeed there is some evidence of a plot or plots against Wilson, involving *ex*-secret service paranoiacs: indeed, 'conspiracy theorists' themselves.[5] But it is very unlikely to have been the cause of his standing down. It was his brain. Wilson's main problem during virtually his whole premiership was to keep his party's Left and Right wings working together, which wasn't helped at a time when the Trade Union movement, which had great influence on the party and power in Britain more generally, was growing more 'militant', encouraging strikes for political motives, and finally ruining any chance Wilson had of settling, permanently, the industrial turmoil in the country by rejecting his Employment Secretary Barbara Castle's ambitious policy ('In Place of Strife') for a new, Sweden-like *kompromis* between management and unions, which might have enabled British industry to flourish as Sweden's had. It would also probably have avoided the industrial turmoil (the 'Winter of Discontent') which brought the viscerally anti-Union Thatcher to power; and the divisions in the Labour Party which followed. These climaxed in 1981 with part of it hiving off to form what it called a new 'Social Democratic Party', which succeeded in splitting the Labour vote but not to any constructive effect. In 1988 the 'SDP' merged with the minority Liberal Party to form the 'Liberal Democrats', who later on joined a very one-sided coalition with the dominant Conservative Party to perpetuate Conservative policies – essentially – from 2010 to 2015.

In the meantime there *had* been another Labour government – indeed, a 'winning' one (three general elections from 1997 to 2010); but one that that didn't seem very 'Labour' to many of the party's members – the Marxist historian Eric Hobsbawm called Tony Blair, the new prime minister, 'Thatcher in trousers'[6] – and which rather blotted at least one of its copybooks by involving the country and its army in the United States' ill-advised, arguably 'imperialistic', and certainly badly-ending invasion of Iraq in 2003. (Harold Wilson, incidentally, when placed in the same situation by President Lyndon Johnson during the Vietnam war, had declined to go along with that.) The Iraq war gave rise to the biggest public demonstration against a government in modern British history, co-ordinated with protests all over Europe, on 15 February 2003. For years afterwards Blair was excoriated by Leftists as a 'war criminal', as well as for 'betraying socialism'. He became the second Labour leader – the first was Ramsay MacDonald – to be placed in Labour's Pantheon of Traitors: if Pantheons can have traitors as well as Gods. (Wikipedia says no. But then traitors can be Gods to some.)

Later the party was also involved in the 'expenses scandal' of 2009 – MPs cheating on the expenses they claimed – less so than the Conservatives, but in a way that affected both parties. People have always complained about politicians; but this incident marked a low point in the reputation of British politics generally, which – as we shall see – may have had a bearing on future policies. Some of this was justified: the stories of MPs claiming for 'duck houses' (a notorious one), cleaning their moats and the like were easily confirmed, and risible; but there can be little doubt that certain elements of the press exploited it for their own purposes. Most newspapers at the time supported the Conservatives, quite propagandistically, and were particularly anxious to avoid the sort of regulation that would limit what they saw as their 'freedoms' to publish whatever they thought would draw readers in, or would chime in with their proprietors' interests and prejudices. Labour was always more likely to introduce such regulation; and also, incidentally – or perhaps not so incidentally – to go along with EU plans to regulate the overseas 'tax havens' that some of the press 'barons' used to siphon their millions of pounds and dollars into. In 2011–12 an official enquiry ('Leveson') was held into a number of egregious sins committed by the tabloid press over the past few years, mainly 'phone-hacking', which actually led to the closure of one of the worst offenders, Rupert Murdoch's *News of the World*, in July 2011. It also recommended the setting up of a new Independent Press Standards Organisation (IPSO), whose independence, however – from the Press – was questioned thereafter.[7] And Lord Leveson was anyway stopped by the government from continuing with his projected 'Part Two', enquiring into press ownership; which most on the Left felt was essential in order to bring their 'bought' press to book. So the role of the Press in British politics did not much change; with effects we shall see when we come on to 'Brexit'.

In the meantime things were happening to Britain's economy and to its society before the time of 'Brexit' which were even more important than the Press. The economy may have flourished under Thatcher, but not spectacularly, and not the manufacturing side of it, which is where the traditional 'working class' was situated, so weakening the formerly solid basis of the Labour Party's and the trade unions' power.[8] Rising stock exchange values did not mirror conditions in the 'real economy', being predicated on financial speculation, rather than on 'making' things. Even those came a cropper in the great 'crash' of 2007–8, from which the banks were only rescued by multi-billion pound government support. (In other contexts that would have been called 'socialism'.) What this event also showed – just as the 'Great Depression' of the 1930s had done, but more so – was how closely allied to American capitalism the British economy was, with the 2007–8 crash, like the 1930s one, originating on Wall Street. Indeed, Britain in the 2000s became almost like a paler carbon copy of the USA, with huge and widening discrepancies of wealth, 'privatization' gathering pace, and the whole concept of its 'Welfare State' – especially the much-loved National Health Service – coming under threat from both British and American corporations.

Of course there were protests; and efforts to pull back. The radical film-maker Ken Loach directed a number of fine films overtly in protest against 'Thatcherism', and one of them, *The Spirit of '45* (2013), reminding the film-going public of what they had lost under it. Danny Boyle's opening ceremony for the 2012 Olympics did the same, but more subtly, and demonstrating an alternative form of 'patriotism', featuring Britain's open borders and the NHS; but without the message being lost on furious Tory MPs. They called all this 'Marxist', without, of course, knowing what Marxism was. In the 2019 General Election the Labour leader Jeremy Corbyn fought on a not-unpopular programme which called – essentially – for a return to the 1960s and 1970s, which may have been rejected at the polls because people thought it meant going back to a politics already demonized in the press (strikes leading to uncollected rubbish, and the like), and to black-and-white TV; and because of the image of Corbyn fostered by the Press. It looks as though 'reactionary' appeals don't work, unless they have 'heroic' ages to enlist voters behind. Boris Johnson was pretty good at that, as we shall see.

Another important trend at this time was the problem of immigration; not so much a problem in itself, arguably – it was repeatedly shown that immigrants contributed more to the British economy and society than they took out of them – but because of local sore-points in particular areas: pressure on housing and education, for example; and because they were perceived as 'altering the character' of parts of Britain, England in particular; especially if they had dark skins, strange accents and 'alien' religious customs, and stuck together in their ethnic groups. They were also seen – rightly – as having been *imposed* on the native populations of these areas, which had not after all ever invited them in. This gave rise to xenophobia and racism on the Right, and among jobless young men in decaying urban areas, who could collectively express their disapproval quite violently. Later this xenophobia was stretched to target Continental European incomers, even the spotlessly 'white' ones, who had come under EU 'free movement' rules; so helping to fuel pro-Brexit opinion and protest. We shall come on to that in a later chapter.

*

Looking more widely, but from Britain's standpoint still, the most important thing to happen in this post-war period was undoubtedly the emancipation – or 'fall' if you like – of the British Empire. That was clearly inevitable, even if certain Britons, like those banded together in the slightly ridiculous 'League of Empire Loyalists', claimed it would be reversible if only their Conservative governments – which oversaw as much of it as Labour did – would only show some 'spunk'. The fall is generally taken to have begun in 1947, with the 'transfer of power' as it was called (because that sounded better than any words implying defeat or loss) to India and Pakistan, followed by Burma, Ceylon and Israel the following year.

But 1947 – another 'revolutionary' turning-point? – was in many ways simply the latest stage in a longer withdrawal from Empire, which went back to the interwar period; or even to 1902, when after its last serious colonial war Britain had agreed to leave the Boers in South Africa to their own (racist) devices. Britain had been giving colonial ground for decades: in Ireland, Egypt, India, the Dominions and elsewhere; with its decline only slowed – as we have seen – by America's and Russia's retreat into isolation after the First War. There was literally no way in its parlous post-Second World War economic state, with colonial nationalism rising all over, usually supported by the new rival empires (though they fooled themselves that they were not really 'empires') of the USA and the USSR, that Britain – however much 'spunk' it might be able to summon up – could hold on to what remained of its empire; without, that is, resorting to means that the liberal tradition in Britain would have deemed unacceptable.

It tried some of those means in Kenya, in defence of the white settlers there, who in most of the empire were the ones who caused the most trouble. The resulting atrocities – which it doesn't require one to be an extreme anti-imperialist to regard as vile – were kept hidden from the newspaper-reading public back home, who were invited instead to focus on 'Mau Mau' atrocities, which were equally real, and fitted in better with (white) people's prejudices about African 'barbarity'. Further atrocities stained the other 'colonial wars' that Britain found itself fighting almost continuously in the 1950s, 1960s and 1970s. Most colonies, however, were 'liberated' far more consensually, and less bloodily. Britain was inordinately proud of this. It confirmed its people's illusion that they had been ruling these countries all along in order to prepare them to rule themselves. The adherence of most of Britain's ex-colonies to the free multi-racial Commonwealth seemed to be proof of that. (Although only, perhaps, by sweeping the colonial atrocities under the rug.)

It was clear whose side Margaret Thatcher was on with regard to all this – she repeatedly dismissed the (South) African National Congress as 'terrorist', for example – but even she was unable to turn the anti-imperial tide back. Indeed, it was under her government that several of Britain's Caribbean colonies won their independence, Hong Kong was allowed to revert to China, and Zimbabwe (ex-Rhodesia), which had not been effectively ruled from London for most of its existence as a colony, was granted majority rule. Thatcher's war with Argentina over the Falkland (Malvinas) Islands in 1982 was interpreted in some circles as a 'colonial' one, which may have been strictly true as the Falklands were a colony, but she had better reasons for fighting that: defence of the loyal islanders against a dictator, for example, and her own reputation as a toughie. By the end of her term in office the old Empire was almost gone. There were still those Falklands, of course, which were more trouble diplomatically than they were worth, and a few scattered 'foreign dependencies' adjudged too small to be able to rule themselves; plus of course the Commonwealth – no longer the 'British Commonwealth' – to cover Britain's imperial shame. Thatcher loathed the Commonwealth: the very idea of eliding the words 'common' and 'wealth', perhaps; and was always quarrelling with it, mostly over the question of sanctions on apartheid South Africa. She was no friend of 'freedom fighters', either abroad or among trade unionists at home. Unless of course they were fighting against restrictions on their individual enterprise.

With the Empire went Britain's status and influence in world affairs, although those may never have been as significant as they are regarded retrospectively. Britain's weakness as a 'world power' was cruelly revealed at the time of the Suez crisis in 1956, when its effort to seize the Canal back from Egypt's Colonel Nasser, in secret cahoots with Israel, was stymied when the USA – at that time on the 'Arab' side – threatened economic sanctions against Britain if it persisted. Nasser won that one, and Britain's prestige plummeted as a result. ('Suez' incidentally was immensely divisive in British domestic politics, indicating the depth of anti-imperial feeling there.) Eleven years later Harold Wilson made the decision to withdraw Britain's troops 'east of Suez', which can be taken as the symbolic marker of its final abandonment of its global role, at least as regarded defence. The United States, incidentally, was none too happy about this, having initially welcomed and supported Britain's contribution to keeping the 'communist' forms of colonial nationalism at bay.[9] From the 1960s onwards, however, it was perfectly clear that Britain had become 'just another nation'; which was one of the reasons behind its first application to join the infant 'European Economic Community' in 1963. Ironically that was blocked by the French President Charles de Gaulle, on the grounds that Britain was too close to the United States – not genuinely 'European' enough – at that time.

In fact de Gaulle's complaint was not all that wide of the mark, and seemed to be borne out by Britain's toadying up to the USA's adventurist and – in one sense 'imperialist'[10] – foreign policies from the 1980s through to the early 2000s. British politicians liked to believe – or to pretend – that their co-operation with America's invasions of Iraq and Afghanistan was as an equal partner, and the fruit of a 'Special Relationship' with their greater ally (and former colony); which would still have made it an independent and 'sovereign' choice, if it had been true. As their Empire was collapsing, or even before, a few imperialists had luxuriated in a dream of a new 'Anglo-Saxon' empire arising from the ashes of the old one, centred in Washington, and taking over the colonies Britain could no longer hold. That would have puffed Britain up, as a major contributor to a new British world order. Before he died, Cecil Rhodes (of 'Rhodesia'), realizing the Empire's weakness and fearing its end, had even set up a secret society with this end in view. Some American conspiracy theorists thereafter professed to believe that the plot had worked, with the US's foreign policy now being subvertly driven by old British imperialists; but there is no evidence for this apart from the number of prominent Americans who won 'Rhodes Scholarships' to study at Oxford. (President Bill Clinton was one.)[11] Short of this, however, a number of Britons seem to have hoped that the alliance might still enable the US to profit from their own past imperial experience: Harold Macmillan for example compared their relationship to that between ancient Greece and Rome; and that the Americans might in particular learn from Britain's mistakes: for example in trying to force British *ways* on their conquered peoples, which had been one of the factors sparking the Great Indian 'Mutiny' of 1857. Unfortunately that didn't happen, with the USA, under the influence of the dogmatic 'Neo-Cons', seeing her role as 'nation-building', along American democratic lines. That of course had disastrous results in Iraq, and then even worse ones – shocking the world – in August 2021; when the Islamist (and cruel) Taliban re-conquered Afghanistan, prompting a panicky and ill-controlled exodus. That was *not* something that had been tried in the British Empire since 1857 – or not before the nationalists had forced it on Britain. (Britain hadn't had the personnel, for a start. And it hadn't been all that keen then on 'democracy'.) So the 'lesson' was wasted. If it had not been it might have helped Britain to retain some of its old imperial kudos. As it was, its perceived subservience to the United States, widely seen as undignified, had the opposite effect; and may also go some way to explain Britain's uneasiness as a member-state of the European Union at the time.

There are 'patriots' today – they are probably just a tiny number of ignoramuses – who don't see why Britain can't become an imperial power again. In some ways, of course, it still is: with its financial influence in the wider world being disproportionate to its size, and with the 'informal' imperialism that goes along with the global domination of its (and the United States') language. Any more than this, however, is so obviously out of the question as not to be worth arguing against here. Patriots who think they can reverse seventy years of imperial retreat will find that they have to reverse an awful lot more. Ever since the 1960s, at the latest, Britons have had to come to terms with the inevitability of their imperial decline, and the need to find an alternative role befitting 'just another nation'; of which adhesion to the European Union was one, but not necessarily the only possibility.

*

Interestingly, it was not Britain's imperial past that dominated people's memories and their culture in the post-War years, with a few exceptions: the Hungarian Korda brothers' empire-set films, for example, and some nostalgic television series about British life in pre-'Transfer' India; but rather the War itself, which became the main staple of 'patriotism' thereafter. Films featuring brave British soldiers, sailors and airmen, led by upper-class Public school-educated officers like those played by Kenneth More, proliferated (usually *minus* mention of all those Polish Battle of Britain pilots); together with a stream of documentary TV programmes about the War – one in 26 episodes, no less, narrated by Sir Laurence Olivier – and the charming comedy series *Dad's Army*, to celebrate (very) ordinary people's contributions on the home front. They may also have given ignorant people the impression that Britain alone had won the War. If it could do that, then nothing was beyond it.

As the War receded in memory, this became its major contribution to the British psyche, with Winston Churchill the sort of 'hero' the British had never had since King Arthur's time. (Lloyd George, their First World War leader, would never do. Besides, his was not as 'good' a war as Churchill's.) In January 2018 the German ambassador to London, Dr Peter Ammon, expressed his exasperation with this, as well he might. He thought it bore much of the responsibility for 'Brexit'. (That was after the famous 'Don't Mention the War' episode of *Fawlty Towers*.) Indeed, the Second World War's domination over Britons' thought patterns is illustrated by the fact that even popular Science Fiction – meant to be set in the future – couldn't escape its tropes; with 'Dan Dare, Pilot of the Future' in the *Eagle* comic – launched in April 1950 – basically a Second World War pilot, in a spaceship resembling a Lancaster bomber with its wings cut off, a fat batman from Wigan representing the loyal and deferential working classes, an enemy (the 'Treens' of Venus) obviously based on the Nazis, led by a Hitler-like figure albeit with a bigger brain than his (the 'Mekon'), who is ultimately defeated by Dan with his typically British ingenuity and his fists (guns in individual combat weren't British), and then allowed to escape, in the interests of 'fair play'. In fact modern 'patriots' might well take a look at 'Dan Dare', the whole strip recently republished in book form, in order to understand the real nature of 'Britishness' as it was imagined in the past. 'Imagined' only, mind.

The Second World War had been a 'people's war' like few others. Even Winston Churchill recognized that – or pretended to – as we have seen. Yet that didn't stop his admirers using him as an example of the leadership they felt had won the War *for* them, and so attaching more credit to the *principle* of 'leadership' (the *Führerprinzip*) than maybe it strictly deserved. This was a departure from the British political norm, with its emphasis on Cabinet responsibility in government, and its preference for collective decision-making. That was Attlee's way, leading perhaps the most successful government in British history; and Harold Wilson's preference, defining 'leadership' – in his memoirs – as the ability to pull people together.[12] This was when the Conservatives, with a totally different idea of 'leadership', were looking for a 'strong' man to lead them, after the 'weak' Edward Heath; which is why they so took to the strong *woman*, when she came along, leading a cabinet otherwise made up of men only, but revelling in her image as 'the only one among them with balls'. Margaret Thatcher professed to model herself on Churchill, whom she called 'Winnie', familiarly, although there's no record of their ever having met. Ever since her time 'leadership' of this kind has been something that a large part of the electorate seems to have hankered after, to the detriment of what might have been better candidates in other ways. Winston Churchill can't be blamed: 'I only gave the roar'; but his image may have contributed to this authoritarian shift in people's political preferences. After that, Margaret Thatcher's very personal victories – or presented as such – over General Galtieri (of Argentina) and Arthur

Scargill (of the National Union of Mineworkers) further cemented the 'leadership' thing; to the detriment, possibly, of proper participatory democracy.

The popular press went along with this, always eager to focus on personalities – heroes and villains – rather than policies and ideas. It is 'people' that make dramas. Because of the material interests of its proprietors, the press focussed most of its ire, much of it defamatory, on 'villains' of the Left, including every single Labour leader after Attlee; which was a heavy burden for the Labour Party to bear throughout the post-War years, although the party can't be said to have greatly helped itself. Nor can the British people: deprived of political education as they were; far more interested in other things: terrorism, football, their jobs and families, where their next takeaway meal was coming from; encouraged to rate 'personalities' through popular game and 'reality' shows on TV (Boris Johnson soared to fame through an amusing albeit bumbling guest appearance on *Have I Got News For You*); easily distracted by, for example, events in the great and thrilling – if somewhat ridiculous – 'soap opera' that was being featured all this time in Buckingham Palace; and with no way of checking the plausible lies spun to them in various media: they, and democracy, hardly stood a chance. Which is something to bear in mind when we come on to the greatest political upheaval of this post-War period, which was of course 'Brexit'.

Brexit fed off all this recent history, as we shall see in Chapter 8. Before that, however, a couple of deviations: first into 'culture', insofar as it bears on British 'identity' and 'patriotism'; and then on aspects of the relations between Britain and Europe, for our whole period.

6

Culture

Many nations' 'patriotisms' focus on their 'high' cultures. Germany is proud of Goethe and Beethoven; Finland of Sibelius; Austria of Mozart; Spain of Cervantes and Picasso; France and Italy of – oh, so many great artists that it would be invidious to pick any of them out. England of course has Shakespeare, whose works have never lost their renown, although for a period they had to be bowdlerized in order to make them palatable. But British patriotism has never focussed on 'art' as much as other countries' have.

This was partly because in the nineteenth century and for a short while afterwards Britain was thought to have rather less *of* it than its Continental neighbours; which was why Britons who valued 'culture', and could afford it, felt they needed to travel abroad to get their artistic 'fix'. Art-themed tours abroad were common through most of Victoria's reign. Often the tourists brought some of the Continent's paintings, sculptures and archaeological treasures back with them (having paid for some of them), to beautify their mansions, or for the benefit of a wider public in art galleries and museums. In some cases this proved controversial later, with the Greeks, for example, persistently agitating to get their 'Elgin' (Parthenon) Marbles *back*. But they were taken originally because the British felt their own artistic traditions were so inferior to the Continentals'. And perhaps because they felt the Greeks didn't appreciate theirs enough.

The Victorians' cultural inferiority was as widely acknowledged at home as it was abroad. It resembled what in Australia is called 'cultural cringe'. At the opera (there were no significant grand operas composed by Britons) singers were only accepted if they were foreign, or if it was thought they were. 'The English artist struggling all but hopelessly against the town's indifference', wrote the novelist Charles Lever, 'has but to displace the consonants or multiply the vowels of his name to be a fashion and a success . . . Mr Brady may sing to empty benches, while il Signor Bradini would "bring down the house".'[1] The same reason explains why Britain felt it had to compensate for its lack of great native composers by importing foreign ones, starting with Handel, and including Haydn, Mendelssohn (Victoria and Albert's great favourite) and Wagner. A little later, when it finally got one of its own – in the person of Edward Elgar – he utterly despaired of the taste of most of his compatriots. Elgar's German friends, who were the first really to appreciate his music, went along with this; as August Jaeger wrote to him once, 'England *ruins* all *artists!*'[2] Another leading composer – Delius – went to work in France. It was the soil, again. It wasn't that there weren't people in Britain who appreciated good music; only that they were convinced they couldn't write or perform their own. That was why they felt they needed to go to Europe for their 'art'. The same applied to contemporary America. Both countries were advanced capitalist economies. Is that where the reason lies?

Although it is difficult and of course largely subjective to try to compare nations' cultural achievements qualitatively, there is an argument for saying that Britain did fall below its Continental neighbours in the nineteenth century in most areas of art. The major exception was literature, especially the novel, where Britain could be said to have dominated; although France ran pretty close here. This was also an area in which its practitioners had a considerable influence *on* the Continent: Dickens particularly, plus Walter Scott and the early nineteenth-century Romantic poets. Britain's musical influence abroad was generally confined to furnishing literary inspiration – Shakespeare especially – and librettos. Turner and Constable – its only major painters of the time – are supposed to have anticipated French Impressionism. The Pre-Raphaelite movement had its equivalents on the Continent, but in itself appears to have had few followers there. 'Gothic Revival' architecture was a Europe-wide movement, with each country providing its own (usually romantic) inspiration, but never quite flourished on the Continent as widely as it did in Britain. Nonetheless George Gilbert Scott, Britain's pre-eminent 'neo-Gothic' architect (St Pancras Station Hotel, the Albert Memorial, and – in another style – the Government Offices) was commissioned to design an important church in Hamburg, now a ruin (its tower and spire unluckily served as a guide for Allied bombers in the Second World War); but otherwise it was rare for the Continentals to employ British architects. And foreigners didn't come to Britain, so far as we can ascertain, to admire the Palace of Westminster or St Paul's Cathedral. Cultural tourism was always one-way.

Although this was widely agreed to be a characteristic of Britain – *Das Land ohne Musik* was the phrase chosen to describe the country in a book published by the German Oskar Schmitz in 1904 (he meant all art, not just music; according to him England simply had no soul) – not all patriots took offence at it. Some, indeed, derogated 'culture' *on principle*. We have come across the middle-class capitalist and traveller Samuel Laing already.[3] He may be the purest example of what we might call 'philosophical philistinism' from that period. His kind is rare in contemporary literature, but only because philistines tended not to write books, regarding them as a waste of their time, by contrast with 'making' things. Not only this, but Laing suspected that 'art' turned young men into rebels and revolutionaries, which for him explained the political ferment going on in Germany when he visited there in 1848. It would be better for them, he wrote, and for their country, if they were put to work in counting-houses, squashing any dangerous artistic tendencies flat; as they generally were in Britain.[4] Laing was certainly not alone in these opinions, if we can judge by the fact that reviews of his books made no mention of them. 'Philistines' also appear, far less positively, as characters in other writers' novels and travelogues, mainly to make the writers themselves look more 'cultured' by contrast. Philistinism didn't die with Laing, of course; Gilbert and Sullivan also savaged the 'arty' people of their day in their 1881 comic opera *Patience: or Bunthorne's Bride*. Jumping much further ahead, one can see Laing's basic thought patterns in the person of 1980s Prime Minister Margaret Thatcher.[5] She of course was a 'patriot' too: and a powerful advocate for capitalism, as it happens. She would make a perfect patron saint for those whose admiration for Britain rests mainly on its history of no-nonsense utilitarianism. Quite apart from her, 'philistines' could have made up a large proportion of British society; and so are worth our taking on board if we want to understand all the various strands that made up Britain's 'national identity' in the nineteenth century, and beyond.

*

Philistinism however was certainly not universal in Britain, even at the times when Laing was writing and Thatcher ruling. *Of course* Britain was never bereft of '*Musik*', in its widest sense, or even more narrowly. It would take more than a chapter in a short book to do justice to all the flowerings of the arts that so enlivened and beautified the nineteenth- and twentieth-century scene in Britain, for just about every class in society from the richest to the poorest: although they were not always the same arts for everyone. As nearly always happens, it was the upper classes who mainly enjoyed 'high' culture: which was only called that, however, because it was those classes that got to define it as 'high'.

Few of the proletariat went to operas, unlike in Italy and Soviet Russia, for example; except to the light 'operettas' of Gilbert and Sullivan, where they sat in the cheaper upper galleries, or 'Gods'. Their musical preference was for the music-hall, which the upper classes wouldn't have thought of frequenting, unless it was to ogle (and much more) at the young female beauties in the cast. Actresses in general had the reputations in Victorian times of being little better than prostitutes, so it was a dangerous profession, reputationally, for well-brought up young girls. (Marie Lloyd's popular song 'The boy I love is up in the gallery' was meant – or read – as a rejection of the sleazy old *roués* in the stalls.) Serious or 'grand' opera was for the upper and the upper-middle classes; as were 'serious' music concerts, albeit with some lower-middles attending them too. The latter could also hear fine choral music in their cathedrals and churches, for which most of the best British early and mid-Victorian compositions were written. Elgar first achieved fame with large-scale choral works, generally written for Midlands and Northern English 'choral societies', long before *Enigma*.[6] (These also had the advantage of requiring large numbers of the sheet music to be purchased, from the royalties on which he made most of the pittance he earned for composing.)

Elgar is particularly interesting from a 'class' perspective, coming as he did from the lower ranks of the middle class – his father was a shopkeeper – which as it happens was the social rank from which most of the undisputed cultural geniuses of Victorian Britain came. (Others were Turner, Keats and Dickens.) We can add to these, three other 'marginal' groups: middle-class women novelists, who weren't allowed to earn a living, and so could concentrate on their writing – a rare advantage for their gender; Irishmen: Wilde, Yeats, Balfe and Shaw; and one Indian (by birth and upbringing), Rudyard Kipling. From this it appears that artistic talent, or success, was only found in the lower-middle ranks or the outside edges of the Victorian social system – very few aristocrats' or bankers' sons or daughters became great artists; which further suggests that that system did not function to support 'culture' of this kind. Which is not to say that the working classes and even the aristocracy could not appreciate the art, especially the novels, produced by all those lower-middles, Irish and women. Dickens was read across almost the whole social spectrum; and although King Edward VII is said to have dozed off during his own Coronation Ode, composed for him by Elgar, the latter's 'Land of Hope and Glory' has always been almost too popular, albeit often with alternative, non-jingoistic words.

What they all thought of the new architecture around them – architecture being the most visible of the art forms – isn't known. There was a battle raging at this time between two particular styles of building, 'Gothic' and 'Classical'; but mainly among the intelligentsia and their patrons:[7] which is why, incidentally, we shouldn't try to infer from Victorian architecture any general attitudes towards, for example, society (Gothic seen as a reaction against modern industrialism), or empire (symbolized by all those Roman columns and architraves). Indeed, it is for this reason that *no* cultural production or fashion should be assumed to reflect Britain as a whole at any time. British society cannot be 'read' from its literature or drama or pictorial art; as neither can the *zeitgeist* of any particular period. This is why we have social historians: to delve beneath the patinas of privilege.

In any case most of the working classes in Britain didn't experience 'architecture' in this way. Here is Dickens's description of his fictional 'Coketown', in his searing novel (there are no jokes in it) *Hard Times* (1854).

It was a town of red brick, or of brick that would have been red if the smoke and ashes had allowed it; but as matters stood, it was a town of unnatural red and black like the painted face of a savage.

It was a town of machinery and tall chimneys, out of which interminable serpents of smoke trailed themselves for ever and ever, and never got uncoiled.

It had a black canal in it, and a river that ran purple with ill-smelling dye, and vast piles of building full of windows where there was a rattling and a trembling all day long, and where the piston of the steam-engine worked monotonously up and down, like the head of an elephant in a state of melancholy madness. It contained several large streets all very like one another, and many small streets still more like one another, inhabited by people equally like one another, who all went in and out at the same hours, with the same sound upon the same pavements, to do the same work, and to whom every day was the same as yesterday and tomorrow, and every year the counterpart of the last and the next.[8]

That reads like an exaggeration; but we know from other accounts (including Engels'), and from some of the surviving old buildings of cities like Manchester, that it wasn't. Even if they went into the centre of their city the workers of Manchester wouldn't have seen much better, until its great Town Hall (by the Gothicist Alfred Waterhouse) was completed in 1877. Architecture was for the social and industrial elite.

Except underground. One of the major building enterprises of the nineteenth century was the great London sewer system that Joseph William Bazalgette built for the Metropolitan Board of Works beneath London, after what was called the 'Great Stink' of 1858, arising from the effluent deposited in the Thames. Bad drainage was also blamed for the London cholera epidemics of the previous half-century. The new system put an end to that, and was credited with saving hundreds of thousands of lives subsequently. Bazalgette, the grandson of a French refugee, should be more celebrated for that. The London Underground Railway – the first of its kind in the world – followed shortly afterwards. These were 'architecture' too. The older Underground stations were quite decorative: Baker Street has recently been restored to its former glory. And Bazalgette even used Gothic arches in his drains.

So far as the more visible Arts were concerned, the 1890s and 1900s saw a turn for the better – or for the worse, if you were a proud philistine – with an 'English Musical Renaissance' (Elgar, Stanford, Sullivan, Vaughan Williams and the Old Etonian Parry); a new native architecture (Arts and Crafts, Voysey, Lutyens, Charles Rennie Mackintosh, Gilbert Scott *fils*) to replace or refresh the stale old 'revivals'; new-style novelists (H. G. Wells, Kipling, Galsworthy, Conrad, Forster, Arnold Bennett and a little later Virginia Woolf); playwrights (Pinero, Wilde, Shaw); and picture artists (Sickert, Sissley, Duncan Grant, Vanessa Bell, Aubrey Beardsley, Art Nouveau). This stronger 'high' cultural life continued through the remainder of the twentieth century. Of course it still might not measure up to that of contemporaries on the Continent. But it was evidence of a rebirth of artistic life in Britain. Laing would have predicted that this would be at the expense of entrepreneurial activity, and at the risk of political ructions; which there certainly were in these *fin-de-siècle* years.

But culture, of course, isn't just 'art'. Middle-taste music flourished in this period and throughout the twentieth century, with jazz, 'light' music (Alfred Ketèlby, Eric Coates), musicals, and a huge flowering of popular or 'pop' music from the 1950s onward. Indeed, what is today known as a distinct 'youth culture' may have had its origins here. (Before, children and teenagers mainly aped their parents.) The new art form of the cinema, followed by television dramas and 'soap operas', was perhaps the most democratic of all the cultural products of the twentieth century; dominated by Hollywood, but with some distinctively British elements: 'Ealing comedies', imperial adventures (usually directed, however, by Hungarian immigrants), war films, 'period' dramas, and James Bond. For reading matter there were 'penny dreadfuls', often featuring rogues – pirates, highwaymen – as heroes; more innocent books for younger children, usually carrying moral lessons (*An ABC for Little Patriots*, 1899, was one); comic papers for all children's ages (*Ally Sloper's Half Holiday, Beano, Dandy*), mostly featuring just picture stories, but some (*Champion, Rover, Hotspur*) carrying densely printed text stories too. Most of these were disapproved of by middle-class parents, who thought they were distracting their children from 'real literature', and were a bit 'common' – the customary word used for the 'lower' classes then. It was to reassure these parents that the Reverend Marcus Morris brought out his new 'comic' *Eagle* for boys in 1951, which introduced them not only to 'Dan Dare, Pilot of the Future' (a space explorer), but also carried a comic-strip version of the life of St Paul. Morris saw *Eagle* as a vehicle for Christian evangelism, but many readers won't have seen past Dan, Digby and the Mekon – Dan's perennial enemy: perennial because Dan could never find it in his gentlemanly heart to kill him. Later Morris brought out a companion paper for girls: girls weren't supposed to be interested in 'space'. It was called *Girl*. The art work for both papers – especially on Dan Dare, by Frank Hampson – was outstanding.

A major cultural activity, however, was sport; indulged in by all classes, but with each class doing it slightly differently. 'Field sports' – hunting, shooting, fishing, anything that involved the violent death of wild animals – were mainly the domain of the upper classes (and some farmers), with subsidiary roles for the peasants. Aspirant bourgeois were sometimes allowed to join in, for cash. Cricket – the most 'artistic' and perhaps the most 'English' of all games – was played by all classes, but with the classes separated, as we have seen. Golf was played by the upper-middle classes, and by the Scots, who had invented the game. There were three kinds of football: Rugby Union, mainly for public schoolboys (in England, not Wales); Rugby League, for the Northern working classes; and Association Football, or 'soccer', mainly for working-class boys, but Eton College played it too. Until recently women weren't allowed – or encouraged – to play any of these games; but had to make do with 'rounders' (baseball or softball, essentially), 'netball' (basketball in the US), and (field) hockey. So there was a strict gender divide, too. Towards the end of the twentieth century the higher soccer leagues became, in effect, an entertainment industry taken over by private capitalists, many of them foreign (Russian in one case), and so ceased representing the working-class areas that had given birth to them; and could no longer be an object of *patriotic* pride. The English national team, with fewer native players to choose from as brilliant foreigners were bought in to replace them, won nothing after its famous (home) World Cup victory in 1966; although it came close in July 2021. Eton also had a game – the 'Wall Game' – which was only played there. Apparently it was pretty rough. All of which demonstrates how important class and money were in nineteenth and twentieth century Britain, and indeed up to the present day; which is another reason why we cannot generalize about 'national' traits, or a British 'culture', at this time. (And we have scarcely touched on Scotland, Wales and Ireland.)

Lastly there was 'intellectual' life, which flourished in Britain throughout our period, but mainly – obviously – among 'intellect*uals*'. Science did best when it could be pursued individually or in small groups, by the likes of – for example – Darwin; Faraday; Galton; Crick, Watson and Franklin; Maxwell; Fleming; Turing . . .; and many others. When 'big bucks' were required, America took over. Britain also had the advantage of boasting four or five of the world's leading universities, which gave researchers the time and leisure to experiment and think. So far as philosophy was concerned John Stuart Mill was probably the only one to hold a candle to the Continentals, and he was different from many of them in being down-to-earth and comprehensible, certainly by comparison with the Germans (and the later French). For 'ordinary folk' who wished to know and discuss what their scientists and philosophers were doing, many nineteenth-century cities boasted 'Literary and Philosophical Societies'; of which only the Newcastle 'Lit & Phil' survives today in its original building: a superb library, in the neo-Classical style. 'Below' them (understood in hierarchical terms, of course), there were dozens of associations set up usually by workers themselves to enable inquisitive and ambitious autodidacts to learn more; culminating in the 'Workers' Educational Association' founded by Albert and Frances Mansbridge in 1903, distributing 'book boxes' to its members every month. This incidentally would have been anathema to most early Victorian Tories (and to Samuel Laing), who feared the repercussions of people's being educated 'above their station'. From their self-interested point of view, they could have been right.

*

There is a lot to admire in nineteenth- and twentieth-century British 'culture', but not of course more than in other cultures of the day. In any case there was little in it that was distinctively 'British', with artists more than anyone being prepared to learn from 'abroad'. Elgar is considered to be a quintessentially 'English' composer; but in his own time he was criticized for being too like Brahms. Other composers sought inspiration from the traditional music of the English countryside; but to this listener's ear one country's 'traditional' music – especially on fiddles – is much like another's at this time. Popular music leaps over borders. (How many people know that 'The Star-Spangled Banner' was based on an eighteenth-century English drinking song?) Turner didn't only paint *British* landscapes, and in most of them it's the skies that distinguish them; with the sky being everyone's. That said, L. S. Lowry's much greyer skies might have been more recognisable to most Britons. The foremost 'national' characteristics in Dickens's novels are the filth, poverty, blackguardism and eccentricity portrayed in them. The very different Anthony Trollope described the England that was behind him, chronologically: the semi-feudal age of mid-nineteenth-century Whiggish politics and the Anglican Church. That, together with those 'period dramas' on television and in the cinema, may have given a false or at least a very romanticized impression of Britain, which, if it serves to fuel 'patriotism', probably does genuine patriotism a disservice. (This is not to say that many of those costume dramas aren't awfully good.) Science was very much an international pursuit. Indeed, cross-fertilization was the rule in all these areas. Even looking back: what would Shakespeare have become if he had stayed in Warwickshire, without the foreign input he got from multi-cultural London and his travelling players; one just returned, as he was about to start work on *Hamlet*, from performing in Helsingør?

British culture is rich, and in many areas – especially Shakespeare – has always had an international reputation. But it is not *peculiarly* rich. And it is worth remembering that for many Britons, from the obscure Samuel Laing to the celebrated Margaret Thatcher, the feature of Britain that made them proudest of their country was its no-nonsense artistic poverty. 'Britain was better than that.' Which is one kind of patriotism; albeit probably not one shared widely among educated – or perhaps any – Britons today.

7

Europeans

Is Britain a 'part' of Europe, or not? Hasn't Britain always been distinct from its Continental neighbours, and better off when it did things independently? – For some patriots – the separatists among them – this is the big question.

On the 'distinctiveness' point: Yes. There have always been features of British society that marked it off from 'the Continent'. (Cricket is one. Driving on the left is another.) Equally important, however, are two caveats. The first is that, apart from cricket, these distinctive attributes were not always the same ones, and indeed were sometimes 'swapped' between Britain and its neighbours – so for example Britain could be more 'liberal' than they were at one time, but less 'liberal' (by the same definition) at another. The second is that insofar as Britain *was* distinct from other European countries, it was no more distinct from them than they were from each other: Germany, to take an obvious example, from France. So Britain isn't *so* different – or exceptionally exceptional; and has not always been, historically, different in the same way. On the other point – 'better off on its own' – we need to explore how much 'on its own' Britain has been in reality in the nineteenth and twentieth centuries. That will be the theme of this chapter.

*

We don't need to go too far back. That Britain was once in the human era geographically joined to the Continent of Europe *via* 'Doggerland', should probably not be treated as a crucial argument in favour of its 'Europeanness' after all this time. What may be more relevant, however, is that Doggerland was replaced not by a 'sea', but by a relatively narrow channel of water, 33 kilometres (21 miles) at its narrowest point, from South Foreland in Kent to Cap Gris Nez in the Pas-de-Calais. The point here being that it was not a huge obstacle to people wanting to travel from France to England, or the other way, either in boats, however primitive, or by simply swimming across; as of course they did, repeatedly (though probably not the swimming), from pre-Roman times onwards. In the nineteenth century the crossing could be an unpleasant experience in rough weather – contemporary travel accounts make a lot of the sea-sickness – but a mercifully brief one: only three hours by sail, reducing to about ninety minutes when steamships came in. As a result, letters posted in London usually arrived in Paris the next day. Communications are important in binding peoples together, and in this regard France was closer to southern England than Scotland was. The result could be seen in the numbers of Europeans who visited or came to settle in Britain (the Census returns don't discriminate) during the nineteenth century: 24,000 in 1821; 50,829 in1851, 84,000 in 1861; 100,638 in 1871; 118,031 for 1881; and 339,436 for 1901, out of a total British population of 12 million rising to 32 million over the same period. Most of these were from 'Germany including Prussia' in 1871 (32,823), and France (17,906). These made up the majority of immigrants and incomers to Britain in this period, aside from Irish (who of course were legally 'British'); with non-Europeans, apart from Americans (7,000+ in 1871), scarcely featuring. Substantial 'coloured' immigration into Britain, usually from the old Empire, only started after the Second World War.

Unfortunately we do not have comparable figures for British visitors to the Continent at this time, but they must have comprised many thousands. Early on they were mainly upper and upper-middle class, travelling there to do 'the Grand Tour' and experience 'the arts', or occasionally for less innocent purposes; but supplemented from the middle of the century onwards by 'lower' middle class people shepherded over to Paris and up the Rhine by Thomas Cook's great new invention: the package tour. Cook's tourists soon earned a poor reputation in Europe, not only among the natives but also among 'serious' visitors, by their loud and boorish conduct. Whether this was fully justified or not we cannot tell; it was obviously to the benefit of the more sophisticated travellers to distinguish themselves from the inferior 'tourists' in this way.[1] But the image stuck, and may have been a factor behind whatever Continental Anglo- (or Brito-) phobia there was. As well as tourists, however, the Continent welcomed hundreds of British professionals there: entrepreneurs setting up factories, doctors, child-minders, artists, even jockeys, and of course diplomats. One of the doctors, Charles Lever, wrote novels set on the Continent, providing one valuable – though not completely reliable – commentary on Anglo-European relations at this level. He despised the 'Cooks Tours' people too.

In Britain the main way people got to meet foreigners in the nineteenth century was as 'industrial' tourists, coming to marvel at the great machines exhibited in the 'Crystal Palace' in the summer of 1851, and at the new-fangled railways, but not at the British art on display; and as refugees from the succession of political upheavals that struck most European countries in 1848, especially, and from the Russian anti-Jewish pogroms of the turn of the next century. Many of these immigrants, or their progeny, later became productive and influential members of British society: Joseph Bazalgette, whom we met in the last chapter; Friedrich Engels; the Rossettis; Gustav Holst; a couple of Eltons; Joseph Conrad; the Marks of Marks and Spencer;

Montagu Burton; several Millibands, Nigel Farage, two-thirds of the 2021 England soccer team, and Emma Raducanu, winner of the US (tennis) Open in 2021. (And that's without mentioning Karl Marx.) It is well known that Britain has always been a country of immigration, in common as it happens with most other European countries, but in this case mainly because it had no 'Alien' or anti-immigrant laws for most of the nineteenth century: incomers didn't even need to show passports. Its population, once one has allowed for some of them changing their names to hide their origins – or to make them more pronounceable: who in Britain would remember Józef [Konrad] Korzeniowski? – reflected that.

As for cultural exchanges – Brits being influenced by Continentals, and vice versa – they were far too many and too complex to list here. In literature, art, music, food, drink, sports, the theatre, political ideology and most other cultural areas, cross-fertilization was the rule rather than the exception. It would have been strange had it been otherwise, with Britain's being so close to 'the Continent', geographically.

*

Closest of all to Britain – just that 21 miles away – was the proud Republic of France, which had been Britain's major diplomatic rival in the years before 1815, and was still its major perceived potential enemy, but nonetheless could be said to be its fondest neighbour too. Once upon a time, of course, they had been the same country, and the 'Angevin' influence could still be seen in Britain's mediaeval church architecture, its aristocracy and the Channel Islands: a little bit of France still under the British crown. France played rugby football, which created another common interest with Britain, albeit more gracefully – less 'physically' – than the latter. (Cricket never caught on, except in a little town in the foothills of the French Pyrenees called Pau, nicknamed *la ville anglaise* because of all the Brits settled there.) French was the second language taught in nearly all British schools that taught any modern foreign languages at all, and was still in the nineteenth century the language of diplomacy. French cuisine was considered to be the *ne plus ultra* by the upper classes, and French styles of dress the most *à la mode* by the modish. The use of French expressions was also considered a sign of *bon goût*. By the British establishment the French were mainly distrusted because of their revolutionary tendencies, which was reasonable in view of their history and some of the hotheads they still harboured, or who in some cases fled to Britain to indulge in conspiracies there. The latter nearly caused a major diplomatic *contretemps* in the 1850s, when France demanded their extradition, but Britain refused on the grounds that it would be contrary to its liberal principles.[2]

There were rivalries between the two nations over colonies, but the most serious of the nineteenth-century ones (Fashoda, 1896) was settled over a bottle of champagne in the desert; and in 1904 an important *Entente Cordiale* between them resolved most other colonial disputes. Another agreement in 1919 shared the Middle East between them after the Great War. In view of this, France should be regarded as a partner with Britain in the great *Europe-wide* imperial enterprise of the nineteenth century, rather than – or as well as – a national rival. The same could also be said of Germany after it entered the colonial race in the 1880s: 'God speed her!', as Gladstone generously put it then. 'She becomes our ally and partner, in the execution of the great purposes of Providence for the advantage of mankind'.[3] So empire pulled the European powers together, rather than dividing them. So far as purely European issues were concerned, Britain kept out of France's losing war with Prussia (1870), but in three of the other major wars of the period (1854, 1914 and 1939) Britain and France fought side-by-side (at least until France capitulated in June 1940). France was also the first European nation with whom Britain was able to sign a free trade treaty (1860). So by and large they could be said to have got on well.

After the 1860s both came to agree, reluctantly in Britain's case (the Queen was a 'German', after all),[4] that the newly-united Germany was the major threat to European peace, against which some kind of collective security was necessary. For Britain the ideal form of this was what was called a 'balance of power' system: not in the way that phrase has been taken subsequently, to describe two great allied blocs balanc*ing* one another – NATO *versus* the Warsaw Pact, for example; but something rather more subtle: five or six European nations of roughly equivalent size and military strength, agreeing – if only tacitly – to come together to resist aggression by any one of them. It was supposed to work almost like clockwork: a threatening step by one would automatically set in motion counter-steps by the others.[5] It was on this basis that the British felt they were able to resist formal alliances with other European countries for European purposes – 1904 was an *entente*, and for *colonial* purposes; which however hid the fact that they were not really 'alone' in Europe, or in a state of 'splendid isolation', as some contemporary patriots put it, but crucially tied to the Continent; as became crystal clear in August 1914, when Germany attacked Belgium, and the wheels of the clockwork fell into place.

Eventually Britain came out of that on the winning side, as it did also after the next World War, thanks latterly to the Americans and the USSR; but not before certain major flaws had come to light in its defensive capabilities, which were perhaps not surprising in view of the nature of its society before then. Victorian and Edwardian Britain was a nation that prided itself on being peace-loving: yes, even in the midst of all those wars against 'natives' in the colonies, most of which appeared 'aggressive' to the natives themselves, obviously, but which were presented to Britons as paci*fying* engagements, reluctantly entered into. Ideologically they didn't like armies – nasty, unproductive and unprofitable things – with the result that the Army they had (apart from the very separate Indian wing of it) was generally poorly officered, by younger sons of the upper classes, and manned by the remaining dregs of society, almost universally despised when they got *out* of their uniforms; short of match practice against 'civilized' opponents; often defeated by the 'uncivilized'; and usually only on the winning sides of any serious battles if it had more powerful and efficient allies fighting by its side. Most of the Army's most celebrated achievements were heroic failures, like the Charge of the Light Brigade in the Crimean War, and retreats, like from Gallipoli in January 1916 and Dunkirk in May–June 1940. Queen Victoria was apparently terribly put out when the Crimean War was brought to an end before her brave boys had had the chance to score any runs. (The Charge of the Light Brigade didn't count.) But that was the British Army for you: at least as it stood in the public estimation; which may have been unfair. The Royal Navy fared much better, being romantic; with a true hero – Nelson – in its locker; and more *British*, with all those British seas around them. For the working classes it also seemed safer. Sailors were unlikely to be deployed against protestors on land.

Wars were the most obvious way in which Britons became 'European' in the twentieth century. Thousands of them are still lying in beautifully-tended war cemeteries in France, Belgium and elsewhere. Those were also – and still are – meant to remind everyone of the terrible price of warfare; against the future threat of which the European Union – under a succession of other names – was set up in 1951. Britain tried to join the European Economic Community in 1961 but was rebuffed by the French President, Charles de Gaulle, on the grounds that Britain was too close to the United States. Britain eventually succeeded in 1972, fairly uncontroversially – the decision was ratified by 67 per cent to 33 per cent in a referendum shortly afterwards – with almost the whole Press in favour of Britain's joining, and most of the opposition then coming from the Left. (The Left saw European union as a Trojan horse for the hated 'global capitalism'. There was something in that.) Thereafter there was always a 'Eurosceptic' element in British politics, with varying and alternating degrees of popular approval, but only finally breaking through in the mid-2010s. By this time it had become mainly a Right-wing, 'patriotic' movement. We shall be coming to that in the next chapter.

*

All European countries, it goes without saying, had interests of various kinds *in* Europe. Most of them, we sometimes have to be reminded, also had stakes in more distant parts of the world where they were trading and *colonizing*. Again, it is worth emphasizing that Britain wasn't the only colonial or imperial European power in the nineteenth and twentieth centuries, with France, Holland, Spain, Portugal, Belgium, Italy, Denmark, Germany for a short time, and even Sweden, all with their noses in the colonial trough. Indeed, it was these common extra-European interests that can be said to have united them, in – as Gladstone had put it – the 'great purpose of Providence for the advantage of mankind'. Leaving aside for the moment the question of whether imperialism really was 'for the advantage of mankind', or even 'Providential', it is clear that this was an enterprise they all shared together, with Britain merely being the biggest of the bunch.

But it could perhaps be said to have invested more than other nations did in its colonial trade, with 'imperial preference', for example, still being an important plank of its commercial policy; originally drummed up by its old imperialists as a step to a world-wide political union of all their colonies, rather like the German *Zollverein* had been, so forging a proper 'empire'. Lack of enthusiasm for this idea from the colonies themselves, however, and changes in the geographical balance of Britain's trade after the Second World War, had made this something of a dead duck by the 1970s. But in any case this – imperial preference – didn't mark it off from its neighbours essentially. France, for example, had similar ties with *its* ex-colonies, which the EEC was able to accommodate.

One other of Britain's foreign interests, however, did crucially mark it off from the other EEC partners. This was its relationship with the United States of America: the one that had stymied its application to join the EEC in 1961. De Gaulle may have been right about that. America represented a different kind of economy and society from the one that was emerging in Europe: more 'free market' and non-interventionist than the more 'social' model that the Continent favoured, and that France's President hoped the EEC would too. The US was also dominating European 'culture' in a way the French had always been more resistant to than the British. That had a lot to do with Britain's and America's sharing a common language (in the main). De Gaulle probably felt more strongly about this than about the awkward economic fit. In the end that difference was overcome, with Britain's going along with, for example, the EU's albeit rather vague 'Social Chapter' that was tacked on to the end of the Maastricht Treaty in 1992. But Britain's 'American' tendencies continued to be suspected by the other Europeans, at the same time as the EU's restrictions on enterprise were resented by Britain's Free Marketist and US-oriented Right; and – exaggerated by the Press – by many people of other persuasions and concerns too. By the latter this was all attributed to Britain's being entrapped in a federation or even a 'Brussels empire' that had taken away its former 'liberty'.

This may have been based on a misunderstanding of the nature of 'liberty' in an international context. Anyone familiar with the histories of Britain's 'informal colonies' in the nineteenth century – the ones that weren't painted red on those world maps, and answering to Whitehall, but were merely *dominated* by Britain in various ways: their production dependent on British markets, for example, or on British investment – will know that these sorts of ties could be as binding as formal colonial ones; and still can be. Britain's accession to the EEC and the EU, therefore, didn't necessarily 'entrap' it, but simply exchanged one trap for another. Ridding itself of its new trap would not necessarily make it 'free-er', but could on the contrary return Britain to another albeit more 'informal' kind of dependency. The particular dependency mentioned in the discussions over 'Brexit' was on the US, the only market big enough to compensate for Britain's loss of the 'free' European one, which might demand concessions that Britain would have resisted if it had had the backing of the EU behind it again. The opening of the NHS to American Health companies, and Britain's accepting 'chlorinated chicken', were the two examples usually quoted. Frying pans and fires come to mind.

*

The answer to the question 'was Britain ever on its own', therefore, is No. As a major trading power from at least the eighteenth century onwards – with foreign commerce accounting for a greater proportion of its domestic product than was the case with any other European country – it was inextricably bound to the latter, and to its own wider-world markets, for all that time. Without them it would have shrunk to nothing; as it nearly did when German blockades cut off much of its trade during the Second World War. Then its people only survived by digging up football pitches and grass verges to grow vegetables, and eating products – canned *snoek*, powdered egg, Camp 'coffee' and beef dripping – they had always rejected up until then. Dependence on imports, of course, didn't necessarily imply dependen*cy*, especially as the dependence was usually mutual, with your suppliers needing your markets too; and especially if you were a big enough market, or had big enough guns, to keep it open. Otherwise you would need *treaties* to keep the relationship going – not only regarding trade but also every other kind of international relationship – which usually involved a degree of 'give and take', the 'give' part of which would be binding. The European Union represented a network of treaties of that kind, originally at any rate, and no more than this while the other partners were content with that: without, that is, the *'closer'* union that was the ambition of some of them, and the great bogey of the Brexiters. While it stayed like that, it involved no more loss of 'freedom' than any replacement system of treaties would involve.

The other question is whether Britain was sufficiently *different* from its European neighbours to justify living apart from them. Of course Britons were always aware of other countries' 'foreignness', as anyone is on first visiting another country, when it is the differences that stand out, before you get used to them. But it is difficult to think of any 'difference' between Britain and, say, France that was greater than those between France and other European countries, or than exist within perfectly compatible marriages. The British Empire certainly wasn't one of them. Cricket may have been; but that was 'only' a game. And Europeans might be persuaded to take it up in time.

8

Brexit

The decision to take Britain out of the European Union, arrived at on the basis of a referendum vote on 23 June 2016, and then implemented – with a few loose ends – roughly four years later, may turn out to be one of the most consequential in its history. (We shan't know for sure until we see how it turns out.) It was certainly more consequential in the short term than Britain's original entry *into* the EEC (as it was then called) in 1972, which was controversial, of course, but approved by a comfortable margin in a referendum called to ratify it in 1975, and remained broadly accepted thereafter. Indeed, it seemed a 'natural' step for Britain to take in the post-imperial world, in the interests of its security, its prosperity (hopefully), and its status in world affairs; and in view of its centuries-long connections with its neighbours, outlined in the previous chapter. Beyond that it would signify that Britain had 'got over' its old pretensions, in a mature and dignified way, and was at last contributing to the original and broader rationale behind European union, which was to ensure that a war like the last two could not break out again. That was what its leading British fan, Prime Minister Edward Heath, had had in mind.

Hence the shocked surprise of many people – perhaps most of them – at the result of the later referendum, which was a narrow but as it turned out decisive win for the 'Brexit' side. (The figures were 51.89 per cent to 48.11 per cent: of people who voted, that is. So a two per cent swing would have swung it the other way.) By all the normal rules of politics this should not have been decisive, because votes on existential questions usually require either 'super-majorities' (i.e. significantly greater than 50–50), or subsequent confirmatory referenda, before they can be put into effect. Indeed, the June 2016 referendum had been billed as an 'advisory' rather than a mandatory one, which turned out to be just as well for the 'Brexiters' (as they were called, or 'Brexit*eers*', which sounded more swashbuckling; or 'Leavers'), after a court ruled that if it *had* been a mandatory vote – like an election – it would have needed to be re-run because of certain irregularities on the Brexit side. (We'll come back to those.) In the end that was gotten over by means of a vote in Parliament – which was after all constitutionally the ultimate arbiter of these things in Britain – to confirm the result anyway.

That was finally put into effect at midnight (Central European time rather than GMT, which annoyed some patriots) on 31 January 2020, when Britain exited the European Union to the accompaniment of noisy celebrations outside Parliament, but by a fairly small number of Brexiters. The latter had originally wanted church bells to be rung all over Britain, as they had been at the end of the last War, but the Church of England was having none of that. And such a display might, in truth, have been seen as provocative, in view of the feelings of just under 50 per cent of the population – maybe more by then – on the other side.

The reasons for this extraordinary result have already – just a few months after Britain's final departure from the EU – been analysed at length, and in different ways, including by the present writer.[1] One explanation could be that it was simply an accident, or a chapter of them. If for example Prime Minister David Cameron had not been so careless in calling the 'Brexit' referendum in the way he did (to calm unrest in his own party, as he thought); or so dismissive of the United Kingdom Independence Party (UKIP) early on: in 2006 he had made a basic error, of taste if nothing else, by referring to them as 'a bunch of fruit cakes, loonies and closet racists', which was obviously provocative, and more dismissive, as it turned out, than UKIP deserved;[2] if the Right-wing press had not been so powerful; or Britain's electoral system not what it was: 'First Past the Post' and all that; or the Brexit leaders not so unprincipled and – it has to be said – clever in their propaganda; or Eton College not so extraordinarily dominant still (or again) in the narrow 'upper' reaches of English society; or England not so dominant in United Kingdom affairs; or the pro-Europeans not so feeble and negative in their advocacy; or the EU not so beastly to Greece in the months before the referendum: then the narrow margin in favour of Brexit might well have turned out the other way. The Parliamentary vote that set the result of this merely advisory referendum in stone was only passed because MPs – many of whom were convinced 'Remainers' – were persuaded that the referendum had indicated the 'people's will', and were nervous of going against it: especially in view of the rank hostility displayed by the other side. All these circumstances made Brexit a very lucky call for the Brexiters; which would seem to corroborate the 'accidental' explanation for it.

Looking for solider and less fortuitous causes, if there is any consensus on the topic it goes something like this. Britons were not really concerned about 'Europe' in the years leading up to the referendum – the topic hardly ever featured in opinion polls – but *were* mightily concerned about other things: economic depression, austerity, inequality, crime, their National Health Service, 'alien' immigration, an out-of-touch 'Establishment', their inability to express these concerns effectively due to the political system (First Past the Post), and of course some more minor gripes, like 'political correctness', which did exist, and in some grotesque forms, but was rather exaggerated by the political Right; and which they were then persuaded to lay at the door of the EU by a Eurosceptic popular press. Why the press was so anti-

Europe is a matter for debate. One reason may be that it saw 'xenophobia' as a promising horse to back in order to win readers. People, they realized, love a good hate. (That goes back to its origins at the time of the Boer War.) Another is that the millionaires who owned the newspapers feared a new EU law that was due to come in shortly that would have closed off the 'tax havens' into which they had siphoned so many of their ill-gotten gains. Or they may have been anti European 'bureaucracy' out of genuine capitalist, or other, principle.

As were some – but not all – of the political leaders of the anti-EU movement. That was clearly true in the cases of the early leaders of UKIP, like its founder in 1993, the history professor Alan Sked, and after him the small group of Europhobic obsessives who had kept the torch burning during the dark years. They included the strangely charismatic ex-banker Nigel Farage, and the Tory MP Sir Bill Cash – who was old enough (just) to remember the last War, and appeared to regard the EU as essentially a continuation of Hitler's 'thousand year Reich'.[3] These were the genuine 'Eurosceptics' in the Conservative Party; organized in what was called the 'European Research Group' or 'ERG' (misleadingly: it did no 'research', having settled on its position *ab initio*), which turned out to be immensely influential within the party, succeeding in getting most of its leading pro-Europeans banished under Prime Minister Boris Johnson.

Whether Johnson himself was a 'genuine' Eurosceptic has been doubted. A journalist originally, he was well known to have penned two *Daily Telegraph* op-eds, one for and the other against Brexit, before calculating that the 'for' one would better suit his ambition.[4] On the other hand, as the *Telegraph*'s former correspondent in Brussels it was he who had originated many of the tall tales about the EU – that it wanted to ban 'bendy bananas' and prawn-flavoured crisps, for example; to regulate the size of condoms to suit poorly-endowed Italians; and to admit Moslem Turkey as a member – which then percolated 'down' to the tabloids, thus fuelling the popular prejudice against Europe. One could never tell whether *he* believed all this. Johnson had a universal reputation (even among his own supporters) as a bit of a fibber.

Which leads on to the next question, which is: why did people vote him into power, in the 'Let's get Brexit done!' general election of December 2019? Explanations for that vary too. One – which however is dangerous for any educated person to suggest, for fear of being accused of 'elitism' – is plain stupidity. There was certainly plenty of that around, probably on both sides of the argument, although elitists tended to stress the ignorance and lack of thought to be found in the Brexit camp in particular. And one of the main determinants of voting in the Brexit referendum – as it was in contemporary American elections – *was* educational level, with the less well-educated voters (as well as the older ones) generally opting for Brexit (and for Trump). This suggests that some responsibility – if you are unwilling to accuse Trump and Brexit supporters of inborn stupidity – could be attributed to the British – or at least the English – educational system's failure to inculcate knowledge of British constitutional history, or – even more crucially – of sheer logic, in the people's schools. ('Public' schools may have been equally deficient in this respect. What can the Greeks and Romans really teach us about politics today?) It was *education* that Disraeli, remember, had relied on in order to wean the 'mob' away from its prejudices, and make 'democracy' in Britain safe: 'we must educate our masters'.[5] That may have been an over-optimistic view. Other factors could have been Johnson's lovable image, as a cuddly P. G. Wodehouse-type teddy bear; and the poor 'leadership' qualities of his main opponent, the almost saintly Jeremy Corbyn, who was monstered by the Right-wing press as most Labour leaders are, but worse, and this time by a section of the Jewish community too. (Because he supported the Palestinians' call for a state of their own alongside Israel, he was portrayed as anti-Semitic, which was demonstrable nonsense in view of his life-long stand against all kinds of racism; but was a smear that stuck.)[6] In fact Corbyn's 'compromise' policy over Brexit – keeping the 'single market' but ditching the rest – might have been the best one possible, and more in line with what the majority of even convinced Brexiters wanted. But he wasn't allowed to put it forward clearly, unsullied by the mud being thrown at him by the other side.

One of Corbyn's major drawbacks was his supposed lack of 'patriotism', made much of by the Right-wing press – his lack of respect for the monarchy, for example shown by the way he dressed at royal and military occasions; his opposition to most of Britain's recent wars; his willingness to talk with terrorists; even the suspicion, which was clearly a gross slander, that he had spied for the communists – complaints based on a crude and superficial view of 'patriotism', maybe (we shall return to this), which was consequently not only rejected but also unfortunately mocked by Leftish and liberal 'elitists'; which mockery may have only provoked the working- and middle-class electors who were supposed to share this form of patriotism all the more. On the Left 'patriotism' was usually over-identified with 'xenophobia', which it did not need to be: there were (and are) better and more positive reasons for loyalty to one's country, as again we shall see; but the Left's patronizing and dismissive view of working-class patriotism may have lost it votes, both in the Referendum of 2016 and in the General Election of three-and-a-half years later.[7] 'Patriotism' has been a potent weapon for the Right ever since Disraeli's time. Its re-emergence now, in the form of the demand for national independence from 'Europe' – usually expressed as 'sovereignty' – may have been a potent factor behind Brexit.

The broader Right in 'high' British politics seized on this opportunity; not so much – arguably – because of its genuine feelings about 'Europe' or 'patriotism', but because it saw that this sudden patriotic animus against Europe could be exploited for other ends. Many Rightists, again, *were* kosher Europhobes, some of them – it must be emphasized – for good and sensible reasons, but others for what could be regarded as dubious 'historical' ones: arising out of their (largely false) memories of what they saw as Britain's past 'independence', or 'splendid isolation', or the myth that it had won the Second World War on its own; or even a certain retrospective reverence for the world-wide Empire that had been so pathetically let go of by the post-War 'Left'. (Wrong again, of course.) Boris Johnson played to this with his vision of the 'global Britain' that he believed (or pretended) could be created, or revived, once it was released from the restraints of Brussels bureaucracy; not an Empire – 'Heaven forfend', he protested;[8] but very close to the early, 'informal' kind. That fitted in well, incidentally, with the way many foreigners regarded Britain's contemporary trauma in any case: simply as an exercise in imperial nostalgia. This was largely unfair – the wider world has always overrated Britain's attachment to its Empire, for understandable reasons: mainly because it was largely how Britain had presented *to them*; but there *were* old imperial nostalgics in Britain, for whom the idea of becoming merely equal to other European nations had always seemed an indignity.[9] This also affected some of the troops. 'We used to rule half the world', was an occasional cry heard among nativist mobs, albeit one not fully supported by history. ('Half' is an exaggeration, for a start.) It is unlikely, however, that Empire nostalgia was pre-eminent in the minds or motives of all that many of the top Brexiters; certainly not a commonly expressed one, at a time when 'imperialism' had so many negative connotations – it was even equated with Nazism – as to seriously besmirch it as a rallying call.

A more rational reason for Conservatives' Euroscepticism, however, although one less widely bruited because it might have had less appeal, was a deep-seated one deriving from the Thatcher era, whose 'liberation' of the British economy seemed to be being obstructed by 'Brussels bureaucracy'. For free market (neoliberal) members of the Conservative élite saw Brexit, quite simply, as a means to 'complete the Thatcher revolution', without outside interference.[10] That may indeed turn out to be its ultimate significance. Such a motive could well have outweighed any feelings about 'national identity' – the line the Right took more publicly – in pointing them to the 'Leave' side. It also coupled them with their friends across the North Atlantic; both philosophically – Britain had invented free marketism but America was its main champion now – and also practically, with the USA's likely requiring Britain to abandon its Europe-imposed 'socialist' trade and labour regulations in any future commercial relationship with her. And Britain would sorely need the American market, if it were to have any hope of replacing the tariff-free trade it had been doing with Europe before the Brexit axe fell.

There can be little doubt that this was a powerful motive for some; rooted in one aspect or part of Britain's 'national identity', and hence 'patriotic' in one – but only one – sense. It should be noted that nearly every one of the leaders of the Brexit revolution was privileged, rich, and with underlying attitudes that to other members of British political society appeared very

'Conservative', albeit in the modern, post-Thatcher, 'free economy and strong government' sense. (In other words, they were not really keen on 'conserving'.) There was a fundamental irony buried in this, in view of their insistence that they were representing 'ordinary people' against the 'élites', on whom they laid the blame for 'Europe' and everything else that was bad. Two of them had been educated at Eton: the prime minister, and his close ally Jacob Rees-Mogg, a caricature upper-class toff, with a whole quiversful of ideas that would have seemed reactionary back in the nineteenth century; as had the luckless David Cameron before them. Prestigious as Eton was, and good on the 'Classics', it may not have been the best place to learn about the realities of British society; or even about Britain's history – and hence its most durable 'traditions'. Most of the rest of the Cabinet had also come from Public (that is, private) schools. (Farage was at Dulwich College – founded in 1619 as 'the College of God's Gift' – before becoming a stockbroker, and then a political activist.)

The political resurrection of these famous old schools in the 2010s was one of the great surprises of the time. It may be worth a brief excursion into *their* history in order to explain this. The 'Public' schools – Britain's 'peculiar institution' – were not always as they are today. Early on they had been meant for ordinary people (boys, that is), which is why they are still called 'public' now, and why they still retain their 'charitable' tax status. By the early nineteenth century, however, they had become finishing schools for the privileged, but effectively run by the boys, which makes sense of *Tom Brown's Schooldays*; and also explains the school *riots* that broke out occasionally, some of them having to be put down by the military. At least these could be taken as evidence of independent thought on the part of the boys. Then, 'reformed' (morally) in the middle of the nineteenth century, the schools entered into their golden age of *service* to the nation, supplying it with prime ministers and bishops to keep it running in a 'civilized' way. For the Empire, expanding and needing people to rule it, they were its major source of 'prefects', as one historian of Indian administration has called them.[11] This wasn't all bad, because the values inculcated in these young stripling rulers were generally *moral* ones, as 'morality' for the upper classes was understood then: in terms, that is, of helping those less fortunate – or 'civilized' – than themselves. Sometimes this involved protecting the colonial *indigènes* from voracious capitalist exploiters, or at least trying to; thereby rubbing down some of the sharper edges of imperialism. For the Public schools' dominating ethos then was, basically, not a capitalist but a 'feudal' one, best expressed in the term '*noblesse oblige*'; which was of course why Margaret Thatcher despised these men so much: the 'Wets', as she called them, mostly with Public school backgrounds, who were such a barrier – temporarily, at least – to her dream of a totally 'dry' – materialist – economy and society.

But this particular Public school ethos in any case seems not to have outlived the decline and fall of the British Empire, which took away much of this particular *raison d'être* of the schools, and hence of the values that had underpinned them. At the time it was widely assumed that it would also make the schools themselves less prominent in at least the higher reaches of British politics and society; with much being made of the much lowlier origins and schooling of a succession of prime ministers from Harold Wilson – replacing the Old Etonian Harold Macmillan – onwards; and including of course Thatcher herself. (But not Tony Blair.) This was supposed to indicate Britain's final emergence into the light of the modern day; when – reflecting what British society had by now become – its leaders would be chosen from the sorts of schools the majority of its people had attended.

Until, that is, 2010; when another Old Etonian entered No.10 Downing Street, so reasserting Eton's grip on British politics; to the surprise of many, who had assumed that such establishments had gone the way of the rest of English feudalism, together with jousting and the *jus prima noctis*, never to return. David Cameron's and then (especially) Boris Johnson's whole demeanour and attitudes reflected their Etonian upbringing, almost embarrassingly for some – Boris's 'jokes' in particular; but did not seem to reflect the old sense of *morality*, or obligation ('*oblige*'), and the better *values* that had been associated with the Public schools in their Imperial days. Those had gone. All that remained were the sense of entitlement that was probably the least valuable legacy of the old Public school system, and the immature school-boyish behaviour that went along with that. In place of the duties and 'obligations' that the schools had once engendered, there were just self-aggrandizement, snobbishness and amorality; which one assumes had been drafted in to replace the older values under and after Thatcher, to enable Eton – and the other Public schools – to survive in a more mercenary age. You needed a lot of – probably ill-gotten – money to be able to send your sons there. It wouldn't do for the schools then to teach those sons to despise the system that had enabled that. And so the 'ordinary' British people got Boris, and Jacob, and Nigel and the rest of them, lording it over them again.

We must beware here, lest we seem to be advancing a 'conspiratorial' explanation for Brexit. A relatively small group of men, all of them from a certain class, exclusively educated, and with highly influential connections, especially among the 'monied' and the Press, seeking to manipulate others by secretive and subversive means (for example the data-mining company 'Cambridge Analytica': managed as it happened by yet another Old Etonian), to a particular end: there are certainly elements of what might be called a 'high conspiracy' here; which should not be dismissed out of hand for fear of being associated with more notorious and ridiculed 'conspiracy theorists' like David Icke, or the people who run QAnon. It should be obvious even to saner folk that people do 'breathe together' (from the Latin, *conspirare*) in order to plot events, and that this sort of thing was involved in the campaign for Brexit in 2016. The question here – as with most other cases of reliably authenticated 'conspiracies' – is the extent to which it was *responsible* for the outcome of the Brexit campaign. *Post hoc ergo propter hoc* cannot be assumed in this case; especially when there are so many other circumstances of the time – some of them listed earlier in this chapter – it could have been *propter*. Ultimately, it may depend on our subjective view of the place of 'conspiracy' in history generally.

That these 'conspirators' could claim to be speaking for 'the people' against 'the Establishment' was one of the curiosities of the Brexit moment. This however is a common feature of modern Right-wing movements: to claim to be the voices of the downtrodden masses against the powers that be, however powerful and privileged they – the Rightists – might be in reality. (In fact Brexit showed how weak what the Brexiters characterized as the 'Establishment' really was. But you needed to believe the opposite, in order to be able to play the 'victim' card.) The name generally given to this is 'populism', and its strength lies in the way it can meet and combat the *Left* wing on the ground traditionally chosen by the latter. *In extremis* it can morph into a kind of Fascism; which is what more and more commentators claimed they saw happening in Britain at this time. Hilary Clinton, the losing Democratic candidate in the 2016 American Presidential election, told a British audience in November 2019 that she felt the UK was heading towards that, too;[12] although it has to be said that 'Fascist' is not a very exact term to apply here: the Brexit movement being not nearly as *statist* as most Fascisms have been – indeed, the very reverse. The pro-Brexit parties, however, starting with UKIP, certainly shared some of the characteristic features of *proto*-fascism; including, as well as their disdain for 'élites', or even for expertise (Michael Gove once famously dismissed gloomy economic predictions by opining that 'the British people have had enough of experts'),[13] their scapegoating of 'aliens' (in this case immigrants); their impatience with constitutional conventions like Parliament's and the judges' powers to hold governments to account: Johnson's Saturnine-looking 'special adviser' Dominic Cummings early on announced plans to break through all that; their appeal to a tribal version of 'patriotism'; their reactionary social attitudes, in the main, particularly their hatred of 'political correctness'; and their lack of conventional morality, especially in the areas of what most people regarded as honesty, veracity, and – to use what had by now become a rather *passé* word – 'honour'.

They also began to incline towards authoritarianism, another characteristic of populism, with the policies of Home Secretary Priti Patel in particular: her 2021 bill to narrow the limits of public protest, for example; which was itself widely protested at the time; and her even more draconian proposal in July the same year to amend the Official Secrets Act to put 'unauthorized' journalistic disclosures in the same category as 'spying', and risking the same penalties.[14] Together with her suggestion that boat captains – even RNLI Lifeboat crew – should be prosecuted if they didn't leave asylum seekers found in difficulties on the high seas to drown, these seemed to indicate that she had not been well schooled in at any rate some of the most liberal supposed 'traditions' of her country. (She had been trained – not at a Public school – as an economist.) Her brand of 'patriotism' obviously had a different focus entirely; and would, if followed through, have resulted in a very different kind of Britain from those to which the more liberal kind of British patriot was attached. All this was done – or intended to be done – under the convenient 'covers' of Brexit and the Covid pandemic; which must be seen as an important – if indirect – result of the former, even if it wasn't a motive. Traditional Britain was, potentially, about to be transformed. It was no wonder, therefore, that so many traditional Britons, and especially English (Scots could take refuge in their own nationality), in public opinion surveys and on the internet, professed themselves 'ashamed' of their country for the first time. In short, the Brexit *process* was undermining many of the foundations on which their old-style 'patriotism' had stood.

Lastly, when it comes to seeking motives and causes for Brexit, it should be remembered that Britain had company in facing this kind of situation; obviously not necessarily in relation to the EU (although there were weaker secessionist movements in other European countries), but in response to similar economic, political and cultural crises. Those responses varied in kind from nation to nation, but followed a similar pattern to Britain's. One was a turn to the Right – to Trump in America, UKIP in Britain, and the *Front National* in France. People's anger was turned against scapegoats who might not really be responsible for their woes, but were easily identified, and disliked for other reasons. This – scapegoating – is another common phenomenon in history. Another was a turn in the opposite direction, to the Left: Occupy, Bernie Sanders, Jeremy Corbyn, Podemos, and the multitude of other quasi-socialist movements that sprang up then. These sorts of dual reaction had historical form, of course, most notably in 1930s Europe. (Historians often brought this parallel up, somewhat worryingly.) Opposites in one obvious way, they also shared a common cause and origin, and in many cases curiously similar philosophies: anti-'establishment', for example. So there must – mustn't there? – be something more behind it; broader, deeper, less 'accidental' and more general factors lying behind what Britons usually see as a characteristically 'British' – *ergo* 'patriotic' – political movement, but which might not be so peculiar to Britain after all. We shall return to this.

*

The immediate political repercussions of this event were shattering. For a start two prime ministers – David Cameron and Theresa May – were forced to resign as a consequence; one political party (Labour) was sorely divided; another which had used to be divided (the Conservatives) was now swallowed up by Brexiters; and a man, the aforesaid Alexander Boris de Pfeffel Johnson – who had previously been regarded as a bit of a joke, partly because that was how he liked to present himself – at last achieved the high position he was well known to have craved since boyhood. Even on the question of Europe, which the July 2016 vote was supposed to have settled once and for all, divisions continued. This was because voters couldn't ever have known what they were voting *for*, which had never been clearly spelled out to them, or even what they were voting *against*, different versions of which were on offer. Had they decided to leave every aspect of their arrangement with the EU, or just its political forms? In particular, did they want to leave the 'common European market'? (Other non-EU countries, Norway for example, remained in that, albeit still needing to abide by the EU's commercial rules.) 'What does Brexit mean?' people asked, quite reasonably; to which Prime Minister Theresa May's Delphic reply, oft repeated, was that 'Brexit means Brexit'. That hardly helped.

So the debate raged on, rancorously. There were large public demonstrations for both sides of the argument; an increase in xenophobic abuse; and what was widely reckoned to be a 'toxic' atmosphere in the country generally. It even turned murderous. Just before the referendum a young 'Remain' MP, Jo Cox, was brutally killed – stabbed and shot – in the streets of her Yorkshire constituency by a Brexiter. For the politicians who had to decide on the final terms of the separation the choice was presented – rather simplistically – as one between a 'hard' and a 'soft' Brexit: the former the choice of the extreme Eurosceptics in the Tory Party; the latter the compromise position adopted by Labour, but rubbished by the pro-Brexit press as 'indecisive', as compromises so often are. (Newspapers thrive on contests, with 'winners' and 'losers': nothing in between.) In the end, and after a series of political shenanigans, the 'hard' Brexiters won. Whether this was truly the 'will of the people', especially after so many elderly Brexiters had died (Covid-19 will have helped here) and been replaced on the electoral lists by young pro-Europeans – the main division in the 2016 Brexit vote had been a generational one – was anyone's guess. Most people by this time seemed to have become bored – if they hadn't been all along – with the whole thing. Apathy – or *anti*-politics – has always been a major factor in British political life, as we have seen. Among more politically-minded people, however, the row continued; with 'Remainers' now metamorphosed into 'Rejoiners', of course.

One of the reasons for this was that 'Rejoiners' still believed that the whole thing had been a 'scam', built on false hopes and 'black' propaganda. A particular object of their criticism was a slogan painted in large letters on the side of the 'Brexit battle (campaigning) bus', seeming to promise an ingestion of £350 million a week into the people's beloved but currently cash-strapped National Health Service, recouped from the savings that leaving the EU would allegedly bring. Could that have persuaded the crucial two percent that stood between 'Leave' and 'Remain' in 2016? It was quite reasonable to believe so. In reality the promise on the bus was based on false figures, and reneged on almost immediately after the result of the referendum was known. Soon after that some of the Brexiters' other 'dirty tricks' – lies, illegal over-funding, improper use of Cambridge Analytica 'algorithms' to influence voters, subvert assistance from supposedly hostile foreign countries, especially (allegedly) Russia – were revealed, but too late to do anything about them. The Brexit side had also claimed that the task of negotiating a new and favourable trade deal with the EU would be 'one of the easiest in human history' – that was Dr Liam Fox, MP, who was in charge of the negotiations for a while[15] – which turned out to be another mistaken prediction, at best.

*

Self-evidently, the main direct result of this affair was Britain's exit from the European Union, and the economic and human repercussions of that. Many of the former were immediate: loss of markets on the Continent; exports being held up by customs checks that hadn't been necessary previously, imports delayed, leading to some empty shelves in supermarkets (these were the things that were felt first); companies and financial institutions relocated abroad; much of this attributed by the popular Right-wing press to malevolence on the part of the Europeans, wanting to 'punish' Britain for leaving them, like in a bad divorce, but in reality the inevitable effects of Britain's no longer being in a common market with them. (One of the advantages of leaving that even Europhiles had expected was that 'Europe' would no longer be blamed for problems back home; but there seemed to be little hope of that.) One of the biggest repercussions was on travel, with 'free movement' being one of the major targets of the Brexiters, without their realizing, apparently, or thinking it much mattered, that this would extend to them too. Britons could no longer work or study on the Continent, or live there without passing bureaucratic obstacle courses which in some cases – retirees on the Costa del Sol worried about this – could still force them out of their sunny homes. Nor could they benefit any longer from free European healthcare: a problem especially, perhaps, for those retirees. The more far-sighted had prepared for this by taking out residency or even citizenship in the countries they wished to work or live in. But for others it seemed not to have occurred to them that Brexit would make *them* 'foreign', too. Stopping 'freedom of movement' was only meant to work the other way around.

But even that gave rise to problems, with foreign doctors, nurses, truck drivers and seasonal workers on the farms having to return to their home countries, even when 'home' for them had been Britain for many years. That was not helped by a clearly ham-fisted Home Office bureaucracy (under Priti Patel), which was repeatedly reported to be sending out expulsion notices in error.[16] Even those who managed to stay complained of insulting treatment at the hands of the natives. Hopefully the numbers of those natives were smaller than of those who rallied round to protect their new 'neighbours'; like the Glasgow crowd of around 200 that physically stopped a Home Office 'Immigration Enforcement' van from seizing some refugees for deportation, in May 2021.[17] That – the protest – seemed much more in line with Britain's older patriotic boast, of accepting all kinds of immigrants. Priti Patel may have been unaware of that.

So far as the middle- or long-term consequences to the British economy were concerned, at the time of writing it is far too early to know whether the wider-world trade deals that Prime Minister Johnson claimed would lie on the 'sunny uplands' that he saw spreading before Britain after Brexit, would fully compensate for its European losses; or whether those deals could be done without compromising the quality and labour standards that Britain had agreed with its European partners before. Neo-Liberals, of course, wouldn't object to that. Even with these shackles shed, however, the sunny uplands could seem rather far away, with the leading Brexiter Jacob Rees-Mogg admitting in June 2018 that the full benefits of Brexit might not be felt for fifty years.[18] (His own fortune had already been squirrelled away to Ireland, so he was well insured.)[19] But then that might have been too pessimistic a view. Until the full implications of Brexit had worked themselves through – 'freedom', fewer regulations, all those new trade deals outside Europe, the final settlement with Europe itself – no-one could know the results for sure. Johnson's bright promise of a spectacular future just *could* be met. If optimistic rhetoric could help it on, Johnson had that in spades.

*

This in fact may be the best way to appreciate and understand the 'Brexit moment'. Concentrating for now just on the 'leaders': there can be little doubt that some of them were genuinely and honestly concerned about the EU, like Sir Bill Cash and Nigel Farage. For some of the others, however, their hostility to the EU, while not being in any way disingenuous, may not have been particularly principled or deep. So far as the broader Right in British politics was concerned, the value of Brexit was that it could be used to rally the angry and disaffected troops to its side, in the Right's campaign to complete the 'Thatcher revolution'. That seemed about to be achieved when the results of the 2019 election came through, leaving Johnson's ambitions victorious and Labour's in tatters. Or, by another (sub-Marxist) way of putting it: Brexit was the horse that just happened to come along, quite fortuitously, to be hard ridden by the Right to victory for late-stage capitalism. (We shall come back to this.) So, for neither the leaders nor their followers was it 'about Europe', essentially.

But it was done; and Britain ended the 47-year marriage with its European neighbours; not at all in a spirit of friendship, certainly not on Britain's side, and on the whole somewhat messily. (The commercial status of Northern Ireland in particular was a serious running sore. The problem here was that it would seem to necessitate a customs barrier between the two parts of the island, so endangering the fragile 'Good Friday' Agreement of 1998 which had brought the so-called 'Troubles' to an end.) Britain formally exited the European Union at the end of January 2020, albeit with a further 'transition' period of eleven months added on in order to enable the country to adjust.

'Independence' celebrations were planned for a future date; but not immediately, because of the divisions and conflicts the whole process had given rise to; and with the 'B' word left off the invitations so as – hopefully – not to rub Remainers up the wrong way. The latter however remained resentful; understandably so in view of the clear chicanery that had played such a part in defeating them, and their doubts over whether a poll of the people taken in the summer of 2016 still represented their real wishes in the 2020s. (Polls taken then suggested not, although the shift was not a great one.) There were moves in Parliament and in the country for a second referendum in order to test this; which was however objected to by Brexiters on the grounds that it would be 'undemocratic' to ignore the first one – 'you lost, get over it!' – and was finally put to bed by the December 2019 General Election result, fought on the slogan 'Get Brexit Done'; suggested to the Tories by Cummings, in order to harness the boredom and exasperation that he sensed the majority of the electorate was beginning to show over the whole issue. That was taken to be the people's final ruling on the matter. But the bitterness continued for months. Right-leaning or 'patriotic' newspapers called Remainers 'traitors' and 'enemies of the people'; a kind of verbal tarring and feathering reminiscent of some of the most authoritarian regimes of the past. On their side, the Remainers claimed – or implied – that Brexit voters were ignorant, stupid, or (at best) conned. All this heightened feelings, and made it virtually impossible thereafter for nervous MPs to think of reversing the result, without risking something very close to civil war. Indeed, in 2017 Nigel Farage spoke of arming himself for the fray and manning the barricades if Parliament obstructed his – extreme – version of Brexit.[20] This seemed far-fetched, in the context of Britain's ostensibly calm and non-revolutionary modern history; but serious domestic conflict could not be ruled out. For 'Remainers', however, the game was indeed lost.

*

So far as Brexit's longer-term impact on Britain's economy was concerned the picture was unclear. (In any case it is unwise of historians to dabble in prediction, although I may take a shot at it later on.) By 2020 few Brexiters any longer believed in the immediate fillip to the economy some of them had promised once Britain had Brexited. Many of the signs – of manufacturing firms switching their operations to the Continent or Ireland, for example; investors doing the same; and suppliers unable to deliver their goods to market due to a sudden exodus of European truck drivers – were not exactly promising for a future island economy standing on its own. This became even clearer when Britain's economy became further wasted by the Covid-19 pandemic. On the other hand, as the more ideological Brexiters emphasized, Brexit wasn't only about trade. It was also about national independence and dignity. Becoming poorer or even littler as a nation might be an acceptable sacrifice if it meant getting these back. According to a poll taken as early as January 2017, 61 per cent of Leavers considered that 'significant damage' to the British economy – and even to their own personal welfare – was 'a price worth paying for bringing Britain out of the European Union.'[21] That was big of them; although it still of course needed to be tested on the forge of real events.

On a personal and social level, relations between the two (or several) peoples were affected in a number of ways. Continental Europeans living in Britain complained of rising xenophobia: not necessarily an effect of Brexit, and indeed generally regarded as one of the *causes* of it, among 'ordinary voters' who felt, rightly or wrongly, that the immigration of cheap and willing labour from eastern Europe was undermining their living standards, and putting pressure on Britain's social, education and health services, especially in the deprived post-industrial north of England. Some of these complaints were hardly evidence-based: many of the jobs that the immigrants had been 'taking' from the natives were those – like seasonal fruit-picking and lorry-driving – that natives were reluctant to do in any case for the wages offered; and a succession of government reports showed that immigration actually added to the viability of the social services – hospitals were highly dependent on foreign doctors and nurses, for example – and on balance boosted the country's coffers. In addition, many of the anti-immigrants seemed not to have known that Britain-in-Europe had always possessed powers to limit incomers' numbers, but had *chosen* not to use them then. But if Brexit did not beget anti-alienism, it clearly encouraged it to some extent. The number of racist attacks in England increased significantly. Nativist organizations like 'Britain First' (it should really have called itself 'England First'; Scottish nationalism being a rather different animal: indeed, the Scots had voted to *stay* in the EU) proliferated and took to the streets threateningly. All this added to the *dis*comfort of many Europeans who had been living in Britain happily and friendlily for years. Many of them feared summary expulsion from Britain by a strict and unfeeling Home Office – the legacy of the immigration-obsessed Theresa May – even if they had family and tax-paying jobs in the United Kingdom. Cases were common, and distressing. Those who were permitted to stay reported feeling unwelcome.

For the roughly three million British who had crossed the other way, to settle for various lengths of time on the Continent, taking advantage of the 'freedom of movement' which to them had been the EU's main attraction, but still they reckoned remaining British, with for example the right to vote in British national elections for their first fifteen years abroad: for these the repercussions of Brexit were equally disturbing. The material adjustments it required could be troublesome: seeking rights of residence which had been automatic to them as citizens of Europe, or even dual nationality (8,000 Britons became Swedes during 2019 alone in order to escape from Brexit, including the present author, and warmer countries will have attracted more); reassuring themselves that they could still retain their British pensions; having to make new and expensive healthcare arrangements to replace their reciprocal rights to medical treatment in their countries of exile; facing longer queues at airports; and needing now, in some cases, to go to all the trouble of applying for visas before travelling back to Britain to visit their families. They also had to cope with the sense of rejection that many home-clinging Brexiters showed towards them and their internationalist spirit; especially after Theresa May's notorious display at the Conservative Party conference of 2016 of her own narrow, pinching nationalism: 'if you believe you are a citizen of the world, you are a citizen of nowhere'.[22] That was regarded as offensive by many British abroad, who did not accept that one could not embrace multiple identities. It could also be seen as – again – un-British; a point made by many of the contributors to a collection of testimonies by British expatriates published in book form in 2017–18 as *In Limbo* and *In Limbo Too*, expressing a range of ways in which Brexit had caused them emotional as well as material harm.[23] In Europe itself there was little evidence that Brexit had greatly affected Britons' relationships with their Continental friends, unlike in Britain; apart from the patronizing sympathy with which they were usually met, which was kindly meant but embarrassing, and the signs of contumely in which their nation of origin – once widely respected in so many ways, if not all – was now held. For the 48.11 per cent – or more, now – it marked a sad decline, national reputation-wise.

A contemporary work of fiction, Jonathan Coe's prize-winning 'Brexit novel' *Middle England* (2018), illustrated this general transformation almost perfectly. Coe first described the mood, as his ('Middle Englander') characters experienced it, at the time of the London Olympics of 2012, and especially after its spectacularly radical-patriotic opening ceremony, choreographed by Danny Boyle (and described in Coe's book): which surprised and was appreciated by everyone save a few Tories, who didn't like immigration and the NHS being featured as objects of national pride. 'England felt like a calm and settled place tonight: a country at ease with itself', wrote Coe. This impression could hardly be sustained just four years later, however, when 'Brexit' had taken hold. By then no-one could any longer regard England – let alone Britain – as 'calm and settled'. This may have been the most devastating – albeit immeasurable – domestic effect of the great 'Battle for Brexit' in 2016–20.

A final one was the way Brexit distracted attention from other important matters that needed to be addressed during these years: the National Health Service, housing costs, homelessness, poverty, policing, fire safety, rising inequality, knife violence, the natural environment, and more; most of which issues *were* debated in Parliament and in the media, but never with the scrutiny they deserved, and always with half an eye on this much bigger elephant in the room. In the 2019 Election the Labour Party tried to draw attention back to these questions in a wide-ranging and apparently popular election manifesto, but without success, at least in the short term. Brexit blotted out everything. Outside the field of Parliamentary politics it was responsible for diverting others from important issues and concerns, including academic historians who felt compelled to waste several years of serious research time commentating on it fruitlessly. While Brexit burned, the rest of the country stood still.

This may have had the calamitous effect of weakening Britain's response to the unforeseen coronavirus pandemic of 2020, which had to be handled by new government ministers, still wet behind the ears, who had been appointed originally (after Johnson's pre-election purge of the more experienced Remainers) for their fidelity to the creed of Brexit, rather than for any administrative wisdom, experience or competence they might possess. Coronavirus also exposed the deep cracks in Britain's social safety-net (in particular in the NHS) that 'Austerity', coupled with the Brexit distraction – both of them the responsibility of the same Right-leaning politicians – had brought about. These were some of Brexit's immediate repercussions, which could be clearly discerned even at the time.

Then, just emerging in the last days of Britain's separation – although it had been augured long before – was the problem of those parts of the United Kingdom whose people had voted *against* Brexit, for very good reasons of their own. Scotland and Northern Ireland were the chief of them, which continued to plague Johnson's government for months. The threat there was that they could both *secede* from the United Kingdom, no less, and return, one way or another, to the EU as separate nation-states, as they had both been in the past. If only for that reason Johnson could not be said – as his election campaign had promised – to have 'got Brexit done' yet; which leaves the story without an ending still. The final stage of that story might turn out to be even more 'existential' than the first.

And then – it needs to be remembered – the British people still had to *pay* for this: both for Brexit, and, on top of this, for Covid-19. That might require a further existential shift, in Britain's economy, politics and society. The hope was that it wouldn't be handled in quite the way that its more recent crises had been. That will be for future historians to chronicle and explain.

9

History

Brexit changed Britain, but to what extent and in what ways cannot (again) be known at the time of writing, in the summer of 2021. One thing it almost certainly did not do was to change the country *back*, to anything it had been at any time in the past.

If this is what Brexiters wanted – and some of them gave that impression: 'Take *Back* Control' – they would probably be disappointed. For a start, history can never be repeated, unless it be, as Karl Marx put it, 'as farce'. There were a lot of farcical aspects to Brexit, gleefully pointed out by 'Remainers': it – the glee – was maybe the only comfort they could draw from it. There were the Brexit-voting farmers and pub owners bemoaning the fact that they couldn't get fruit-pickers and bar staff anymore; British foreign holiday-makers and retirees suddenly realizing that 'third country' status applied to them too; Brexit leaders claiming that they had never said that things would get better after Brexit only to be caught out by quotes from their pasts; some objectively 'silly' politicians directing the whole proceedings: I'm sorry, but one doesn't need to be particularly partisan to characterize Johnson, Rees-Mogg, Mark Francois and Nigel Farage this way – or was this just a clever ruse to lower people's guard? – and many more: all noticed by most observers, but to little effect, as the die had already been cast.

Secondly, and more profoundly, the 'take back control' slogan was predicated on the assumption that it was the EU that had limited that 'control' while Britain was a member of it, which rested on a mistaken view of the nature of the EU: that is, as a dominating *imperium*, rather than an association of nations with Britain taking an equal part in its decision-making, a bit like the Commonwealth used to be regarded. Behind this lay a further misunderstanding of the nature of *alliances*, which the EU was basically a network of, and of their relationship, in this case, to what the Brexiteers regarded as their national 'independence'. The simple point here is that no nation, unless it's a 'superpower' like the USA, Russia or China, or like Britain was conceived to be in the nineteenth century – and arguably not even in their cases – can afford to go it alone either diplomatically or commercially, without help from others; which was what the EU was supposed to have given Britain in the 47 years it had been a member of it.

It followed that Britain and its people had no *less* 'control' over their fate and fortunes as part of the EU than they had ever had in the past. Indeed, in many ways their membership had offered them more freedom: free-er travel obviously, freedom to work abroad, a bigger choice of markets, the opportunity in combination with their allies to negotiate more favourable terms with those markets (in May 2021 the British government triumphantly announced a new trade deal with Iceland, Norway and Liechtenstein, which turned out to be less favourable than the terms with those countries it had had as a member of the EU); more influence in foreign policy; and – although this was impossible to measure quantitatively – more 'status' and 'respect'. To repeat: 'control' is not only a function of 'independence', and treaty obligations – such as those the EU required – are not the only way of limiting it. A one-man or woman team will not win many football matches. As many 'Remainers' pointed out, if the losses arising from its coming out of the European common market could only be compensated by Britain's having to submit to the unwelcome demands of the American food, pharmaceutical and health industries, the country could end up with rather less 'control' in practical terms than before. Imperial historians call the latter 'informal empire'. Ask any citizens of a former British colony whether their political 'emancipation' necessarily made their economies more 'free'.

*

Actually it is not at all clear what historical condition the Brexiters wanted their country to go 'back' to, if this *was* how they saw things. It cannot have been the 1960s and 1970s, unless they were socialists, as some were, fearing the impact of the 'market-driven' EU on their ambitions for 'social democracy in one country'. For Conservatives or the reactionary-inclined, who made up the majority of Eurosceptic leaders in 2016, their Golden ages had been earlier. The Second World War was a common reference point: Churchill, Dunkirk, the Battle of Britain, standing alone against Hitler; or, further back, Victorian times, or the buccaneering First Elizabethans.

Most of them – like everyone; this not just a tilt at the Brexit side – knew very little about Britain's history in any case. What they did know, from school long ago and then from popular TV 'period dramas' and documentaries, was usually played out in terms of *personalities*, which of course are far more cinematic and hence attractive and exciting than broad historical 'trends' or 'infrastructures' or 'material factors' can be. (Shakespeare's plays are based on this. Coincidentally, Johnson was supposed to be writing a book about Shakespeare at the start of his premiership; following his biography of Churchill, whom Shakespeare might well have written a play about if he had been alive then. That too would have centred on Churchill's personality. Shakespeare tells us very little about the crisis of feudalism under Henry V.)

Which brings us at last to the question of *agency*. Many of the leading Brexiters, especially the Public school-educated, seem to have been still imbued with the very old-fashioned view of history as having been moulded by 'great men'; or 'Titans' as Jacob Rees-Mogg called them in the subtitle of his *The Victorians* (2019). 'As Britain prepares to liberate itself from the European Union, it is essential that we remember the spirit, drive and values of the Victorians who forged modern Britain, as we consider our future as a nation.' That is taken from the book's 'blurb'. This view of historical causation – deriving ultimately from the Victorian Tory Thomas Carlyle's book *On Heroes*, published in 1841 – would get little backing from serious historians today. (One wonders what sort of British history Rees-Mogg and Johnson were taught at Eton – if any. Or did they *only* study the 'Classics'?) Of course, we serious historians might be wrong. We still need to see – again, this is written in the summer of 2021 – how 'Titanic' (in Rees-Mogg's sense, not the ship's) Boris Johnson turns out to be.

Rees-Mogg's historical reference point is obviously the nineteenth century, which was Margaret Thatcher's too. One of the motives behind Brexit for the more ideological Brexiters was – as we have seen – to 'complete the Thatcher revolution': which they attributed *to* Thatcher personally, in true 'heroic' style. In fact Thatcher can be seen to have been very much a creature of her time, anticipated by other events in recent British history (and even John the Baptists, like the old nationalist – and another Classicist – Enoch Powell), and swept up by the same winds that were blowing fiercely on other countries contemporaneously, notably the USA and Chile, and were just beginning to ruffle the feathers of more social democratic countries all over the world. (Even Sweden was affected.) That is one reason for not regarding it as a particularly 'British' phenomenon, or a reason for calling those who followed Thatcher's way British 'patriots' particularly. This was the way *she* saw it, of course – 'we have regained our heritage,' restored 'the character of the British people', as she claimed[1] – but that applied, if it applied at all, to only one class of Briton, in a country whose 'national identity', as we saw in the first chapter, embraced and indeed gloried in far more variety than that.

'Completing the Thatcher revolution', however, can be expressed another way. If we focus on 'broad currents' in history, rather than personalities, the universality of this trend – what became called 'neoliberalism' – might suggest that it had something more, and more international, lying behind it. Thatcher's influence beyond her own national boundaries might be one, of course. (She certainly had world-wide admirers, including President Reagan in the USA.) Another possibility could be a global 'conspiracy' of some kind, engineered by powerful groups of people with no real loyalty to any country, but only to their own profit, and with the means of manipulating other countries' economies – and Thatcher – in their own interests. These are dangerous waters; but still the idea that 'international capitalists', of whatever race or religion or none, are holding countries to ransom must remain a possibility in our search for the *fons et origo* of 'Thatcherism' and of its revival in the form of Brexit. It fits rather better than other 'conspiracy theories'; such as those that put the blame on extra-terrestrials, or unreconstructed Nazis, or reptilian shape-shifters, or God. (During the Brexit debate one Brexiter, dressed as a leprechaun, was photographed with a placard proclaiming that Nigel Farage had been 'sent by Christ to get Britain out of Europe and fulfil Bible prophesy'.) All nonsense, of course, and possibly not seriously intended; but signs of one of the effects of the Brexit debate, which we shall come on to later.

On the other hand there is an alternative explanation, which the present writer is more inclined towards, but not with any degree of certainty. This is that Karl Marx was essentially right. Marx is generally seen as a communist, and therefore an anti-capitalist, which of course he was, in spades; but his communism was based on an analysis of the capitalist system, founded on the philosophies of the great liberal thinkers of the past, which held 'free trade' to be the great liberal*izing* factor of their time: but which (the theory) simply stopped there. Marx agreed with them about liberal capitalism, and its huge improvement over the economic systems of the past; and indeed that it was an inevitable 'stage' in the development of all national economic systems, which was why he applauded the contribution imperial Britain had made in introducing it to India, as the necessary step in the latter's evolution to modernity. 'Socialism', leading to 'communism', was the next stage after that, but only to be achieved after the capitalist stage had worked itself out. That was why he didn't hold out much hope then for true socialism's arising in Tsarist Russia, which was far behind other countries in its capitalist development. According to his analysis Britain, as the first into capitalism, should have been the first to evolve out of it and into socialism; but it soon let him down. Before a viable socialist revolution could be fired up, capitalism needed to progress through all *its* stages, which would become more and more burdensome to ordinary people, and less and less viable even on its own account. In Britain, the late nineteenth century and early 1900s, to be sure, saw its economy struggling; but only to be alleviated – wrote Lenin afterwards, based on J. A. Hobson's work[2] – by the 'new imperialism', which forced open new overseas markets and sources of raw materials for British industry, which was undergoing a crisis of 'over-production and under-consumption' at the time. That was the way capitalist economies normally and naturally collapsed: destroying themselves through their own 'internal contradictions', at first gradually, while they could find temporary sticking-plasters to stop the bleeding, and then in a rush – 'the revolution'. For a true Marxist the lesson was, or ought to have been, not to seek an end to capitalism prematurely, which could have all kinds of unfortunate consequences (like Soviet Russia), but to encourage capitalism to develop to a point where it would implode of its own volition. A *very* elaborate 'conspiracy theory' might see Margaret Thatcher as the knowing agent of this development in Britain's case, secretly brainwashed by the USSR to fulfil Marx's prophesy, and to speed up the 'red in tooth and claw' capitalism that would eventually bring it to its end. Brexitism – 'completing the Thatcher revolution' – was a stage in that. – No, of course not. A Marxist would say it didn't need her or the Brexiters to bring capitalism down. But if she had known . . .

Nonetheless later events in the years just before Brexit could be regarded as symptomatic of the death-throws of late-stage finance capitalism, predicted by Marx, albeit somewhat delayed. The great banking collapse of 2007–8 was one obvious example; surrounded as it was by other events and trends in Western society pointing to a crisis of *confidence* in capitalism, at least, among those who weren't immediately benefiting from it. Those trends included huge and growing discrepancies in wealth between rich and poor (so much for 'trickle-down' theory); enforced 'austerity'; even 'global warming', caused by uncontrolled production, and potentially leading to the death of the planet; and the 'populist' response to all this, not only in Britain, in the form of Brexit, but also in the USA, by then the world's most developed capitalist economy, in the form of 'Trumpism' and all that went with it. If true, this properly establishes Brexit's place not only in British history, but also in that of the world.

*

Looked at from this global perspective, Brexit cannot be regarded as particularly 'patriotic', if patriotism is seen as an allegiance to one nation and its 'values' in particular. Thatcherism – one element behind Brexit – certainly represented some of those values, at a couple of periods in Britain's history; but it was emphatically not the only one, or peculiar to her, or the most important, or the one that represented all or even most of the different 'Britains' listed in Chapter 1. Nor was the other value or 'tradition' that Johnson seemed to be appealing to in many of his journalistic flights of fancy.

> By Global Britain I meant a country that was more open, more outward-looking, more engaged with the world than ever before. It meant taking the referendum and using it as an opportunity to rediscover some of the dynamism of those bearded Victorians; not to build a new empire, heaven forfend.[3]

'Heaven forfend', indeed; but his words will have warmed the heart-cockles of old imperial nostalgics, as well as of the Thatcherite Right. They will also have cemented the illusion that 'empire' was a peculiarly 'British' characteristic, which of course it wasn't at all. Indeed, we have seen that imperialism was one of the things that had bound Britain to nearly every other European coastal nation over most of the nineteenth century, occasionally in competition, but without their ever having come to blows as a result: until – by one reading of it – the War of 1914. There is nothing peculiarly 'British' here.

As well as this, an emphasis on capitalism and imperialism glosses over rival British traditions of socialism and *anti*-imperialism, which were arguably at least as important and just as *British*. We have met some of them in this book. Working-class solidarity, standing in stark apposition to Thatcher's individualism, was one. Aristocratic paternalism was another, and, allied to that, a hierarchy of 'class'. The idea of a Britain which welcomed, or at least tolerated, immigrants, and especially refugees, was a third. Then there were the fond notions of a British empire ruling other peoples for their own good and not for Britain's alone (these, remember, were ideas only, not necessarily actualities); of a country that had a great literature but otherwise didn't care much for fripperies like art, though that became less of a characteristic in the twentieth century; a stable nation (usually contrasted with France), and one whose governing classes were persons of honour and probity, reflected in Britain's non-partisan civil service; whose middle classes were enterprising and hard-working, and 'lower' classes generally loyal, albeit with a few eruptions of public feeling, but no gross violence; with free speech, a free press and a right to protest enshrined either in law or in a deliberate absence of law; with a strong resistance to authoritarianism, of either the Left or the Right; a far more liberal police than most Continental countries had, and 'secret' and political policing non-existent (until the 1900s); a country cursed by poor food (but so what?) and with an inordinate taste for tea; sporty; characterized by great humour (from *Punch* to *Monty Python*), eccentricity, 'muddling through' or 'busking it' (a term sometimes applied to Boris Johnson), and – less flatteringly – by *le vice anglais*; overall a country that was pretty 'free', but in ways that transcended the narrow freedoms of the 'market'; with a civilized political discourse; a bureaucracy composed of honourable people not afraid to 'speak truth to power'; and a broadly tolerant religion, except in one or two parts of the kingdom: in other words a nation characteristically 'hybrid' in so many ways, but with common human decencies which were expressed aptly in the game that was one of England's greatest contributions to world civilization: 'it's just not Cricket, you know!' These were Britain's national characteristics as it wished others to see them (not necessarily as they were), and some of the objects of its deepest self-regard and, yes, 'pride'.

*

How did 'Brexit' impact on these? What was left of the 'traditional' Britain afterwards? – Brexit itself may have been less important in this regard than the *process* by which it came about, which might – again, we cannot tell for sure yet – have affected the country quite radically. This was because a number of what had been thought to be basic principles of British political life were sidelined, torn down or revealed to have been illusory in the four or five years following the 2016 referendum vote, including some of the obstacles deliberately placed there by tradition in order to put a brake on 'bad' or ill thought-out or highly marginal decisions by the 'democracy'. In order to 'get Brexit done' after the vote in June 2016, Johnson had illegally prorogued Parliament, lied to the Queen, sought to undermine the courts, got rid of those of his own senior MPs he considered to be obstructive, and sacked or moved on senior civil servants who tendered advice he didn't like. In order to win the original referendum he and the Brexit side generally had used techniques of persuasion which were widely taken to go beyond what had generally been considered acceptable in British politics, including blatant lies. Most of the popular press – never very reliable as news sources – now turned into sheer and unabashed propaganda sheets for the Right, naming and shaming those who opposed Brexit, and even the Law Lords, as 'traitors', no less. (Hence Britain's low status in contemporary 'press freedom' surveys.)[4] The Labour leader in the 2019 General Election, which was called by Johnson in order to legitimize the purely 'advisory' Brexit referendum vote, was traduced in the same way that 'Leftists' were traditionally traduced in the 'tabloids', but at an even greater pitch. Jeremy Corbyn may have been a 'loser' in any case; but the dishonest campaign waged against him on the grounds of 'anti-Semitism', which was entirely unfounded, may have 'done for him' in the end.[5] If Britain had conceived of itself as a fair and honourable democracy before this, afterwards that reputation could no longer be sustained.

What effect this would have on public life after the 2010s was unpredictable. Some of those on the Right talked of 'reforming' the entire British constitution in order to remove some of these fly-blown impediments to governments getting their way; otherwise known as seeking 'efficiency' (not usually a very 'British' objective in itself). The Conservatives' 2019 Election manifesto hinted at this. 'After Brexit we also need to look at the broader aspects of our constitution: the relationship between the Government, Parliament and the courts; the functioning of the Royal Prerogative; [and] the role of the House of Lords'; all this in order to put right what the Conservatives claimed was 'a broken Parliament that simply refuses to deliver Brexit'.[6] Among the leading advocates of 'efficiency' was Dominic Cummings, widely believed to be the genius, evil or otherwise, behind both the Referendum vote and Johnson's elevation to the premiership, and for a time Johnson's chief Special Advisor ('Spad') in government, until the two of them fell out and Cummings had to leave. But that wasn't the end of him; unfortunately for the prime minister – although it didn't seem to harm him in the short term. Clearly millions of electors didn't much mind. 'But he's a card, isn't he?' 'At least he got Brexit done.' And 'at least he isn't Corbyn'.

Cummings's revenge was a vicious attack on Johnson – and others in government – before a Parliamentary Committee in May 2021 for repeatedly, as he claimed, lying over their handling of the coronavirus pandemic that began sweeping over the world shortly after their election victory. At most other times that undoubted scandal might have marked the end of Johnson's prime ministerial career; but on this occasion it didn't – for a while at any rate. This may have been due to another effect of the Brexit 'process'; which was to *accustom* people to political dishonesty, and get them to accept it; even applying it to transparently honest and honourable politicians like Jeremy Corbyn: 'they're all the same'. This may have anaesthetized people against the charges of dishonesty, corruption and inefficiency brought against Johnson, and encouraged him and any others with political ambitions to continue playing the same game. (They also, of course, had the success – up to a point – of the notoriously deceitful Donald Trump in America to encourage them along this path. Johnson and some other leading Brexiters, like Nigel Farage, were quite pally with Trump.) This may have altered the basic rules of politics in Britain to favour the unprincipled; much like relaxing the laws of cricket would be to allow cheating. (Trump apparently regularly cheated at golf.) If this kind of thing were to become accepted, then it would make honest politics (or games) that much more difficult. If that was one of the side-effects of the Brexit imbroglio of 2016–20, it was – and remains – a crucially important one.

Another effect of the *process* of Brexit was to boost Right-wing and authoritarian thinking in Britain, almost to the level of 'fascism'. We have already seen Hilary Clinton raising this danger to Britain in 2019 with specific reference to the Brexiters.[7] In Britain a certain degree of *proto-fascism* could be said to be represented by the exaggerated nationalism of many 'ordinary' Brexiters, especially those gathered in 'patriotic' crowds or mobs; the distrust of élites and 'establishments'; the demeaning of 'experts' and 'intellectuals'; the calls for 'action' rather than discussion; the appeals to an earlier – albeit mythical – national 'purity'; the hostility to immigrants, even poor and persecuted refugees; dubbing people in authority 'traitors' because they didn't agree with you; the overt hostility to progressive or 'politically correct' or 'woke' ideas (some of them admittedly silly); a particular and somewhat tribal view of 'patriotism'; and of course the racism that lay behind much of this new temper of the times, now broadened out to include, for example, Poles and Romanians as well as 'blacks'. Two successive Home Secretaries, Theresa May and Priti Patel – both with surprising origins in this context: the first the daughter of a clergyman, the second of Ugandan-Asian immigrants – were prominent in taking up arms against the immigrant 'threat'; May coining the phrase 'hostile environment' to deter immigrants from coming into Britain unlawfully, and Patel – well known for her far-Right views – responsible for measures and proposals aimed against them which frequently went against the requirements of humanity, and on a couple of occasions against the Laws of the land: before of course the government had had a chance to 'reform' the latter, which was one of her fervent wishes. In 2021 – as mentioned before – she even proposed prosecuting boat captains who dared to rescue immigrants in danger of drowning on the high seas. That of course would also contravene internationally-agreed maritime law. Whether or not these measures were justified then, they clearly offended against one of nineteenth-century Britain's fondest principles, of 'free immigration': an essential pillar of its self-identity and thus its 'patriotism' at that time; which is not to say that it was right for the twenty-first century, but only that what Britain felt was admirable about itself had fundamentally changed since the time of Marx, Mazzini, and all those enterprising Jewish immigrants in London's East End. Countries evolve; which may be a reason not to base your 'patriotism' on your country's past.

In all these ways it could be said that the process of Brexit and its aftermath were unpicking the best – or at least the most characteristic – aspects of 'Britishness', as they appeared in history; although of course the Brexiters didn't see it like this. One other way these events can be regarded, however, is not as *changing* anything, essentially, but as revealing how things had always been. Beneath Britain's bright liberal exterior lay a darker core which liberals had either not seen or had brushed under the carpet, confident perhaps that they were old sins that had been largely washed away. The events of 2016–21 disabused them of that, bringing to the surface of politics, and even of everyday life, 'British' – but not exclusively British – qualities that now seemed as significant, at least, as the contrary ones they had once been most proud of. Fascism – or proto-fascism – was not an aberration, but something that, in one form or another, had infused the British 'character' for years: once diverted into 'imperialism', perhaps, although not – as has been suggested in Chapter 3 of this book – into every aspect of that complex and sometimes quite 'liberal' phenomenon. The same applied to the large-scale corruption that was revealed in the early stages of the Covid-19 crisis; and – in particular – to the racism that may still have been more endemic to Britain than liberals had fondly thought. A mob reaction to the failure of three 'black' players in the England football team to score in a penalty shoot-out in an important international cup-final in July 2021 was supposed to have shown evidence for the latter; although, to be fair, this was soon countered by anti-racist demonstrations by the footballers themselves, and messages of support for the black players by thousands of 'better' Britons. But the stain on Britain's character remained. So far as 'history' was concerned, an awful lot would need to be swept under the carpet in order to present a clean picture: some unnecessary wars (but not the Second World War), the horrors as well as the triumphs of industrialization, colonial atrocities of the worst kind, religious hypocrisy, and much more. For those who had always refused to believe that their own – or any – country was essentially 'better' than others, this could be seen as welcome, if somewhat depressing, evidence. For more traditional 'patriots', of course, unless they were the proto-Fascist type, it should not have been so reassuring. But for everyone the 'Whig interpretation' of Britain's past history – the one that presented it as 'improving' decade by decade, which will have encouraged optimism in people, so *dis*couraging political unrest – could no longer be relied upon.

Indeed, such was the confusion into which the Brexit process had thrown the British body politic that almost nothing could be relied on. Politicians certainly couldn't be, in the light of the well-publicized lies of some of them, and the inadequacy of Johnson's post-Brexit government, composed not of the wisest and most experienced Conservatives in the main, but of young-ish new ministers appointed purely on account of their loyalty to the Brexit project, and 'shown up' badly by their response to the Covid crisis in 2020–1. (If that disaster hadn't arrived, there's no knowing how they might have coped with Brexit itself. As it was, they had Covid to blame for any failures.) Popular trust in politicians may have reached its nadir in these years; and the *mis*trust have morphed into something even more dangerous: a widespread disbelief in anything that was presented to people by 'authority'. For many it was the great lie on the 'Brexit bus' that did it; for others the revelation of the *too* clever work of Dominic Cummings in engineering the referendum vote; and their disappointment at the immediate effects of Britain's withdrawal from the EU, which were not at all what they had been promised. The hostility was not only directed at Tories. No politician could be trusted: again, 'they're all the same'. Some took refuge in 'conspiracy theories' to make a different kind of sense of what was happening, which is a sure sign of the breakdown of the political process anywhere. (It happened in the contemporary USA too.) The Victorians, incidentally, had been well aware of this danger, which is why they had valued public honesty and transparency so highly. Hence their honourable and impartial civil service, now directly undermined by Johnson's government; and the other 'checks and balances' incorporated in the (unwritten) British constitution, which looked like going the same way. Without public trust, countries can easily fall into anarchy, or worse.

For the political Right, proto-Fascist or otherwise, this opened up opportunities. They didn't need to listen to 'the democracy'; they could manipulate it. This was easier for them than it was for the Left, because – in Britain – they had a partisan press behind them; and the press was an essential ally and manipulator. (Usually; in July 1995 however Tony Blair managed to get the media mogul Rupert Murdoch on to Labour's side after flying to the other side of the world to persuade him. But this just emphasizes the *power* of the media.) For many politicians, especially perhaps 'career' ones – who went into it out of personal ambition rather than to 'do' anything for their constituents or for the country – politics had always been something of a 'game', where winning or losing were the only considerations, and any new 'winning' technique was therefore worth pursuing, whatever its relationship to the *issues* they were supposed to stand for. Of course this had always been so to an extent. All parties from the dawn of Britain's political history had tried to get their messages across by means of propaganda. The difference now was that the means of propaganda had become so sophisticated as to be almost undetectable by most voters; and that the most sophisticated of these means were almost exclusively in the hands of the political Right. The problem for the Left was either how to combat them, or whether to adopt them for its own cause. In either case there were bound to be implications for Britain's 'democracy'.

*

At the end of this process – whenever it comes – it may be difficult to recognize the Britain of the pre-Brexit era; or the *myth* of pre-Brexit Britain, *possibly*, which had underlain many Britons' loyalty and indeed 'patriotism' in the past. For a start, Brexit marked a true 'revolution', in a country that had prided itself since the mid-seventeenth century on not requiring revolutions, apart from slow, gradual ones like the 'industrial' one of the early years of the nineteenth century. Britain had generally resisted 'extreme' forms of politics too, seeing off its 1930s Fascists, for example, and its communists, only now to be visited by a political tendency widely regarded, as we have seen, as 'proto'-fascist, at the very least. The sacred 'Union' between England, Wales, Scotland and Northern Ireland was coming under threat. So were traditional guarantors of 'moderation', like the separation of powers and judicial scrutiny. Age-old conventions like not lying to Parliament were simply disregarded by Ministers with impunity. A good half of the national press had changed from being genuine '*news*papers' to Right-wing propaganda-sheets. Civil servants were no longer respected for their objective advice, and often had to endure bullying on account of it (for example from Priti Patel at the Home Office); and were increasingly being supplemented by 'Special' and partisan 'Advisors', or 'Spads'. Ministers were abusing their powers to enrich themselves, party donors and their friends, like mediaeval barons distributing largesse. Fond 'British' traditions like tolerance towards refugees, minimal policing, saving people from drowning, and the right to protest – even simply loudly – had now become almost totally reversed. Politicians no longer attracted the kind of respect that many of them had had in previous years. Even cricket, after a number of scandals involving betting 'fixes' and 'ball-tampering', was hardly 'cricket' any more. And football – 'created by the poor, stolen by the rich', as one popular banner put it[8] – was clearly no longer the 'People's Game'. If 'patriotism' involves respecting the history and traditions of your country (which it needn't, of course: Sweden as we have seen bases its own on Sweden's aspirations),[9] the Brexit years can hardly be considered in that light.

Obviously this wasn't all Brexit's doing; and indeed Brexit was as much a product of the situation as its cause. The seeds of just about every one of these new plants can be discerned in Britain's past history, complex and uneven as that was. Most of the excesses of the 2010s were built on what might be considered 'traditional' British values, albeit alternative and minority ones, and only heightened now. Corruption was nothing new; as neither were lying, racism, mobs, Scottish separatism, authoritarian tendencies on the Right of politics, imperialism and free marketism (obviously), and even cheating at cricket. (W. G. Grace was notorious for that.) 'Spads' began with Harold Wilson, and the general denigration of civil servants with the TV series *Yes Minister* – the only comedy show the notoriously humourless Margaret Thatcher liked. The 'yellow' press went back to Rupert Murdoch's empowerment in 1981 by Thatcher, and before that to the turn of the twentieth century. Race riots began in the 1950s.

As well as all this, most of these developments also had their *international* equivalents; which may give a clue as to their genesis. For a start, Brexit was only one of a number of nationalist and so-called 'populist' movements arising in Europe and the Americas in the 2010s. So if they were nationalist, they were at least international in their nationalism. This suggests that something broader than simple British 'patriotism' lay behind it. The same had been true, of course, of European Fascist parties in the 1930s: fiercely nationalistic but also parts of a trans-national trend. In that earlier case economic depression had much to do with it; and the same – or similar – may have been true in the 2010s. Our 'Marxist' would have a material and logical explanation for it, of course: it marked the final breathless struggles of a doomed capitalist system, no less. Among others, however, a crisis on this scale could not be relied upon to provoke such *rational* reactions – if not necessarily reasonable ones – which might explain Brexit in Britain; as well as, for example, Trumpism in America.

In Britain it appeared *very* irrational; not only the policy itself – Brexit – but also the contortions of the people who saw it through. This too might be seen as 'typically British' – eccentricity, humour, nonsense and so on – but in the past these traits had generally not been allowed anywhere near *government,* which had been conducted on far more sober lines. (That was Falstaff's comic-tragedy: to be dismissed when prince Hal became king.) Now the clowns had been allowed out of the circus, and set on the country as a whole: with Boris Johnson as the chief jester, the role for which he was best known before his elevation,[10] but followed closely by the unlikely genius behind 'UKIP', Nigel Farage, and the languid and top-hatted Etonian 'toff' Jacob Rees-Mogg. Some of their colleagues appeared equally Monty Pythonesque: the very odd-looking Michael Gove, for example; and the short, fat and unfortunately named – for the chair of one of the major Europhobic pressure-groups – Mark Francois. Of course one shouldn't count politicians' appearances, names and eccentricities against them; but foreigners simply could not take these men seriously. If Johnson and Co. thought that by their 'Titanic' personalities they were restoring 'respect' for a Brexit Britain, they were deluded. But it seemed they didn't really care; or simply blamed foreigners, for *never* liking them.

This really was a very great departure from British political tradition, and hence a blow to any kind of 'patriotism' that had that tradition at its core. It may have had something to do with the fact that true 'aristocrats' were no longer in charge of the 'head' of our 'hybrid': Johnson and Rees-Mogg talked like aristos, and had been educated like them, but weren't really top-notch, class-wise. (They weren't 'old Norman', for a start.) Most of the more traditional upper-class Tories – Thatcher's 'Wets' – were banished from the Conservative party, electorally, in 2019. The remainder were mainly posh capitalists – fairly posh, anyway. The Civil Service had been bullied into demoralization, with several high-profile resignations under Johnson, and submission to the 'Spads'. Two key and generally much-valued British institutions of recent years, the National Health Service and the British Broadcasting Corporation, were coming under attack, from under-funding, privatization and some said Americanization in the former case, and from revenue cuts and 'soft' government censorship in the latter. If any institutions could be said to epitomize later twentieth-century 'Britishness' – not Thatcher's sort, of course – they could well have been the NHS and the BBC. ('Traditions' don't have to go back to King Arthur. If they did – the Round Table and all that – it might not be all that bad.) The Brexiters, and those who rode on the backs of them, were certainly not 'patriotic' in this sense. But then we should probably not put too much weight on that claim of theirs. The more negative attitude of 'xenophobia' (or at least xeno-scepticism) probably expressed their philosophy better. This of course also had its roots in British history; although the other sort of British patriot had been hoping that it had rather dried out in the European sun. Which backs up the suggestion hinted at (only) here: that possibly one of Brexit's effects was to reveal what Britain was *really* like, underneath.

Or – maybe – just *England*. The Scots and Northern Irish were different, albeit each in a very different way: Scotland as a historic nation of its own, and a 'proud' one; British Northern Ireland not wanting to be a separate nation – that was the whole point of it – and resistant to independently joining the rest of Ireland, which was still a member of the EU. Both these parts of the UK had voted *against* leaving the EU in the 2016 referendum, Scotland because it was historically more Europhile than England (and welcomed EU-immigration, for example), and Northern Ireland because Brexit was bound to harm Britain's trading and other relations with the Irish Republic to which it was conjoined. (Wales might have voted 'Remain' also, claimed its nationalists, if it hadn't been for the English retirees and holiday cottage-owners living there.) In Northern Ireland's case there were fears of the new post-Brexit dispensation's sparking a recurrence of the 'Troubles' between the two communities living there which had so devastated the province in the 1970s and 1980s; or even of a re-united Ireland – the North joining up with the South. In Scotland it made the possibility of secession from the UK, last rejected in a referendum in 2014 by 55 per cent to 45 per cent, more likely. Both of these would be real game-changers. For members of the Conservative Party – since the 1880s, at the latest, when it had been officially re-named the Conservative *and Unionist* Party – the integrity of the whole United Kingdom was always supposed to be one of its core values. Prime Minister Theresa May shed tears over it – 'my beloved Union' – on the day she announced the resignation that had been forced on her, in great part due to the Irish difficulty, in July 2019.[11] Without Scotland and Northern

Ireland Great Britain would be reduced to a 'Little England', almost literally. (To repeat: the 'Great' was always meant to refer to its size and plurality, rather than to anything more boastful.) Yet surveys seemed to show, extraordinarily, that a majority of English Brexiters would be willing to accept these losses, in return for 'taking control' of their English rump.[12] Now that *would* be both unhistorical, and surely unpatriotic, so far as *British* patriotism went.

*

But then so was the whole Brexit position, in many ways. Its main ostensible agenda – that is, disregarding the deeper and broader reasons behind it – was basically un- (or at least *a*-) historical. UK 'independence' was a chimera, based on a misunderstanding of Britain's historical relationships with the continent of Europe, the Commonwealth, and the world, and the nature of 'treaties'; as well as on unrealistic expectations for the present. Those especially who looked back to their Empire for guidance about the future – 'Heaven forfend!' – should not have done. The world had changed mightily since Britain last ruled over palm and pine; which in any case, so far as *effective* rule was concerned, was a lot shorter than many people assumed. (Some imperial historians would push the beginning of the 'Decline and Fall' of the British Empire back to 1858, or 1902 at the latest.)[13] Also, the material conditions that had favoured Britain's original empire-building – its striking industrial and commercial leadership in particular – were obviously long past resurrecting in the twenty-first century. The old empire had ridden on the back of a successful economy, and in open seas, which could hardly be said to be the situation now. The basic point is this: that the British Empire, whether conceived 'formally' or 'informally', had been built up from the bottom, and in the context of the special international conditions of its time; which in 2016–20 – and presumably thereafter – simply did not exist. It also – *pace* Rees-Mogg – was not essentially built by 'heroes', but by circumstances. Besides this, it had always had the British '*anti*-imperial' and anti-racist traditions to contend with: two others of Britain's proud original contributions to history, albeit rather forgotten today. The old empire therefore, in whatever guise, was a false trail to follow in the twenty-first century; a part of Britain's history that bore almost no relevance to these new times.

As did most other things in its history. History moves, in its own way; and people and nations need to move with it. It should be broadly irrelevant to the present day. And this advice comes from a professional historian.

10

Patriotisms

Britain has an extraordinary history; never more so, perhaps, than over the last five or six years. (This is being written in the summer of 2021.) Whether that merits any special pride being taken in it, or feelings of 'patriotism', let alone pride in what Britain has latterly become, must be doubtful. Patriotism doesn't need to be founded on past history, and for some countries whose pasts are even more problematical than Britain's this might not be a good idea in any case. For Britons such a history – one that will make them feel good about themselves – must be selective, for everyone will surely acknowledge that any nation's history is a mixture of the 'good' and the 'bad', however those qualities are defined. Besides, countries and societies *change*, so that what they are today may have little or no equivalence in their pasts. This book has demonstrated this by reference to a number of features in which Britons took great pride in Victorian and early twentieth-century times – indeed, were considered to define their 'national identity' then – but are now entirely gone. The Empire is not the only or even the most important one.

Beyond that, and in connection especially with Britain's relationship with the continent of Europe, which is the major 'national' question at the time of writing, to say that its history is 'extraordinary' is not the same as saying that it is 'exceptional'; or, rather, that it is more 'exceptional' than any other nation's is. In many ways, indeed, Britain has marched in close formation with other countries – 'imperialism' was one example; present-day 'populism' is another – which suggests that forces outside it or its leaders' control may have had a hand in it. My choice among those forces would be the global advance of capitalism; but there are other possibilities. They too must undermine the notion that Britain has been entirely responsible for its own past history, which should be an object of 'pride' – or, conversely denigration – for that reason. 'As flies to wanton boys are we to the gods; They kill us for their sport.' Well, not quite (King Lear was rather depressed when he said that); but there is a great deal in what Britain is conceived to have achieved in recent times which should rather be seen as the results of forces beyond its control: Lear's 'gods', or late-stage capitalism, or even accident. We have seen how influential the last of these was in the five or six years leading up

to Britain's departure from the European Union. Which is another reason
for not crediting the Brexiters' claim that they were essentially returning
their country to its place in 'history'. In fact in most ways they were
wrenching it away from that.

*

Still, if you want to base your patriotism on your nation's (or nations')
history, you are of course welcome to; but this book might suggest better
ways it could be done. It needs to be acknowledged, first, that Britain's
history has been bound up with other countries' histories from the start,
right through to the present day. To recapitulate: it began with Europe, in
relation to which it started as an integral part – connected via 'Doggerland'
– but then became separated by a very short distance when Doggerland was
inundated (we presume), and so Continental Europeans needed to get into
boats to visit its shores. Which they did, in several waves of invasion and
settlement, up to the Normans, who put their stamp on the country in
several – and not always very nice – ways. Thereafter Britain was able to
repel or deter any further attempts at forcible invasion – the 'Battle of
Britain' is the final iconic event here – but not the immigration of foreigners
who came in peace, and the influx of ideas. The same was true the other way
around, with Brits visiting and influencing the European Continent.
Throughout its existence the history of Britain has been essentially the
history of Europe, writ small. All histories of it as a nation should begin with
that.

There can be no doubt regarding its 'European-ness'. Again: Britain
shares roughly the same physical and climatic conditions with other
European countries. It is separated from them only by two narrow bands of
sea, the English and the Irish Channels. Its pre-history went along with
theirs, albeit with the ancient Brits usually lagging a little behind. They
always traded with one another, often over large distances, and expanded
into neighbouring territories at different periods, but with roughly similar
results. About half of Europe came under the Roman Empire for three or
four centuries. After that almost the whole of Europe, including the British
Isles, was 'visited' (to put it mildly) by the Vikings. Not that any of this
should greatly influence us today. Most of it was far too long ago to be
considered relevant to the question of Britain's relationship with Europe
now, and rightly so. We cannot allow cavemen and the beastly Danes to cast
such a long shadow. Only to Israelis can history that far back appear
'relevant'. And theirs was written by God.

At the end of this 'dark' period Christianity came to envelope the whole
continent, bringing with it the Europe-wide religious civil wars which all
broke out at roughly the same time. Parts of Europe succumbed to militant
Islam, but only for a while (so far). All countries had cultural (Classical)
'Renaissances'. Extra-European exploration and trade started out from a
number of European centres, and nearly every coastal European nation

amassed an overseas empire. The 'industrial revolution' began in one or two places, mainly northern Britain, together with the various forms of modern capitalism, but soon spread overall. Other revolutions affected most European nations, including Britain, even if they didn't topple them. Scholarly and scientific co-operation was common, and invaluable on all sides. Artistic and architectural styles were Europe-wide, especially in the Middle Ages, when 'Romanesque' and then 'Gothic', with its pointed arches, were – with a few national variants – common to all. Today Shakespeare, Mozart, Sherlock Holmes and Kurt Wallander are known everywhere, and regarded – surely – as parts of *Europe*'s heritage. Modern organized and codified sport began in Britain, but everyone plays football today, and to the same sets of rules. (Cricket of course is the big exception; but there's still time.) Then the major ways of organizing societies, and the ideologies connected with them – feudalism, theocracy, democracy, nationalism, liberalism, socialism, feminism, imperialism, fascism – put down roots everywhere, although in different degrees and stages depending on local material circumstances. Almost every country feels it is 'free-er' than others, with 'freedom' being a slippery concept. 'Neoliberalism' has hit us all. Most countries have perpetrated 'atrocities' of one kind or another, if not at home (*vide* Germany), then in their colonies. We are all affected by American culture, itself influenced by European to a considerable degree; and by what today is called 'populism'. We were all floored by the great global pandemics, from the Black Death through to Covid-19. We've all shared the burden – or privilege – of incorporating foreign refugees into our societies, albeit some more begrudgingly than others. Most European countries were involved in some way or other in the twentieth century's two World Wars: Italy on both sides; and in many of the Continent's bouts of terrorism. Britain was particularly involved with the Continent in two other ways: sheltering refugees, and tourism. So there are important ways in which we can all talk of sharing a common 'European' history, from way back up to the present day, despite the Europeans' internecine quarrels and battles: which is another thing they share together, in a way. Britain is not so 'different', or as 'exceptional', as many Britons seem to think. If that was their reason or excuse for wanting their independence from the EU, it was a shaky one. But of course it doesn't have to be. Even close relatives can fall out.

Naturally, there *were* differences between Britain and its Continental neighbours in the period covered by this book. They included their conceptions of 'freedom', especially economic, but that didn't long outlast the challenges of the twentieth century; the particular *beneficence* of Britain's empire – allegedly, and ignoring all those atrocities – but (again) empire itself was something it had in common with other European nations; its 'splendid isolation': but that was always a bit of a myth; and its proud philistinism, which was really only a Victorian thing. Other things might be added, like Britain's fairly relaxed state Church; the 'Public' schools: all very well in their time, perhaps, but still exerting an unexpected influence on

British politics; its people's wandering urge; their utilitarianism; their poor food; and their principled stand against Hitler. These did mark it out for a time, but no more (yet again) than any of the nations of the Continent was marked out from all the others. And this should not have stopped Britain co-operating – joining, or even federating – with other nations if it was to the advantage of all of them. Indeed, this could only augment and enrich its essential and multicultural 'Britishness', by one way of looking at it. Britain was always *outward-looking*, the very opposite of 'parochial'; as part – it could be argued – of its national identity. Maybe Boris Johnson's 'global Britain' ambition will reprise that? Or not.

One other effect of these early shared historical experiences was to make Britain *multi-cultural*, and even multi-national, in ways explained in Chapter 1. There is no single 'national characteristic' to describe the country. Even 'whiteness' won't do, since the influx of Asian and African immigrants in modern times. (In any case the rest of us aren't white, but cream-coloured or pink. And colour almost never denotes identity; unless of course 'apartheid' is imposed on people.) Formally speaking – to recapitulate again – the 'United Kingdom' is made up of three separate 'nations' and a 'province', each with its own distinctive traits. It also comprises a multitude of 'cultures', based on origins, class, religion, politics and locality. This crazy-paving of peoples has gone through a great deal in the last two hundred years (the period covered in this book), sometimes separately and fissiparously, at other times together. It is this that makes British history so fascinating to study, but also so difficult to distil into something that might merit any sort of 'patriotic pride'. Unless, that is, you can feel pride *in* its complexity; which – I suggest – is probably the best way to go. And – to be fair to Britain's new 'patriots' – is the way implied in the new national song that was suggested by them to be sung in schools in June 2021: 'One Britain One Nation'.[1] (Although the idea of making all schools adopt it might be seen as 'un-British' in itself. The Brits don't usually go in for 'patriotic' shows.)

*

Alternatively, one can choose one's focus of national pride and patriotism from a number suggested by Britain's past. Not all these are consistent or compatible with one another, which is why one needs to make a choice, or else to abandon the attempt. Broadly speaking, they can be divided into two sorts, corresponding with the two 'sides' conventionally taken up in modern politics: 'Right' and 'Left'. On the 'Right' side of the account are the Empire (of course), Britain's military and naval victories, the Union flag, the Royal Family, the Church of England, the Public schools, statues, 'family values', 'discipline', 'imperial measures', blue passports (actually black, now), patriotic 'shows' (like a new Royal yacht Johnson decided the nation needed, even if the Royals didn't), and one particular kind of 'freedom' – Margaret Thatcher's sort. On the 'Left' side might stand the other sorts of 'freedom' that Britain has at times been associated with: of expression, religion, protest, sexuality, anti-slavery and foreign immigration, all of them objects of national pride at various times in the past; plus internationalism, *anti*-imperialism (invented by the British, as we've seen) and the Commonwealth; certain institutions like the Trade Unions, the Welfare State, the NHS and the BBC; egalitarianism, at least as an objective; a reluctance to be too 'patriotically' showy; liberal 'progress' (the 'Whig interpretation'); and, yes, the multi-culturalism that (again) has always been a part of its identity. (Shakespeare and cricket can go on either side of the divide.) All these can be harnessed to 'patriotism', of one kind or another.

In fact one of the rare common strands in modern British history has been the *conflict* between these two different conceptions of what Britain stands for: between rival perceptions of 'patriotism', in other words. Leftists don't usually like to admit to 'patriotism' because of the way the word has been appropriated by the Right (we saw how that happened under Disraeli); and also because it is supposed to mean that they can't be 'internationalist': 'if you call yourself a citizen of the world you are a citizen of nowhere.' But if you want to love your country because of *its* internationalism you should surely be able to. For people in either of these categories there should be enough pickings in the history recounted in this book to feed their national pride. And if you are a politician, it might well improve your chances with your 'naturally' (apparently) patriotic working-class constituency if you can make this clear. But in order to be *useful* patriots they should not neglect the other sides of their pictures. Tory patriots, for example, should be aware of the harm the Empire did; and Left-wing anti-imperialists of its occasional benefits (like cricket). Above all, however, they need to be aware of *how things happen* in history: not by the individual volition of heroes or Hitlers, but by circumstances usually outside the control of either. Jacob Rees-Mogg: take note.

This applies to one of Britain's proudest boasts in the nineteenth century, although not one much respected today, which concerned the asylum it was able – 'able', mark – to afford to Continental political refugees, even those who would be categorized now as 'terrorists', which the rulers of the countries they fled from regarded as dangerous, but turned out not to be. Marx's and Engels's long sojourn in England, where they plotted the downfall of their host's capitalist economy, must be regarded as a feather in the nation's cap by radical patriots, and even possibly by the other sort. It was enabled partly by popular pressure, albeit fuelled by people's feelings – partly principled, partly xenophobic – against the repressive European regimes Marx et al. had been forced to flee from. Other achievements of the time that could be admired on the Left were the successive extensions of the franchise and of civil rights for minorities; the abolition of colonial slavery; moderation of the penal code; a deliberately soft approach to policing, which disallowed 'secret' policing – spies – absolutely; the nation's contributions later to international law and to the founding of the League of

Nations; and self-government for colonies as members of a free and equal 'Commonwealth'. Right-inclined patriots liked to claim credit for many of these – they showed how 'enlightened' the ruling classes were, which was a fair enough point – but they were mainly forced on the Right by the Left. Rightists were more likely to take pride in 'heroes' like Nelson, Wellington, Churchill and Thatcher, their nation's gung-ho imperial adventures, its booming economy (this is in the nineteenth century), the Union of Britain and (later Northern) Ireland, 'two World Wars and one World Cup' (to repeat a notorious England football chant), and the Queen. What both sides tended to forget – if they wanted to celebrate Britain – were the other sides of some of these pictures: the horrors of its industrial towns and cities, invariably noticed by foreign visitors; 'wage-slavery' in the great new factories; the crime and prostitution that so many poor people had been forced into; the persecution of early and even later trade unionists; avoidable disease and deaths; the sufferings of the Irish part of their 'Union' and of tens of thousands of their colonial subjects; the downright atrocities; and the general incompetence of the British Army after Waterloo, unless it was fighting 'natives' armed only with spears. Still, there may be enough there to piece together a moderate degree of patriotic 'pride'. So long as we don't forget that not all these admirable characteristics – free immigration for example, manufacturing industry, the ban on 'spying', World Cup success, and the British Empire – have survived to the present day.

*

Indeed, the present day – the early years of the twenty-first century – has revealed, or given rise to, a very different sort of Britain from any of the ones that are celebrated in history. A liberal Victorian transported there now would be favourably impressed by some things, no doubt, especially in technology and medicine, and possibly by the general health of people and women's rights; and would immediately recognize certain institutions, like Parliament, the Conservative Party and Eton College, albeit with a smidgen of surprise, perhaps, that the last of these had lasted so long, as part of the present age's detritus from the past. But he or she would also be mightily shocked by, for example, surveillance cameras in the streets – unconscionable in the nineteenth century; the decline of manufacturing industry; the gap between rich and poor (free trade was supposed to have ironed that out); violent political and religious extremism; the descent into the lowest gutter of the national tabloid press (that's not going to get me a good review in the *Daily Mail*!); blatant lying by politicians; possibly the poor *quality* of Britain's ruling class generally; the 'hostile environment' for immigrants and protesters (that would shock our Victorian visitor to the core); Theresa May's claim that you couldn't owe allegiance to both your country and 'the world'; 'diving' in football (or is that mainly by foreign players?); state-subsidized arts; the attenuation of the once proud Royal Navy; and – probably – the tendency towards what might be called 'authoritarian misrule' in the present day. (Or of a few years ago, if you are reading this later on.) Not all of this, to repeat, was the *fault* of anyone, or even of the nation collectively, and certainly not of Brexit alone, which was more a symptom than a cause. It may even be that Brexit could prove to be the cure for some of it, if its more optimistic advocates are right. The point is, however, that a 'patriotism' founded on Britain's past history is unlikely to be a reliable guide to its future; as is probably true of any country's 'history'.

In particular, we must be aware of Britain's history's being hijacked by 'populists'. There is no way that it can be seen to have been leading to *this*. Britain today is at a genuine *disjuncture*. My advice to readers of this book, therefore, is to base their attitudes and especially their politics on *current* circumstances, rather than on Britain's – probably misremembered – past: as I'm sure most of them do. We are what we are, not what we were.

Besides, there is much in present-day Britain to be attracted by, if not necessarily proud of (if we didn't personally contribute to it), or 'patriotic' on account of it. Each of our choices, no doubt, would be different, depending on which of the many 'Britains' we represented, but any of them could make us love our country more. My own very personal choices – the things I miss living abroad – are: not the predictable fish and chips and Marmite, which you can get in Sweden if you look hard enough for them; but steak and kidney puddings (not pies, which I can get from Taylors and Jones in Hantverkargatan, Stockholm: highly recommended); Marks and Spencer food halls; cricket, as must be obvious from some of the asides in this book; English country churches, even though I'm not a church-goer; being served in little shops by middle-aged women who ask me 'what can I do for you, young man?' (I'm 80); the humour of ordinary people; Essex, my beloved native county, especially the northern part of it; Hull and the East Riding of Yorkshire, where I mainly live when I'm not in Sweden; Cambridge, my old university town, mainly for the architecture and memories of sunny days on the river; Elgar played live – you might have thought that would make the other sort of 'patriot' of me, but no; and the fascinating *complexity* of the British and imperial history I write about for a living – but I can do that from abroad. So far as that history is concerned, I personally admire (without necessarily being 'proud' of) Britain's part in the Second World War; Shakespeare, Dickens, Turner and Elgar; the achievements of many of its immigrants and offspring of immigrants (like the English men's football team); its liberal progress during most of the past two hundred years until recently; the NHS and BBC; Britain's past reputation for tolerance and moderation in many respects (if not others); its radical (including anti-imperial) traditions; the more liberal aspects of its imperialism, few as they may have been; and the fact that it didn't fight to cling on to its Empire as long as some other colonial powers did.

But I recognize that this is a selective picture, and that other 'patriots' will disagree. Each person's love of his or her country is different. We can love the same country for very different reasons; and also love other countries *as well as* our own. Among my own non-British loves are Sweden, naturally; France, culturally; Australia, bigly; and the 'liberal' bits of the USA. Plus humanity at large, of course, even if by Teresa May's 'patriotic' calculus that means I'm 'a citizen of no country at all'. OK; that's probably more than readers need to know of my personal preferences; but it might help reassure them of my feelings towards the country I may have seemed to have denigrated here, and persuade them that love of country need have nothing to do with 'patriotism' as understood by people like Lia Nici, mentioned in the Preface: the 'Queen and Flag' sort. *Or* with 'history'; which again in my view – even as a historian – should be kept well clear of it.

*

Finally, with regard to the British history sketched out here, readers should be aware that my brief account of it – despite all my efforts – may not be totally reliable. But then history is bound to be controversial anyway. This is partly because it *is* complicated. In fact the rich complexity of Britain's history in particular is one reason why many of us – not only me – like to study it. In doing so, we often find ourselves pitched against 'fake' or oversimplified versions of it, especially popularly, which can be irritating if we care for historical 'truth'. If we believe historical *un*truth to be potentially dangerous – used to draw unreliable lessons to guide present-day policies, for example (like American neo-Cons did to justify the invasion of Iraq in 2003) – then it is incumbent upon us professional historians, in the public interest, to correct the misunderstandings, mistakes and lies. There are plenty of those coming from British politicians today. Not that we usually get very far with this. The 'general public' doesn't usually want to be bothered with our sort of scholarship. Besides, 'fake' history is often more beguiling than the truth. 'Never mind the history; feel the myth.'

This is not to say that genuine 'truth' is ever simple, or can be finally established objectively. Swedish schoolchildren, admirably, are taught from very early on to respect what is called *källkritik*, or going back to original sources before accepting a proffered opinion; but even the most authoritative *källor* can be falsified, hidden or destroyed. Who for example was knowledgeable enough to get behind the lie on the 'Brexit Bus' in 2016? It is important to be aware of this possibility; so long as it doesn't cause us to distrust *all* evidence, which can lead on to unfounded 'conspiracy theorizing', and thence to a kind of intellectual anarchy. 'I'm a free American, and so can believe whatever I like', as I heard one contributor to an American radio phone-in programme declare after being picked up on an obvious falsity. (He had claimed that the London Blitz was in retaliation for the Allied bombing of Dresden.) His kind seems to have proliferated in very recent years, encouraged, of course, by a recent American President who side-stepped the problem of his own untrustworthiness by labelling all the facts adduced against him as 'fake'. Countering this is difficult, especially in the face of those who distrust scholars automatically, as 'élitists' who have their own agendas, *as* élitists, to interpret things in certain ways. These days it is not easy to persuade the general public of even the most certain and self-evident 'facts'; especially when they are deliberately distorted by leading politicians and their 'Spads', who seem to regard politics as a game, to be simply won or lost, with any tools – including lies – that come to hand. This may be the crucial political battle to be fought today. Citizens need to trust their governments. Otherwise 2020 (and thereabouts) will be seen to mark a crucial stage in delinking Britain from one of its proudest historical traditions, albeit one sometimes more honoured in the breach, of government honesty and probity. What price 'patriotism' then?

And that doesn't bring an end to the problem. Material facts are one thing; interpretations something else. Because of the aforesaid complexities of history – causes uncertain, motivations mixed (and in any case not necessarily identical with causes), background factors not always clear, trends and developments interweaving constantly and confusedly, and our selection of the most significant ones very often based on our general philosophies and predilections, as well as our interests and preferences (readers of this book will have noticed some of these) – we can't be sure about anything. All I can say in defence of the observations and analyses offered here is that they are *consistent* with the known evidence; and that, if they are wrong, they will not be as wrong as some. And they may be largely irrelevant – *history* may be irrelevant – in any case; except of course to correct *a*historicisms. And that (yet again) comes from a professional historian.

*

In conclusion (to this part of the book, anyway): some of the above may be thought to be controversial, or even 'biased'. I'm sure it is both. It must be obvious to readers that I was opposed to Brexit from the beginning, for a number of reasons: my personal European connexions; my Left-wing tendencies; possibly my status as an intellectual and hence an 'elitist' – although if you knew more about my background you might start to doubt that; but mainly – I would claim – my life-long study of British history, which you will probably find makes most professional historians more Europhile than UKIP's founder, a historian himself. (Incidentally, I wasn't so pro-Europe *before* the beginning: that is, at the time of the referendum in 1975, when I *think* I may have voted *against* British membership. But circumstances change.)[2] History today doesn't prove that Brexit was wrong; but it offers very little evidence for its being right either. It's the misleading views of Britain's past which are sometimes martialed to justify the Brexit position that this book has tried to unravel; and, of course, the form of 'patriotism' that has been based on, or bolstered by, these.

It is probably my pretty dismissive view of the politicians who have led us into our present situation of 'authoritarian misrule' that will be most held against me as indicating 'prejudice'. But I don't see why, if these people can be objectively shown to be foolish, or dishonest, or malevolent, even contemporary historians shouldn't say so, if they believe it helps explain the events of their day. In my view – and I'm treading dangerously here for a historian, by making a prediction – Britain's present government (in the summer of 2021) may well be seen by future chroniclers as being one of the most incompetent and corrupt in the whole of British history; measured against (as I have measured it) those that went before. That is one of my reasons for arguing that Brexit marked a *disjunction*, a sharp break from British 'traditions', rather than, as Brexiters liked to claim, a means of returning to them. The evidence of lying, chicanery, incompetence and corruption on the part of Boris Johnson and his loyal ministers has been revealed so clearly by trusted journalists (even Conservative ones),[3] by courts of law in one or two cases, and even by their own admissions, as to make it highly unlikely that 'history' will come to their rescue in the coming years. If this is so, then a present-day historian must take it all on board; if only in pursuance of his or her secondary duty – that is, after simply chronicling events – to try to *explain* them. The peccadillos of its leaders may not be the major reasons for the state Britain finds itself in today, as we have indicated; but they can point us towards the real agencies of change.

Beyond that it is up to our politicians, and those who give them legitimacy – that is, the electorate – to learn some lessons from the great historic disjunction that was Brexit; helped on, hopefully, by a more reliable view of Britain's past. Historians can only diagnose, not prescribe. The diagnoses made in this book, however, might suggest a number of *areas* for possible treatment – even perhaps surgery – in order to bring back to health a political and social situation which is clearly largely broken, whichever way we look at it. That may turn out to have been the major contribution of this whole Brexit business to Britain's history: to reveal in no uncertain terms the weaknesses of its so-called 'constitution'. We know that Boris Johnson, probably under the influence still of Dominic Cummings, is contemplating major constitutional surgery with the aim of making British government more *efficient*. But it is arguable that this is not the main problem with it, and that Britain's governmental system also needs to be made more responsive to an enlightened democracy: sometimes at the cost of 'efficiency' if the latter means getting wrong things done more quickly. That would require at least a look at Britain's FPTP voting system; at its press and other media; at its education at all levels, from Eton (certainly) 'down' – introducing *political* but non-partisan education, perhaps, and classes in sheer logical thinking; and at the role of the Civil Service, returning it to its old 'Nolan' Principles, and what it at least aspired to be before the invasion of the 'Spads'. Distrust of government and of politicians also needs to be looked at. The advertising and propaganda 'industries' could be examined, and perhaps legislated for in some – hopefully liberal – way. Then, it might be useful to enquire more carefully and sympathetically into some of the social and economic grievances, quite apart from ignorance, which can turn 'electorates' into 'mobs'. All these factors have been instrumental – or at least enabling – in Britain's recent history, and especially in the latest stages of it. Genuine 'patriots' should surely be looking into all this. Otherwise Britain could sink even further into an essential 'unBritishness'.

Of course, if 'patriots' are *not* particularly wedded to their 'history', and don't derive their 'patriotism' from it, then that is fair enough. There are other possible focuses of true patriotism than the musty past. It would be understandable for a patriot, and for patriotic reasons, to want to found a '*New* Jerusalem' in Britain, rather than to return to the old one, real or imagined. Surely this is what fired the patriotism of those servicemen and women in the Second World War who voted for a radical Labour government afterwards: the desire for a nation they *could* feel patriotic towards. History can serve as a guide to future action, especially in indicating what to avoid, but should never be used – even accurate history – as a model. This applies to Leftish 'golden ages' as well as to Right-wing ones, and was probably why Jeremy Corbyn was doomed to failure, in his desire to take the country back to the social-democratic 1960s – a highly 'patriotic' ambition in itself, surely – if Labour had won the General Election of 2019. History moves on, and almost never back. You don't dress in Rees-Mogg's notorious top hats and double-breasted jackets to prove your love of your country as it *is*. You can do it as an affectation, or a joke, or if you're playing the villain in a nineteenth-century melodrama. But not with any relevance to the present day.

If it *were* possible to resurrect the past history of Britain nowadays, it would probably take a very different form from what many of its self-styled 'patriots' may think. Obviously the Empire would be a feature of it, and also the industrial dominance that underpinned it. But who can see either of those re-appearing in the post-Thatcher years, even if Rees-Mogg's 'Titans' were to return to the scene? Neither of the originals was built by 'Titans' in any case, but by circumstances largely – 90 per cent, say – beyond any individual's control. (There lies Rees-Mogg's, and many other Right-wing patriots', fundamental error.) Other 'Victorian virtues' that would need to be re-embraced in order really to honour Britain's 'traditions' would include the free admission to the country of *all* immigrants, minimal policing, absolutely no private 'surveillance', and certainly no MI5. The 'Public' schools – our neo-feudal lordlings, so surprisingly rehabilitated in recent years – would need to move out of our way; or else return to teaching a more honourable – genuinely feudal – morality, '*noblesse oblige*' and the rest, than they appear to be doing today; as well as – probably – better and more *serious* history. (That's judging by Boris Johnson and his Old Etonian chums in the government: only a small sample, admittedly.) The Civil Service would be allowed to give independent advice. Victorian non-virtues, equally characteristic but less welcome in most people's view, would be workhouses, the death penalty, philistinism, and invading poorer countries for commercial gain. All these were crucial elements of Britain's 'national identity' all those decades ago. Most of them are either unattainable now, or not particularly attractive if they could be attained. To base a present-day 'patriotic' agenda on them would seem to be a distortion both of history, and of the needs of the present.

Why Britain has fallen as low as many conceive it to have done over the past five years, certainly in terms of international prestige but also among a newly 'ashamed' sector of its domestic population, has largely of course to do with Brexit, which was supposed to elevate the country, but on false premises (as well as 'promises'); but the damage goes back further than that. Some of the reasons have been vaguely suggested above in this chapter: a broken and imperfectly democratic political system; the apparent increase in lying and corruption in public life, and the public's acceptance of this; 'hidden' and not-so-hidden 'persuaders', like our lowly-ranked Press; poor political education; foreign (mainly Russian) interference, and the malign example from the other side of the world of Donald Trump; widespread scepticism of just about anything, but especially all authority, not only governmental but also 'expert', further undermining trust, and often generating wild 'conspiracy theories'; simple ignorance and stupidity, if an over-educated 'elitist' is allowed to suggest something so patronizing; and on the other hand the sheer Machiavellian cleverness of those who wished, for their own reasons, to lead the stupid astray. Lastly, we need to find a place for 'accident' in history, especially in the run-up to the referendum of 2016. All these will be readily recognized in the Brexit era (from the referendum onwards), and have been made much of by the many critics of the Cameron–May–Johnson governments, who probably comprise a majority as I write. Indeed, it is possible that no Tory government and set of ministers in British history – certainly since Neville Chamberlain's – has been as widely traduced as Johnson's. Whether this will make any material difference to the situation before the next planned General Election in May 2024 probably won't be known before this book goes to press. Johnson's government then had a Parliamentary majority of 80; which – under the FPTP system of voting – didn't at all reflect its position in the country more generally. And apparently the old rogue has many supporters in his party still: 'he's a card, isn't he?'[4]

That however is still just a short-term analysis. Just as Britain's rise as an industrial and imperial power in the nineteenth century can't be explained in terms of individual movers and shakers ('Titans') alone, or even to any significant degree, nor can its rapid fall from grace – if this is how it turns out – in recent years. One major long-term factor often suggested is the burden and then the decline and fall of Britain' overseas Empire, to which the new 'Europe' was supposed to act as a palliative, or an alternative source of prosperity and global influence, and was so regarded by many of the 'Commonwealth' – i.e. 'internationalist' – brand of imperialists, who hadn't so much minded the marginal loss of sovereignty that free co-operation with other countries entailed; but seems to have been resented by those – usually but not always elderly – who couldn't abide the indignity of being just 'subjects' of another empire, as they regarded the Brussels set-up, themselves. Whether the reaction against the EU really was greatly influenced by these people's residual imperialist feelings must – as has been suggested before in this book – be highly doubtful. 'We used to rule half the world!' was a *rare* slogan even among the more thuggish Brexiters (as well as being wrong). But imperial decline and the rise of other Powers towards which the British had used to feel superior must have left some people, who cared about these things, at least slightly discombobulated. The extent of this can't be known, because there is no reliable way of measuring discombobulation.

A more likely possibility, however, is that one thing people *were* affected by was Britain's perceived economic decline after the end of the Empire, whether or not the two trends were connected. And especially by the decline of its manufacturing industry by contrast with finance, which of course couldn't employ so many laid-off car workers or coal miners; thus transforming the British economy in a fundamental way. Margaret Thatcher's brutal way of addressing that must be adjudged a medium-term failure, though we have seen that many Brexiters disagreed. Their occasionally stated motive for Brexit, to allow them to 'complete the Thatcher revolution', also hints as a much more powerful factor behind the whole affair.

That has been suggested here already. If Marx was right, albeit a little premature, unrestrained capitalism is bound to encounter self-made crises which will destroy it in the end. The trade depressions of the twentieth century can be seen as evidence of these recurring crises, as can the financial crises of the early 2000s, and foreign wars, imperialism and 'austerity', chosen as they might have been as means of stopping or delaying them. A gentler way of dealing with the problem might have been Social Democracy, or Keynesianism or Welfareism, aiming to rub down the sharpest edges of late-stage capitalism, and so to rein it in before the final Armageddon. This was actually practiced in several European countries after the Second World War, especially the Scandinavian ones but including Britain under Attlee and Wilson, and to pretty good effect; before it was destroyed – or self-destructed – itself. For a very short while in 2019 Social Democracy seemed to be on the cards for Britain again, signalled by Jeremy Corbyn's new radical – but also reactionary – Labour Party; until it came a cropper in the General Election of that year, seeming to destroy all hopes of halting the progress of the Leviathan in this way. So the monster marched on; *possibly* inexorably, if this analysis is sound. Personally, I hope not.

Right or wrong, because people do not recognize this or other underlying imperatives of modern history, they resort to other measures to counter its effects on them, which typically include, for example, scapegoating, proto-fascism and electing clownish personalities as leaders. Of course other countries were experiencing this too, or something like it, which again suggests that it was an international trend. This may not be the whole explanation for the Brexit and post-Brexit *débâcles*, or even the primary one; but it connects the stupidities of Britain's leaders then with a broader and possibly more rational historical pattern. Historians don't like irrational or 'accidental' history; which may be why I'm rather attracted – although not entirely persuaded – by this idea. Again, like most of the other explanations offered in this book, the best I can say for certain is that it *fits*.

What bearing this may have on 'patriotism' is for readers to decide. If 'great' events in Britain's past history have been the result of external causes, then obviously they are nothing to be 'proud' of, even if it made sense anyway – which it doesn't – to feel 'pride' in something that happened before your time. You can be grateful to be British, or American, or French, or whatever but not 'proud' of it: unless it was a nationality you chose, and – ideally – you have done something yourself to make it prideworthy. As someone who very late on 'chose' Sweden for my second nationality I feel I qualify for the first, but not – yet – for the second. The same applies to the thousands of immigrants who have settled outside their 'mother' countries, and many of whom and their progeny *have* worked to do their adopted countries proud, from the British Royal Family (arguably) to two-thirds of the 2021 English football team. But this may be a purely 'academic' point, or even an over-semantic one.

In any case people obviously do feel pride in being 'British'; and – insofar as that merely means *admiring* their homeland – with some justification. There are undoubtedly worse countries to live in: even for minorities and women. It is also arguable that there are nations whose peoples have committed more egregious crimes than the British have, although the latter's 'other island' (Ireland) and empire – although not all of it – must put it pretty high up the league of international wrongdoers. There are admirable qualities in Britain, even aside from cricket, although arguably fewer than there used to be. Britain's much-lauded toleration, stability and various forms of 'freedom', for example, are coming under serious pressure as this book is being written; but hopefully will survive as historical memories, at least, which other sorts of 'patriot' than the 'Flag and Queen' kind can rediscover and build on in the future. Theirs won't be the unconditional – 'right or wrong' – patriotism that many on the Right seem to demand of Britons, or that traduces other nations, or reads 'inferiority' into what are merely other peoples' differences, or disqualifies patriots from being 'citizens of the world' too. This book is for them; and is why it has the word 'Patriot' in the subtitle. Patriotism needs to be reclaimed from Dr Johnson's 'scoundrels'; as also does the history of that complex and gloriously multicultural entity called 'Great Britain'.

For the best sort of 'patriotism' – the most constructive sort – doesn't, or shouldn't, depend on *pride*, in your country's past history, or in anything else about it. Patriots can love and support their countries while still criticizing them; perhaps even *aided* by their criticisms, which – as with wayward children – can arise from their love, and inspire them to try to improve their countries, if they have the means. This brief – and admittedly selective – history of Britain, and especially of the English part of it, should supply plentiful material for this more discriminating kind of loyalty; as well as undermining some of the false historical foundations for the 'loyalties' of some of those who *call* themselves 'patriots'; which was my original – and I maintain 'patriotic' – aim.

Afterword

(January 2022)

The problem with publishing a history book that finishes so close to the events it describes is, of course, that there has been no time to see how those later events will pan out; or even how they will have panned out in the short period between the book's writing and its publication. A certain degree of hindsight will be necessary before we can know which recent trends will turn out to have been the dominant or lasting ones in the years to come, or even to seem significant just six months later. With 'accident' having apparently played such a large part in recent British politics, this could be a particular problem today. This book was completed in the late summer of 2021, which came at the end – or at the beginning, or in the middle: who can tell? – of a short period of almost unprecedentedly rapid change in British history, whose culmination cannot yet be foretold with any confidence. It also came at a time when the main domestic actors in the drama – and one overseas one, Donald Trump – appeared so frankly preposterous to probably over half of the British population, and to just about every foreigner, as to defy the 'rational' explanations that serious historians generally like to give to events. (Obviously I'm not unbiased; but you don't need to be partisan to see the risible sides of Johnson, Rees-Mogg and Farage.) Whatever the Fates and Boris Johnson (still prime minister as I write) or his successors may have in store for us, the only thing we can be fairly confident of is that it will be unlike anything Britain as a nation has experienced before; however much certain politicians would like to return *to* those past experiences: whether they be the rollicking days of the first Elizabethans, the imperial glory (or whatever) of the Victorians, the social democracy of the post-Second World War years, or the austere discipline (for some) of the Thatcher and post-Thatcher eras. It will be different.

Also, it won't be 'patriotic', in the (limited) sense of adhering to any kind of essential British 'identity' or 'values' that can be established historically; for those were *ever* changing, as this book has tried to show. This indeed is probably true of most countries; with 'patriotism' in nearly every case being simply a tool for weaponizing support for one out of any number of competing national traditions, in the self-styled patriots' own sectional interests. Peace or War? Right or Left? Queen or Democracy? Morality or corruption? Union flag or Trade Union banners? Peers or Plebs? Obedience or Protest? Uniformity or Multiculturalism? Secure borders or Open ones? Progress or Reaction? Art or Utility? Empire or Anti-imperialism? – Which of these are the most distinctive traits of Britain's past? All of them have their roots in its history, one of whose leading characteristics is its complexity; and so are equally worthy of – if this is what you are after – patriotic 'pride'.

As well as this, any of them could rise to the top in future years, and so be adjudged, together with their historical precedents, to be more essentially 'British' then, depending on how Britain fares hereafter; which will also of course be affected by world-wide events and trends mainly outside its – or any nation's, even the 'super' ones' – control. Climate change – or the denial of it – will clearly have an impact, for a start. So *may* 'populism', in a number of guises. Or Islamicist terrorism. Or the global collapse (yet again) of capitalism. Or another pandemic. Or the Second Coming of Christ the Redeemer. (As a dedicated sceptic, I wouldn't rule anything out.) Whatever it is, I probably won't be around to analyse its historical genesis. That will be a treat in store for my younger readers.

*

At present – at the beginning of 2022 – very recent events seem to suggest just three possibilities for Britain alone, insofar as it or its politicians are in control of its fate. The first is the Armageddon that is predicted by the most pessimistic quasi-Marxists, with uncontrolled late-capitalist economies self-destructing, and possibly taking the planet along with them; or alternatively being replaced by new Stalinist régimes. Personally, as a middle-class liberal with much to lose under *this* régime, I hope not; but it cannot be denied that capitalism (or today's version of it) is looking somewhat under siege today.

Along with this scenario the Brexit debate – not necessarily Brexit itself – revealed a depth of not merely reactionary but also racist, sexist and frankly authoritarian opinions in British (or English) society that had always been there, but half-hidden by social conventions ('political correctness') that had made them embarrassing to express openly, until the newly-emergent political Right clad them in a patina of respectability, justified – quite reasonably and indeed liberally – on the grounds of 'free speech'. One can see something resembling a post-capitalist 'Fascism' emerging from this; especially if Brexit doesn't produce the 'goods' its leaders have promised, and people are not reconciled to this by their new British-blue passports and their 'sovereignty'. Brexit itself was fuelled by the kinds of resentment and prejudices that are characterized today as 'populism', but in the twentieth century were typically associated with overt Fascism: anti-alien, anti-establishment, anti-expertise; a parallel that many present-day observers of a historical bent have noticed and regard as deeply ominous: even if they don't anticipate death camps and invading other countries in Britain's case.

(Britain anyway has got past the latter stage.) You can be *fairly* Fascist without being a Hitler; and it is just possible that Brexit has opened the floodgates to this milder kind. In which case this is the aspect of the whole recent crisis that will be adjudged to be the most significant by future historians of Britain. Or of England, if Brexit provokes the other parts of the kingdom to hive off. Now that really would put paid to 'patriotism': patriotism, that is, of the explicitly 'Great British' kind.

A second alternative is the Brexiters' much brighter vision of Britain's future, based on *reviving* capitalism through 'taking back control' and so freeing enterprise from Brussels bureaucracy, thus inaugurating a new age of prosperity, international influence and renewed respect for the 'Global' – or even 'Galactic' – Britain of Boris Johnson's pleasant dreams; thus *returning* Britain to a more glorious stage of its 'history'. That however might take another fifty years, as Jacob Rees-Mogg has suggested, to show through. So obviously it would be unfair to expect signs of it to appear in the interval before this book hits the market. All bets on this must still be on. Although it should also be said that the signs in the meantime – over the last few months (up to late January 2022) – have not been exactly promising, with empty shelves in food markets; shortages of motor fuel; an exodus of foreign fruit pickers, nurses and lorry drivers; no new 'global' trade treaties that anywhere near compensate for the free trade with the remaining EU that Britain has given away; some prized freedoms missed (to travel, for example); the Conservative Party sinking in the polls partly as a result of people's disappointment with the results of Brexit (but also various scandals); Britain's actually *losing* 'respect' abroad, by most accounts (and in this expatriate's experience); and Britain's main Brexit negotiator, the neoliberal Lord (David) Frost, throwing in the towel in January 2021. But only time will tell. (Seriously.) And according to surveys many Brexiters believe that these losses, even if permanent, will have been an acceptable price to pay for the restitution of what they call their 'sovereignty'. In which case, what right have the Remainers (or Rejoiners, now) to cavil?

As a third and final alternative future, the British might yet *re-consider* their decisions of 2016 and 2019; probably not in order to reverse them, which might be unlikely – would the other Europeans want Britain back? – but in order to negotiate trade agreements with the remaining EU which would still curb their freedom to produce and trade independently, but would also open up that huge free market again to them, on terms – quite expensive ones, but arguably worth it – similar to Norway's, so re-joining a European customs area but without its political chains; or, by another way of looking at it, without Britain's being able to influence its rules. That indeed was what very many Brexiters had been led to understand they were voting for in 2016, before the whole Brexit cause was hijacked by its extremists; and roughly what the Labour leadership was offering in 2019, if only its message had been allowed to get through. It may also be what Opposition leader Sir Keir Starmer was hinting at when he pledged, in a speech in January 2022, that a new Labour government would endeavour to 'make Brexit work'.[1] In order to enable that, however, a whole lot of other changes might have to be made: the defeat of Johnson's government, obviously; but also some reforms to the British 'constitution', such as it is, and especially the parliamentary voting system sanctioned under it; to the press, almost the most 'unfree' in Europe, as we have seen; to the reputations of Britain's rulers: that of course must mainly rest on the latter's own shoulders, but the press bears a lot of responsibility here too; and to Britain's educational system, especially at what is deferentially considered to be the 'top'. This may well be too much to hope for.

If so, there can be little doubt that the events of 2016–21 will be seen to have marked, rather than a return to Britain's 'patriotic' past, on the contrary a radical break from it; meaning that Britain's previous history could no longer be mined in support of what the country had become. Some of that was rooted in its past, but in versions of it ('traditions') that were contradicted by others; and with other aspects of Britain's situation being pretty new, and the unusual degree of trickery, deception, corruption and dishonesty – added to incompetence – that Johnson's government manifested in its first months in power being almost entirely so. For those of my generation, probably the luckiest in British history – post-war, welfare state, free higher education, 'progressive' in so many ways – but also possibly the most naïve, it has all been a mighty shock. Hence the special hostility directed at Johnson's government, months and possibly years after the dies had been cast in 2016 and 2019. 'You lost: get over it', the Brexiters continually demanded of the 'Remainers', as if this whole thing had been merely a game; but in the political circumstances of the time there seemed little chance of that. It may well remain so, and Johnson's government become notorious in future accounts of Britain's history as one of the most immoral and incompetent ever: a bit like King John's. That is, if I'm not being too influenced by my own political prejudices; and if no worse government arises hereafter. Which it could well do, if the present situation comes to be accepted as normal – 'politicians are all the same' – and the electorate ceases to care. That would be the most significant legacy of all of these recent events in British history, and the most disappointing, democratically.

*

The few short months between the completion of this book and its departure to the printers afforded no certain clues about which of these three scenarios would come to pass. Britain's economy, and also incidentally its response to the coronavirus pandemic (strongly criticized by a cross-party Parliamentary committee in October 2021), are generally reckoned to have lagged considerably behind those of most of its EU neighbours' in this period; but that could of course be attributed to the necessary adjustments that would need to be made anyway in its transition to its new post-Brexit situation, even if that turns out to be as bright as the Brexiters were claiming. (Some of those Brexiters, especially their press, blamed their difficulties on European 'spite'.) Empty shelves in supermarkets, partly due to the absence of foreign lorry drivers but also affected by the pandemic, continued. There were sporadic rows with French trawler owners over fishing rights in the English Channel, provoking a stern Foreign Office 'summons' to the French ambassador in the late autumn of 2021, which the xenophobic British press latched on to delightedly; and loose talk of a 'trade war'. In October that same year the Government seemed to permit the spillage of sewage – including faeces – into seas and rivers; about which the EU would doubtless have had something to say, if Britain had still been a member. Much of this, of course, except the sewage, had been predicted by the 'Remain' camp long before, but scornfully dismissed by the Brexit side as 'Project Fear'. Could it be that Gove's much derided 'experts' had after all been right? These were the things that seem to have most affected the bulk of the population; apart from in Northern Ireland, where the flaws in the Brexit settlement still worried nearly everyone, as they threatened the fragile peace between the two communities there (the 'Belfast' or 'Good Friday' Agreement) made in April 1998.

Reputationally there can be little doubt – although it is difficult to cite chapter and verse for this – that after Brexit foreign countries' respect for Britain continued to plummet. That was to some extent due to the 'Boris' factor, with Continentals finding it difficult to take Johnson seriously. His reputation was hardly enhanced by an unfortunate speech he gave to the Confederation of British Industries in late November 2021 – losing his place, waffling on about 'Peppa Pig's World' (Peppa Pig was a popular children's cartoon character), and making '*brrrm-brrrm*' noises in reference to one stage of his career as a motoring journalist; all this was reported in the Swedish press, and presumably elsewhere. Johnson's next egregious scandal, 'Partygate', was also splashed across foreign newspapers. 'It is very sad to see a great country, with which we could do so much, led by a clown', as the French President Emanuel Macron was reported to have said (in private) in December 2021.[2] That may simply have indicated a cultural mismatch. (Britain's brand of humour has always been *sui generis*.) A related victim – in Britain anyway – was the school that had produced Johnson and several of his henchmen, and was held responsible for the privileged and irresponsible values, and jokes, that these men appeared to have been stuck with in their Lower Sixth (or even Fifth) forms. Eton and Britain's other 'Public' schools may have performed a valuable role in the nineteenth century, as we have seen – keeping its colonial 'prefects' honourable and serious, for example – but lost that usefulness when the 'honour' and seriousness seem to have drained out of them, to be replaced – in Johnson's case – by self-interest, a sense of entitlement, a poor education, especially historical, triviality, and gamesmanship. Again, it is difficult to be sure about this; but Eton College had been getting a lot of stick in the months before this book appeared, and it is difficult to imagine its ever regaining the respect it had once had. Will this mark a final end of the aristocratic (or quasi-aristocratic) 'head' of

Britain's hybrid political beast, described in Chapter 2 of this book, after its many years of overt and hidden influence, and its surprising re-emergence into the light – or dark – of day in the 2010s? Or will the new Grammar or even Comprehensive generation of leaders, augured earlier on by the very serious and pretty honourable Wilson and Thatcher, make a comeback? Only time – and the British electoral system – will tell.

In foreign and commercial affairs there were disappointments for the Brexiters, including more difficulties than they had anticipated in getting a trade deal with President Biden's USA. Biden, with his Irish forebears, was particularly critical of the mess Johnson seemed to be making of the Irish part of the Brexit deal. In any case none of Britain's other new commercial treaties, actual or potential, measured up to the big one it had just lost, and were no better, even, than many of those the EU had already negotiated with the same countries. With regards to 'security', the Brexiters received a bit of a boost with a new treaty signed by Johnson with respect to the Pacific region ('AUKUS': Australia, UK, USA), which annoyed both France and China, but might be considered to be in line with Johnson's 'global' and even Anglo-Saxon (or 'Anglospherical') imperial nostalgia, negotiated as it was with two of Britain's ex-colonies. Paxman's 'harrumphers' will no doubt feel a thrill at the sight of all those White Ensigns fluttering again in the China seas.

On the domestic front, the popular divisions that the Brexit process had either created or opened up between 2016 and 2021 showed no signs of diminishing during this subsequent period, despite Brexiters' continually urging Remainers to 'get over' their loss. That was difficult – again – in view of the *way* they had lost: cleverly or 'cunningly', according to your semantic preference. The so-called 'toxic' public discourse continued, in the newly popular 'social media' in particular. Further revelations of dubious practices on the 'Leave' side of the 2016 vote, including *suspicions* of Russian interference – suspicions only, as the results of an inquiry into this were withheld from Parliament – increased the Remainers' sense of grievance, whilst apparently doing little harm to those whose side had benefitted from this derring-do. They still insisted they had been right. (Psychologists attributed this to the natural reluctance of anyone to admit that he or she was wrong.) Further revelations, not directly Brexit-related, could be said to have given credence to the Remainers' suspicions of the leading Leavers' underlying motives: such as the 'Pandora Papers', leaked to the public in October 2021, detailing the extent of their material interests in the foreign tax havens that had been imminently threatened by the EU (it looked as though for them the country had got out just in time); and a whole slew of 'corruption' charges, mainly against Tory politicians, in early November: provoking Johnson to protest, at a news conference that month, that 'I genuinely believe that the UK is not remotely a corrupt country', even though no-one had claimed it was. (It was not the 'country' but only Johnson and his allies who were being accused.) But it made one think: perhaps

Britain always *had* been institutionally corrupt? Could this have been a feature of its 'identity' all along, alongside – or even coming before – democracy, tolerance and all the more bruited ones? One could dig out plenty of examples, if one chose to look, and defined 'corruption' loosely: party funding, Oxbridge entry,[3] purchasing peerages, and the 'bought' Press, for a start. There is a case to be made – although it hasn't been made here, maybe missing a trick – that, *pace* Boris, 'corruption' has been a fundamental aspect of Britain's history all along.

As well as all this, the tendency towards authoritarianism – one of the genies released by the rub of the Brexit lamp in 2016–21 – was confirmed in a score of ways: Priti Patel's continuing along her illiberal path – by excoriating Human Rights lawyers after an asylum seeker blew himself up in a taxi in Liverpool in November, for example;[4] a Justice Secretary proposing 'overhauling' the Human Rights Act itself in October 2021;[5] veiled threats against the much-prized English jury system, when in January 2022 a Bristol jury let four young statue-destroyers off scot free on the grounds that the statue – commemorating a slave-trader – was more offensive than they were; and every signal emanating from the Conservative Party Conference of October 2021 indicating that Johnson's government was serious about making national decision-making more 'efficient', to the detriment of Parliament's, and the Judiciary's, balancing and scrutinizing powers. 'Authoritarianism' wasn't even confined to the political Right, with the new overhauled Labour party's excommunication of dissidents like Corbyn – over the issue of Palestine – indicating that it was biting there too. In the field of 'culture' – indeed, what were called the 'culture wars' – universities, state schools, the BBC, universities and even comedians were put under pressure to modify what was perceived to be their 'left-wing' and 'un-British' biases; a Conservative minster (John Whittingdale) called for more 'British' content on TV;[6] and Conservative 'trusties' were elevated to key management positions in many of these fields. This looked very much like state-directed censorship. Of course these trends might not last. And none of them seemed to have much adverse effect on the government's popularity, with opinion polls giving it marginal majorities over the main Opposition party for most of this period: although not over *all* the Opposition parties – or at least their voters – counted together, and less and less so as time went by. But that hardly mattered, under FPTP; and with a new General Election not expected for a couple of years.

Pro-Europeans rested their diminishing hopes on these Opposition parties' coming together in a kind of 'Popular Front' against the Government, and on Labour's coming down more firmly on their side. (That posed problems for Labour, much of whose working-class constituency was known to be Brexitly-inclined. Hence Starmer's clever compromise.) Otherwise there were faint signs of hope in the air for the Left, if one looked abroad: Trump's defeat in America, of course, and a series of Leftward shifts in national elections in Scandinavia – Labour's original 'Shining City', remember – in the autumn of 2021. Britain had never been totally impervious to Continental political trends, so some of this might seep across the North Sea. And it might not even depend on the Opposition(s). Even the Conservative Party, 'extreme' as it seemed to have become in the Brexit era, might be forced to 'moderate' under the even more extreme pressure of events, by becoming more 'communitarian' in its social politics, as had happened before in Britain's history: for example, after the Second World War.[7] There were early signs of this in Chancellor Rishi Sunak's Autumn 2021 Budget, taxing and spending in a very 'old Labour' way, in order to compensate for the 'austerity' of the past decade; and signifying what one junior Minister characterized as a 'philosophical shift'. (Sunak protested, however, that he was still a 'small State' man at heart.)[8] For a while Johnson took up the promising progressive catchphrase of 'levelling up', to the same end. If he could be believed – and his axing of a promised high-speed train route in the long-neglected north of England in November 2021 raised immediate doubts here – this might place an obstacle on the Government's Right-ward path. (Or perhaps not? After all, the 1930s had shown that Fascism could live with a certain kind of 'socialism'.) So far as the European Union as an institution was concerned, the wider break-up that some Brexiters had hoped for, and even predicted after their own success in Britain, didn't (yet) come to pass, with Britain's experience seeming to act as a deterrent to other members, rather than as an example to follow. So all was not 'lost'. Or, for that matter, 'won', viewed from the other side of the fence. On that side the Brexiters could still look forward to their much-heralded and hopefully inspirational 'Festival of Brexit' to come, 'celebrating the rebirth of the UK as an independent nation' – a particular foible of Boris the showman – but at one stage re-christened 'Unboxed', which sounded rather less celebratory.[9] And at the time of writing it is not at all certain that this will happen, under any name; or, if it does, that it will be unchallenged.

More vital and worrying, although less easily defined, was the descent into *unreason* that the Brexit debate had revealed: with 'experts' devalued; evidence – even sometimes of people's own eyes – disregarded; many politicians abandoning 'truth' for whatever *un*truths they thought they could get away with; and people holding to the most unlikely views: such as that Jeremy Corbyn was 'anti-Semitic'; or that Johnson was 'doing his best'; or that all Brexiters must be 'stupid'. Reason played very little part in the great debate over Brexit in 2016, even though there were rational cases to be made on both sides; with opinions more often based on underlying prejudices, other issues entirely, *ad hominem* views, and tabloid newspaper headlines, rather than on even cursory attention to the facts. By most accounts the depth of unreason revealed in Britain did not begin to rival that in the USA, with large slews of the population there turning against any kind of intellectual authority, and embracing the wildest possible 'conspiracy theories' in its place: 'I'm a free American, and can believe what I like';[10] but this was undeniably part of a global trend, that affected other countries and peoples too. Therein may lie the greatest current peril to democracy and decency, as it did in the 1930s. It is probably rooted in the material crises of our times, and the growing sophistication of the propaganda industry. The solution to this *must* lie in the teaching of critical but constructive thinking, explicitly, in schools. But governments – of any colour – don't generally favour that. ('Critical? You might get them criticizing *us*.')

However, in all these regards these *are* of course early days. It is still not at all clear (in January 2022) in which direction Britain will go in the next five – let alone fifty – years, or where it will land up eventually. Will it be on the Right-hand political shore, or the Left? As a proud 'Global' Britain, or a group of struggling offshore islands? Or possibly – but less likely – back again with its European friends? Opinion polls in the autumn and early winter of 2021 were indicating popular majorities – if only slender ones – favouring that, and regretting Brexit. This was widely attributed to Boris's 'shine' at last beginning to wear off. Alternatively, would Britain become truly 'sovereign' after Brexit, or simply riding on America's coat-tails? If Britain returned to its Victorian history, as many Brexiters apparently wanted, would it be to the 'glorious' part of that history: wealth, freedom, empire; or to the inequalities and poverty that had marked the underside of those 'Titanic' days? (A booming billionaire class and 'food banks' for the poor were perhaps the most genuinely 'Victorian' features of this new, post-Brexit age.) Would Britain remain the 'United Kingdom' it had been since 1707, or become re-divided into its constituent nations? And where, for that matter, will the entire world be if global warming continues as it is? That might depend on possibly the greatest event – or the most disappointing one – of these later months: the International 'COP 26' Climate Conference held in Glasgow in November 2021. (When its report was eventually published, on 13 November 2021, opinion was divided as to its effectiveness.) And of course this would affect Britain too; especially, as it happens, the low-lying areas of England – Essex, Cambridgeshire, Hull – where I lived when I was there.

This level of uncertainty was another new feature of the times. A few years earlier, when Britain's history seemed to be following a fairly regular albeit oscillating pattern of development, the near future had been at least fairly predictable, within certain bounds: with Tories alternating with Labour, and both parties adapting in their periods in the wilderness to the new challenges of the time; and – perhaps more importantly – broadly agreeing on what the debate between them should be about. In the early 2020s that was no longer so. 'Labour' and 'Conservative', with their respective histories, hardly represented the major divisions in the country any longer, certainly over 'Brexit'; with the Conservatives originally divided over Europe, until UKIP and the ERG more or less swallowed them up; and Labour so riven over the question as to raise questions about its very future as a force in politics, for a while. This wasn't a unique situation in British history, incidentally, with foreign policy often splitting the parties, especially

Labour, and 'imperialism' having played a similar political role just over a century previously to the one that 'Europe' is playing today. (The argument then was over the 'Boer' War.)[11] Then all the main parties survived, albeit with the most 'on the fence' one (the Liberals) showing some pretty deep scars afterwards. (No modern lessons should be inferred from that.) The Tory Party in particular, the most 'imperialist' of them, suffered hardly at all in the long and medium terms. It had always managed, from Disraeli's time onwards, to harness popular 'patriotism' on foreign policy issues to its cause. This was another example of that. Conservatives professed to fear the 'mob', understandably. But maybe they needn't have done.

Looking more broadly, the uncertainty that surrounds Britain's political progress at this time may seem to confirm the importance of the factor of 'accident' in its history. That won't be welcome to history scholars, who generally like to find 'rational' causes for events. The reason we can't know much today is that we can't even guess how the cards will pan out after they've been dealt; or (in this case) what part the Joker card – or Macron's 'Clown' – might play. The present period represents a genuine historical disjunction, with little firm connexion with past, 'historical', stages, and even efforts to restore those stages – reviving 'global Britain', for example, or even post-War social democracy – probably bound to fail. It's in the lap of Lear's gods. So it looks as though there is no rational explanation for any of it. History is – presently – a mess; and is looking all the more messy in view of the 'clownish' appearance – after a fairly impressive 'Rise' in the nineteenth century (to 'patriots' at least, and seen in 'power' terms), and a moderately dignified 'Decline' in the twentieth (to more enlightened 'patriots') – of Britain's sudden early twenty-first century 'Fall'.

Even if one had come to terms with the inevitability of that Fall, as most people clearly had, there were more dignified ways of landing than this 'clownish' one. (Joining the EU had been believed to be one.) Hence the embarrassment to be British, and even shame, that many Britons felt directly after Brexit, undermining the patriotism that many of them had genuinely felt towards the Britain – or how they remembered it – of old. Some of them even resettled abroad as – in effect – 'refugees' from Brexit; despite the pull of Lia Nici's 'flag and Queen', and the seduction of their new navy-blue passports, and of the engraved 'crowns' now (in January 2022) restored to their British pint-sized beer glasses. Johnson and the other Brexiteers held these up triumphantly as the fruits of Britain's new 'sovereignty', but they were clearly trivial; and in any case had never been disallowed by the EU.

*

So it was all very confusing; except that there *are* general historical theories that might make sense of it; especially those resting on the behaviour of the general populace at this time, based on crowd psychology (Gustav le Bon and his successors);[12] on analyses of 'dominant discourses'; and on studies of education, gender relations, propaganda and the press. There are also of course 'conspiracy theories', some of them fairly credible, others quite mad; 'great men' theories, like Rees-Mogg's 'Titans' one; explanations based on generalizations about 'human nature' – selfish, ignorant, or whatever; and, I suppose, religious ones: remember the placard-carrier who proclaimed that Nigel Farage had been sent by God?[13] If we want to make sense of the muddle of recent events, we are not limited for choice.

The broad explanation favoured by the present author is the one suggested already in this book, albeit only tentatively. That is the quasi-Marxist one that has slowly grown on me during my fifty-plus years' study of British and imperial history: the one that sees capitalism in most of its forms needing, due to its 'internal contradictions', to grow redder in tooth and claw, and in various different ways, in order to survive. The rich Brexiters who rode the global neoliberal wave fit that pattern, following on from Thatcher and the austerians who came after her, all of them desirous of 'completing the Thatcher' – i.e. late capitalist – 'revolution'. This whole episode has derived from a natural – and possibly inevitable – stage in a capitalist process, which followed its own internal logic, without direction from the outside – least of all by politicians – so long as it was permitted to take that course by the people who were supposed to be in control of events, but really weren't. 'We have the *guts* to change the United Kingdom', Johnson told his party conference in October 2021; but more may be required for this than sheer 'guts'. I was brought up in a period when we thought we *could* control the process – modify it anyway, to benefit society – through what is generally known as 'social democracy': the 'third way'. But then came Thatcher (or, rather, the build-up of the late-capitalist forces behind her) to unleash the monster, and so to create, indirectly and involuntarily – who can tell what her position would have been today on this issue? – the conditions that made Brexit possible. That however is just a hypothesis, and at one level of explanation only. I can't prove it, and don't want to seem to be pushing it. It doesn't crucially affect the other points and arguments in this book. All I *can* say, is that it broadly fits. It could even make sense of the 'clowns'.

Otherwise it is important to realize that Britain – to return to the theme of my first chapter – has had not just one but several histories, any of which might serve as a guide as to how it is now, and what it might become. Some of those histories are actually mutually contradictory: featuring both imperialism and anti-imperialism, for example; capitalism and social democracy; colonial atrocities and imperial paternalism; militarism and pacifism; art and philistinism; open doors and closed ones; racism and multiculturalism; progress and decline; Boris Johnson and Jeremy Corbyn: all of these representing 'traditions' that are firmly based in Britain's past, with none of them really deserving to be privileged over the rest. If we want to 'use' history for present political purposes – which is not recommended – then the best kind to choose would be one that acknowledges the essential diversity of Britain's experiences over time, and consequently the error of focussing on just one or two of them. The latter is bound to misrepresent the true history of Britain, even if that history were not frequently misunderstood – as it often is – by those wanting to harness it to particular projects of theirs.

This book has endeavoured to correct a few of those misunderstandings – the 'we used to rule half the world' one, for example; Rees-Mogg's ringing endorsement of the 'Titans' of Victorian times; the myth of British 'exceptionalism'; and the crude thinking of the young Leftist statue-spoilers of Bristol – with the object of bringing Britain's history down to earth again, and restoring to it some of the context which is essential for an understanding of how we British were then, and what we are today. *Context is all*. That is the main lesson that history should be teaching us, about any aspect of any country's past. And secondly, in connection with the particular subject-matter of this book: that today's British context is significantly different from any of those of *its* past. To repeat a point made earlier: we are where we are, not where we were; and in any case where we were is – and always has been – 'contested'.

NOTES

Preface

1 See https://www.theguardian.com/commentisfree/2021/mar/21/must-we-wave-the-flag-at-every-little-thing-now-good-or-bad.

2 This refers to an incident in Bristol in June 2020 when protesters pulled down a statue of the seventeenth-century slave-trader Edward Colston. See https://www.bbc.com/news/uk-england-bristol-52962356.

Chapter 1

1 Easily the best modern work on Britain's and Britons' perceived 'identities' is Peter Mandler, *The English National Character. The History of an Idea from Edmund Burke to Tony Blair* (Yale University Press, 2006).

2 See https://www.nhm.ac.uk/discover/cheddar-man-mesolithic-britain-blue-eyed-boy.html.

3 David Cannadine, *Ornamentalism: How the British Saw Their Empire* (Allen Lane, 2001).

4 Quoted in Jane Ridley, *Bertie: A Life of Edward VII* (2012).

5 Maureen Holland, 'His father keeps a shop', in *CMUSE*, July 2015.

6 John Finnemore, *Famous Englishmen* (1901), pp. 3, 5.

7 See Bernard Porter, *The Absent-Minded Imperialists* (2004), p. 257 and fn. 3.

8 As told to me – about the 1960s – by my former wife Deirdre O'Hara, from an Irish Catholic family.

9 https://johnmajorarchive.org.uk/1993/04/22/mr-majors-speech-to-conservative-group-for-europe-22-april-1993/.

10 See Martin Weiner, *English Culture and the Decline of the Industrial Spirit, 1850-1980* (1981).

11 From 1914. See https://en.wikipedia.org/wiki/Your_King_and_Country_Want_You.

12 Nicola Rippon, *The Plot to Kill Lloyd-George* (2009).

13 Porter, *The Absent-Minded Imperialists*, p. 211.

14 See http://www.statistica.com/statistics/520954/brexit-votes-by-age.

15 Professor (of History) Alan Sked.

16 Rudyard Kipling, 'The English Flag', 1891.

17 Quoted in Rosemary Ashton, *Little Germany: Exile and Asylum in Victorian England* (OUP, 1986), p. xii.

18 G. J. Harney, in *Star of Freedom*, 18 September 1852.

19 See for example the anonymous *Anteckninger anledning af an Resn till England*, (Stockholm, 1835).

20 Gladys Storey, *Dickens and Daughter* (Frederick Muller Ltd, 1939), pp. 21–2.

21 David Sanderson, 'Why Shakespeare's King Lear sounds even better in German', in *The Times*, 20 September 2019.

22 Quoted in Peter Fleming, *Invasion 1940* (1957), p. 192.

23 See https://www.rescue-uk.org/article/little-known-history-fish-and-chips.

24 See for example (from Norway): https://sv.nytid.no/imperiet-kan-slå-tillbaka-efter-Brexit/; and https://www.prospectmagazine.co.uk/world/the-myth-of-brexit-as-imperial-nostalgia.

25 Jeremy Paxman, *Empire: What Ruling the World Did to the British* (2012).

26 John Mackenzie, *Propaganda and Empire* (1984); Porter, *The Absent-Minded Imperialists*.

27 Ibid (both books).

28 From the song 'Rule, Britannia!' by James Thomson, set to music by Thomas Arne, 1740.

29 *The Times*, 28 February 1853.

30 Bernard Porter, *The Refugee Question in mid-Victorian Politics* (1979), *passim*.

31 Ibid.

32 Remembered, but not noted at the time, unfortunately.

33 Quoted in Leon Radzinowicz, *A History of English Common Law*, vol. 1 (1948), p. 28n.

34 See Bernard Porter, *The Refugee Question* (1979), pp. 114–15.

35 Another example, I'm afraid, of my not being able to provide a reference because Covid 19 has separated me from the notes I made from the original police report.

36 Bernard Porter, *The Origins of the Vigilant State* (1991).

37 Bernard Porter, *Plots and Paranoia* (1989), ch. 7.

38 Samuel Laing, *Notes of a Traveller* (1842), p. 349.

39 'Now, what I want is, Facts. Teach these boys and girls nothing but Facts. Facts alone are wanted in life. Plant nothing else, and root out everything else.' From the beginning of Dickens's *Hard Times*, published in 1854.

40 See Weiner, *English Culture and the Decline of the Industrial Spirit, 1850-1980*, *op. cit.*

41 https://www.theguardian.com/society/2016/jan/18/nye-bevan-history-of-nhs-national-health-service.

Chapter 2

1 William Blake, 'Jerusalem' (1804).

2 The sources for these figures can be found in B. R. Mitchell, *British Historical Statistics* (CUP, 1988).

3 Martin Weiner, *English culture and the decline of the industrial spirit 1850–1980* (CUP, 1981).

4 Words by Cecil Frances Alexander, first published in her *Hymns for Little Children* of 1848, and usually sung to a tune composed by William Henry Monk in 1887.

5 One example is the 'Avenues' area of Hull.

6 See https://en.wikipedia.org/wiki/Gentlemen_v_Players.

7 Mill's developing thought on this can be followed in the *later* editions of his *Principles of Political Economy* (first edn 1848); and his (posthumous) *Autobiography* (1873).

8 Cobden in Manchester, 15 January 1846; *Speeches on Public Policy* (1870), vol. 1, pp. 362–3.

9 Sheridan Gilley, 'The Garibaldi Riots of 1862', in *Historical Journal*, vol.16 no. 4 (1973).

10 Palmerston in House of Commons, 1 April 1852, in *Hansard*, 3rd series, vol. 119, cc. 511–12.

11 See *London Review of Books*, 4 October 2001, for a range of comments on '9/11', some of which were read as taking this view.

12 See Bernard Porter, *The Refugee Question* (1979), pp. 58, 128.

13 Obituary in *The Economist*, 14 February 1998.

14 See Bernard Porter, *Critics of Empire* (1968); 2nd edn, 2008.

15 Bernard Porter, *The Origins of the Vigilant State* (1991).

16 Ibid, p. 169.

17 See Craig Stewart-Hunter, 'Combat Motivation during the First World War', in *Inquiries*, vol. 3 (2011).

18 See Christopher Andrew, *The Defence of the Realm* (2009).

19 Gill Bennett, *The Zinoviev Letter: The Conspiracy that never Dies* (2020).

20 Kay Halle, *Irrepressible Churchill* (1966), pp. 52–3.

21 Martin Gilbert, *Winston S. Churchill, The Prophet of Truth* (Heinemann, 1976), p. 450.

22 Paul Addison and Jeremy Crang, *Listening to Britain* (2010).

23 Churchill speech of 30 November 1954.

Chapter 3

1 This chapter roughly summarizes my *The Lion's Share* (6th edn, 2020); and the much shorter *British Imperial: What the Empire Wasn't* (2015).

2   J. A. Hobson, *Imperialism: A Study* (1901).

3   See Bernard Porter, *British Imperial* (2018), pp. 40, 77 *et passim*.

4   *Daily Telegraph*, 25 May 2019 (by Simon Heffer). For other (mainly hostile) reviews, see https://booksinthemedia.thebppkseller.com/eviews/the-Victorians.

5   J. E. C. Wheldon, head master of Harrow, 1885–98.

6   John Bright and Thorold Rogers, ed., *Speeches on Public Policy by Richard Cobden* (1870), vol. 2, pp. 315–16.

7   See my *Britain Before Brexit* (2021), ch. 3.

8   See H. Maxwell-Stewart, in https://www.bbc.com/travel/article/20120126-travelwise-australias-penal-colonies-roots.

9   See https://en.wikipedia.org/wiki/United_Services_College.

10 Anthony Kirk-Greene, *Britain's Imperial Administrators 1858-1966* (2000), p. 180.

11 Charles Wilson, *The History of Unilever* (1946), vol. 1, p. 167.

12 See Bernard Porter, 'How did they Get Away with it?', in *London Review of Books*, 3 March 2005.

13 David Anderson, 'Guilty Secrets', in *History Workshop Journal*, no. 80 (2015).

14 Bernard Porter, 'Who was the Enemy?' in *London Review of Books*, 21 May 2015.

15 Quoted in Eric Stokes, *The English Utilitarians and India* (1959), pp. 45–6.

16 J. K. Paasikivi, *Meine Moskauer Mission 1939-41* (1968), p. 243.

17 See Richard Price, *An Imperial War and the British Working Class* (1972).

18 Originally published as *Die Grundlagen des neunzehnten Jahrhunderts*.

19 Kipling, Milner (educated in Germany), J. Ellis Barker (né Eltzbacher) . . .

20 Benjamin Kidd, *The Control of the Tropics* (1898); Karl Pearson, *National Life from the Standpoint of Science* (1901).

21 On 'flags', see Eddy Izzard's great sketch: https://www.youtube.com/watch?v=_9W1zTEuKLY.

22 My *Absent-Minded Imperialists*. But see also Mackenzie's riposte, 'Comfort and Conviction: a Riposte to Bernard Porter', in *Journal of Imperial and Commonwealth History*, volume 36, 2008; and my reply to that in *ibid.*, vol. 39 (2011).

23 *Supra* p. 39.

24 See my *Critics of Empire* (1968).

25 See my *Empire and Superempire* (2006).

26 See, for example, Ramachandra Guha, *Rebels Against the Raj. Western Fighters for India's Freedom* (William Collins, 2022).

27 See *Critics of Empire*, ch. 4.

Chapter 4

1   See https://bernardjporter.com/2016/02/29/first-past-the-post/.

2   See FIFA, *History of the Laws of the Game* (2016): via Wikipedia.

3   Ian Cobain, *The History Thieves. Secrets, Lies and the Shaping of a Modern Nation* (Portobello, 2016).

4   Official Guide to 'Unparliamentary language', at https://www.theyworkforyou.com/glossary/?gl=20.

5   See https://closeyeroll.wordpress.com/2016/12/03/dennis-skinner-did-not-call-half-the-tories-crooks-and-how-to-verify-other-quotes-from-parliament/.

6   Ian Blackford in House of Commons, 28 April 2021.

7   See https://inews.co.uk/news/politics/labour-mp-dawn-butler-kicked-out-of-the-commons-chamber-for-calling-boris-johnson-a-liar-1116819.

8   https://www.theneweuropean.co.uk/brexit-news/nigel-farage-on-the-civil-service-and-military-49688.

9   In 1947 he gave an emotional and inspirational speech on the need to unite Europe; but he also made it clear that Britain and its Empire should not be a part of it. This has often confused propagandists.

10 See Hugh Cudlipp, *The Prerogative of the Harlot: Press Barons and Power* (1980).

11 H. John Field, *Towards a Programme of Imperial Life* (Clio, 1982), chs 4 and 5.

12 See Alan Lee, *The Origins of the Popular Press 1855-1914* (1976); and Stephen Koss, *The Rise and Fall of the Political Press in Britain*, vol.1 (1981), ch. 9.

13 https://rsf.org/en/ranking; compiled by 'Reporters Without Borders', 2020.

14 *Leviticus* 18:22; which puts homosexuality on the same 'abominable' level as eating shellfish.

15 https://www.standard.co.uk/hp/front/downfall-of-the-bigots-6349125.html.

16 *Supra*, p. 26.

17 *Supra*, p. 148.

Chapter 5

1   Sidney and Beatrice Webb, *Soviet Communism: A New Civilisation*; originally published in 1935, then shortly afterwards reprinted, shrewdly, with a question mark after the title.

2   Margaret Thatcher, 'Don't undo my work', in *Newsweek*, 27 April 1992.

3   See Bernard Porter, 'Though not an Historian Myself', in *Twentieth-Century British History*, vol. 5 no. 2 (1994).

4   Interview in *Woman's Own*, 31 October 1987.

5   See Steven Dorril and Robin Ramsay, *Smear! Wilson and the Secret State* (new edn, 1992).

6 Quoted in Michael Hanagan and Behrooz Maazami, 'Introduction to a 1995 Conversation with Eric Hobsbawm', in *International Labor and Working Class History*, no. 83 (2013).

7 See *Wikipedia*: https//en.wikipedia.org/wiki/Independent.

8 Eric Hobsbawm, 'The Forward March of Labour Halted?', in *Marxism Today*, vol. 22 (1994).

9 See W. R. Louis and R. E. Robinson, 'The Imperialism of Decolonisation', in *Journal of Imperial and Commonwealth History*, vol. 22, 1994.

10 See Bernard Porter, *Empire and Superempire* (2006).

11 See Carroll Quigley, *The Anglo-American Establishment* (new edn, 1981); and. https://www.americanrhodes.org/news.

12 Harold Wilson, *Final Term* (1979), p. 234.

Chapter 6

1 Charles Lever, *A Day's Ride* (1861), ch. 42.

2 Quoted in Jerrold Northrop Moore, *Elgar. A Creative Life* (1999), p. 452.

3 *Supra*, ch. 1.

4 Samuel Laing, *Observations on the Social and Political State of the European Peoples in 1848 and 1849* (1849); and *Observations on the Social and Political State of in Denmark and the Duchies of Schleswig and Holstein, in 1851* (1852).

5 References to her philistinism in the literature and journalism of the time are legion. No-one disagrees. Google 'Thatcher' and 'Philistinism'.

6 These included an *Ave Verum Corpus* and other religious choral works (1887); several part-songs; *The Black Knight* (1889–92), *From the Bavarian Highlands* (1895–6); *The Light of Life* (1896); *Scenes from the Saga of King Olaf* (1896), *The Banner of St George* (1897), *Caractacus*; and then *The Dream of Gerontius* (1899: the year of the *Enigma* – orchestral – *Variations*).

7 See my *The Battle of the Styles* (2012).

8 Charles Dickens, *Hard Times* (1851), ch. 5.

Chapter 7

1 Bernard Porter, *Britain Before Brexit* (2021), ch. 3.

2 See Bernard Porter, *The Refugee Question in mid-Victorian Politics* (1979), passim.

3 Quoted in W. L. Langer, *European Alliances and Alignments* (1931), p. 308.

4 See p. 4 *supra*.

5 See my *Britain, Europe and the World. Delusions of Grandeur* (1987).

Chapter 8

1 See Bernard Porter, *Britain before Brexit* (2021), chapter 14; some of which this chapter reproduces.

2 *Daily Telegraph*, 5 April 2006.

3 See Richard J. Evans, 'The Myth of the Fourth Reich', in *New Statesman*, 24 November 2011.

4 *Guardian*, 16 October 2016.

5 Supra, p. 62

6 This is still a hotly and indeed rancorously debated issue. An extended discussion of all sides of it, with sources, can be found in https://en.wikipedia.org/wiki/antisemitism in the UK Labour Party.

7 See Vernon Bognador, 'The fury of elite Remainers is making them increasingly anti-British', in *Daily Telegraph* 28 August 2021.

8 Quoted in Stuart Ward and Astrid Rasch, *Embers of Empire* (2019), p. 3.

9 The 'imperial' dimension of Brexit is more fully discussed in the final chapter, 'Brexit and the Empire', of my *The Lion's Share*, 6th edn. (2020).

10 See Simon Jenkins, 'Complete the Thatcher Revolution', in *Spectator*, 30 September 2006.

11 Philip Mason, *The Men Who Ruled India* (1992).

12 *NBC News*, 14 November 2019: https://www.nbcnews.com/news/world/hillary-clinton-warns-u-k-headed-fascism-over-lawmaker-abuse-n1082031 (accessed 29 August 2020).

13 Michael Gove interview with Faisal Islam on Sky News on 3 June 2016: https://www.youtube.com/watch?v=GGgiGtJk7MA (accessed 29 August 2020).

14 See https://www.theguardian.com/commentisfree/2021/jul/20/proposed-secrecy-law-journalism-spying-home-office-public-interest-whistleblowing.

15 'Ten politicians who claimed Brexit negotiations were going to be easy', in *Independent*, 30 March 2019: https://www.indy100.com/article/brexit-easy-nigel-farage-theresa-may-david-davis-boris-johnson-8846041 (accessed 29 August 2020).

16 See https://www.theguardian.com/politics/2017/aug/23/home-office-apologises-for-letters-threatening-to-deport-eu-nationals.

17 https://www.theguardian.com/uk-news/2021/may/13/glasgow-residents-surround-and-block-immigration-van-from-leaving-street.

18 'Brexit benefits? You'll have to wait 50 years,' says Rees-Mogg: *New European*, 23 July 2020; https://www.theneweuropean.co.uk/top-stories/jacob-rees-mogg-interview-with-channel-4-news-1-5619425 (accessed 29 August 2020).

19 See https://www.independent.co.uk/news/uk/politics/brexit-jacob-rees-mogg-scm-ireland-city-move-eu-withdrawal-dublin-a8398041.html.

20 Tom Peck, 'Nigel Farage would pick up a rifle if Brexit is not delivered', in *Independent*, 17 May 2017: https://www.independent.co.uk/news/uk/politics/

nigel-farage-brexit-rifle-pick-up-uk-eu-withdrawal-ukip-leader-liberal-democrat-a7741331.html (accessed 29 August 2020).

21 'Greater number of Leave voters willing to risk their own or family members' jobs than those unwilling, poll finds'; in *Politico*, 8 January 2017: https://www.politico.eu/article/uk-voters-believe-economic-damage-is-price-worth-paying-to-get-their-way-on-brexit/ (accessed 29 August 2020).

22 *Independent*, 5 October 2016.

23 Elena Remigi et al, eds, *In Limbo* (2017) and *In Limbo Too* (2018).

Chapter 9

1 Above, ch. 6.

2 V. I. Lenin, *Imperialism: The Highest Stage of Capitalism* (English version, 1917).

3 See https://www.telegraph.co.uk/politics/2018/07/15/rest-world-believes-britain-time-did/ Quoted in Stuart Ward and Astrid Rasch, *Embers of Empire* (2019), p. 3.

4 Reporters without Borders, *World Press Freedom Index 2020*: https://rsf.org/en/ranking_table (accessed 29 August 2020).

5 See above, ch. 8.

6 *Our Plan. The Conservative Manifesto* (2019).

7 See *Times*, 14 November 2019.

8 See https://www.leftvoice.org/football-created-by-the-poor-stolen-by-the-rich/.

9 Above, p. xxx.

10 See, for example, his appearances on the popular comedy-quiz TV show 'Have I Got News for You', accessible on YouTube, 15 November 2008, 13 September 2009, 23 November 2015, *et passim*.

11 On www.youtube.com/watch?v=_t25xAp270o.

12 Alain Tolhurst, 'Grassroots Tories would sacrifice the Union if it meant Brexit being delivered, new poll reveals', in *Politics Home*, 18 June 2019: https://www.politicshome.com/news/article/grassroots-tories-would-sacrifice-the-union-if-it-meant-brexit-being-delivered-new-poll-reveals (accessed 29 August 2020).

13 1857–8 was of course the date of the Indian 'Mutiny', and 1902 marked the end of the (second) 'Boer' War; both of which indicated serious weaknesses in Britain's ruling capacity, which were to persist. For an account of British imperialism that sees it mainly as a response to perceived decline, see my *The Lion's Share* (6th edn, 2020).

Chapter 10

1 See https://www.onebritainonenation.com; and, for the song itself, https://www.youtube.com/watch?v=eRIP0vBtcBg&t=27s.

2 That of course was a vote in favour of preserving the status quo, which is the opposite of what Brexit sought to do. I was also, I remember, a strong 'Commonwealth' man at the time, contrasting the multi-racialism of that organization with what I took to be the 'white man's' club represented by the EEC. But I'm not wholly certain of the way I voted in 1975.

3 Peter Oborne, *The Assault on Truth: Boris Johnson, Donald Trump and the Emergence of a New Moral Barbarism* (2021).

4 See https://www.newstatesman.com/politics/2021/07/boris-johnson-liar-and-chancer-popular-why.

Afterword

1 See https://www.dailymail.co.uk/news/article-10367563/Keir-Starmer-vows-make-Brexit-work-insists-patriot.html.

2 See https://metro.co.uk/2021/12/02/emmanuel-macron-called-boris-johnson-a-clown-and-uk-a-circus-15701518/.

3 I resigned my Cambridge Fellowship on account of this: my College's deliberately prioritizing Public school over Comprehensive or even Grammar school applicants. See https://bernardjporter.com/2021/11/18/corruption-on-high-table.

4 See https://www.independent.co.uk/news/uk/politics/priti-patel-asylum-lawyers-liverpool-b1959306.html.

5 See https://www.independent.co.uk/news/uk/politics/dominic-raab-human-rights-act-review-b1932579.html.

6 See https://www.thetimes.co.uk/article/we-want-more-britishness-on-tv-john-whittingdale-tells-broadcasters-xwqwbr67z.

7 See Julian Coman, 'Labour, take note', in *Guardian*, 12 October 2021.

8 *Times*, 28 October 2021.

9 Andra Maciuca, 'Tory MPs deflated . . .', in *The London Economic*, 21 October 2021.

10 Supra, p. 134.

11 Bernard Porter, *Critics of Empire* (1968), chs 2–4.

12 Gustave le Bon, *Psychologie des Foules* (1895).

13 Supra, p. 116.

FURTHER READING

There are many general histories of modern Britain, of which Jacob Rees-Mogg's *The Victorians* (2020) is probably the least reliable, but illustrates a certain way of thinking on the topic. More highly recommended are two books by David Reynolds, *Island Stories: Britain and Its History in the Age of Brexit* (2019), and *Britannia Overruled: British Policy and World Power in the Twentieth Century* (2000). On the domestic front, Nick Cohen, *Waiting for the Etonians: Reports from the Sickbed of Liberal England* (2009) was perceptive for its time; and Peter Mandler, *The English National Character: The History of an Idea from Edmund Burke to Tony Blair* (2006), is the leading work on English 'patriotism'. 'Imperial' nostalgia is examined in Stuart Ward and Astrid Rasch, *Embers of Empire in Brexit Britain* (2019). On the misunderstood topic of 'patriotism' in the Second World War, Paul Addison and Jeremy Crang, *Listening to Britain* (2011) is highly enlightening.

All these books can be supplemented – and partially counterbalanced – by Ian Cobain's *The History Thieves: Lies and the Shaping of a Modern Nation* (2016). Robin Ramsay, *Conspiracy Theories* (2006), sensibly discusses that contentious topic. For the Empire, John Darwin's *The Empire Project* is the latest and best general history, largely supplanting my own *The Lion's Share* (6th edn, 2020). My other books on foreign policy, anti-imperialism, policing, political refugees and culture are cited in footnotes (*Britain, Europe and the World*, 1983; *Critics of Empire*, 1968; *The Refugee Question*, 1979; *Plots and Paranoia*, 1989; *The Battle of the Styles*, 2011); to which might be added *British Imperial* (2015), a distillation of the main themes of *The Lions Share: Empire and Superempire* (2006), comparing British and American 'imperialisms'; and my two collections of mixed essays, *Empire Ways* (2020) and *Britain Before Brexit* (2021), which elaborate – especially *Britain Before Brexit* – on themes in the present book.

INDEX

academia 8
accident 138, 143
Acheson, Dean 8, 12
advertising 60
Afghanistan 46, 78
Africa 40–1, 45, 76
alliances 92, 113
Amritsar 53
anarchists 14, 28, 32, 64
Anglophobia 90
'Anglosphere' 77, 148
anti-imperialism viii, 51–3, 117–18, 126, 131, 133
anti-semitism 100, 119, 150
apathy 67, 106
Arabs 41, 45–6
architecture 23, 56, 82, 85, 91, 129
aristocracy 1, 3–4, 22–3, 58, 64, 84, 91, 118, 124, 147
army 48, 92–3, 132
    see also military
art and the arts 9–11, 17–18, 24, 32, 81–8, 90, 118, 132
asylum, see immigrants
atrocities (colonial) 45–7, 53, 76, 121, 129
Attlee, Clement 34, 44, 60, 65, 69, 72, 79–80, 139
AUKUS 148
austerity 98, 112, 117, 139, 143, 150
Australia 42–3, 53, 134
authoritarianism 66–7, 69, 72, 79, 104, 109, 118, 120, 123, 132–3, 135, 144, 149

balance of power 92
Baldwin, Stanley 60–1
banking and investment 18, 49, 117, 139

Battle of Britain 35, 78, 114, 128
'battle bus' 106, 122, 134
Bazalgette, J. W. 85
Belgium 52–3
Bell, Steve 59
Bevan, Aneurin 18, 60
Biden, Joe 148
Blair, Tony 19, 46, 49, 60, 72–3, 103, 122
Blake, William 21
Bletchley Park 35
Boy Scouts 7, 32, 51
Boyle, Danny 74–5
Bray, Steve 19
Brexit 1, 8, 49–50, 54, 58, 60, 71, 74–5, 80, 97–112, 133, 143–54
Britain 1–19
British Broadcasting Corporation (BBC) 125, 131, 133
British Union of Fascists 33, 60
Britishness, see national identity
Bush, G. W. 46

Callaghan, James 72
Cambridge Analytica 103, 107
Cameron, David 59, 98, 102–3, 105
Canada 42
capitalism 10, 18, 36, 42, 45, 49, 52–3, 62, 69, 74, 82, 87, 102, 108, 115–17, 127, 129, 144, 153
Carlyle, Thomas 22, 115
Cash, William 99, 108
Castle, Barbara 73
Catholicism 5–6, 14, 19, 25, 27–9, 63
Chamberlain, Houston Stewart 50–1
Chamberlain, Joseph 60, 66
Chamberlain, Neville 34, 138
Channel crossing 89–90
Channel Islands 91

Chartism 22–3, 31, 55
China 40, 43, 46–7, 113
Christianity, *see* Religion
Church of England 1, 24, 64, 88,
    129–30
Churchill, Winston 29, 34–6, 42, 46,
    57, 60, 66, 69, 79, 114, 132
Civil Service 30, 56, 58, 118–19,
    122–3, 125, 136
    Colonial 44
civilizing mission 41
class 2, 4–5, 24, 33, 71, 84, 118
climate change 144, 151
Clinton, Bill 77
Clinton, Hilary 104, 120
Cobden, Richard 26, 42, 52, 66
Coe, Jonathan 111
colonial nationalism 45, 77
comic papers 86
commerce 10, 17, 21, 39–40, 107, 109,
    128, 145
Commonwealth 13, 35, 48, 76, 113,
    126, 131–2, 138
communism 33–4, 36, 69, 77, 116
concentration camps (South Africa)
    45–6
Congo 52–3
Conservatives and Conservative party
    1, 6, 12, 14, 21, 24–5, 27, 30–1,
    34, 49, 58, 62, 64–5, 67, 73, 79,
    102, 105, 114, 119, 125–6, 132,
    136, 145, 151
conspiracies and conspiracy theories
    72–3, 77, 103–4, 115–16, 122,
    134, 138, 150, 153
Cook, Thomas 90
COP 26 (Climate Conference), 151
Corbyn, Jeremy 75, 100, 105, 119,
    137, 139, 150
corruption (political) 59–60, 65, 67,
    73–4, 120, 123, 136, 146, 148–9
Council house sales 71
Covid-19 x, 105–6, 112, 119, 121–2,
    129, 144, 146
Cox, Jo 106
cricket 1, 24–5, 86, 89, 91, 95, 118,
    120, 123, 129, 131, 140
Crimean War 16, 29, 93
crowd psychology 152

culture 81–8, 130
Cummings, Dominic 104, 109, 119,
    122, 136

Daily Mail 33, 132
Dan Dare 79, 86
Darwin, Charles 63
decolonization 12–13, 19, 52–3, 55,
    75–6, 101, 126, 138–9, 152
democracy 13–14, 19, 36, 53, 55, 58,
    62, 78, 118, 122–3, 136, 146,
    151
Denmark 4
depression (trade) 30, 34, 139
Dickens, Charles 10, 17, 82, 84–5, 88
Disraeli, Benjamin 4–5, 25, 30, 60, 62,
    100, 131
dissent 18
Doggerland 2, 89, 128

education 4, 24, 51, 64, 99–100, 136,
    146–8, 151
Edward VII, King 4
Elgar, Edward 4, 5, 82–4, 87, 133
Elgin (Parthenon) Marbles 81
emancipation 14, 25
emigration 42–3, 110
Empire 5, 8, 10, 13, 75, 95, 102, 113,
    118, 127, 130–3, 137, 140, 151
    see also imperialism
Empire Day 43
Engels, Friedrich 9, 28, 85, 131
England 98, 105, 110, 123, 125, 141,
    145
Eton College 44, 57, 86–7, 98, 102–3,
    115, 132, 136–7, 147
Europe and Britain 65, 80, 89–112,
    127–8, 147
European imperialism 93–4, 127,
    129
European Research Group (ERG) 99,
    151
European Union (EU; *also* European
    Common Market) 42, 48, 70,
    74–5, 77–8, 93, 97–112, 150
Eurosceptics 93, 114
evolution 63
exceptionalism ix
experts 120, 147

fake history 134
Falklands (Malvinas) War 12, 71, 76, 79
famine 27
Farage, Nigel 3, 58, 99, 102–3, 108–9, 113, 116, 120, 124, 143, 153
fascism 33–4, 46, 50–1, 58, 104, 120–1, 123–4, 129, 139, 144–5
Fawlty Towers 79
'Festival of Brexit' 150
Finland 81
First Past the Post (FPTP) 56, 58–9, 98, 136, 138, 146
food 11, 118
Fox, Liam 107
France and French 2, 12, 21, 26, 41–2, 47, 77, 81, 89, 91–2, 105, 118, 134, 147
Franchise 56–8
Francois, Mark 113, 124
free market and free trade 16–17, 22, 25–7, 31, 40, 43, 65, 69–72, 94, 101, 132
freedom, *see* liberalism
freedom of movement 107, 145
Frost, Lord (David) 145

gender 6–7, 14, 79, 84, 86, 152
General Election, December 2019 99–100, 109, 119, 137, 139
General Strike (1926) 31, 33
Germany 11, 13, 18, 31–3, 36, 47–8, 60, 79, 81, 89
Gilbert and Sullivan 82–3
Gladstone, W. E. 16, 30, 60, 93–4
Glasgow 107–8
globalism 49, 93, 145, 151–2
Gove, Michael 104, 124, 147
government 22, 55–67
'Great Britain' 11, 126
'Great Crash' (2007–8) 74
Great Exhibition
    1851 9, 28
    1951 18
Great Labour Unrest (1911–14) 31
'great men' 41–2, 115
Greece 98
Green Party 56
Gulf Wars 19

Heath, Edward 70–2, 79, 97
Heseltine, Lord 4
Hitler, Adolf 10, 34, 99, 114, 130–1
Hobson, J. A. 39–41, 51, 53, 116
Home Office 107, 120, 123
    see also Theresa May; Priti Patel
homosexuality 19, 35, 63–4, 72
Hong Kong 40, 76
Human Rights legislation 149
hybridity 22, 118, 124, 147–8
Hyndman, H. M. 25

ideology 8
immigration 2–3, 14–15, 27–8, 75, 90–91, 98, 104, 107–8, 110, 118, 121, 128, 130–2
imperialism 1–2, 5, 7–8, 11–12, 25, 29–33, 36, 39–54, 61, 66–7, 75–7, 91–4, 101, 116–17, 123, 127, 129, 132, 143, 152
imperial
    nostalgia 101, 148
    preference 94
In Limbo 111
independence, *see* sovereignty
India 29, 40–2, 44–9, 52–3, 63, 75, 84, 92, 102, 116
Indian Mutiny 29, 45, 74
Indirect Rule 45
industrial
    revolution 21–2, 39
    unrest 5, 31, 33, 72
industry 9–10, 18, 21, 23, 29, 73, 121, 132, 137
inequality 25–6, 132
informal empire 78, 94, 114
internationalism 3, 65, 111, 124, 131, 138
Iraq and Iraq War 46, 53, 73, 78, 134
Ireland and Irish 2, 3, 5, 15, 27–8, 36, 39, 41, 47, 53, 58, 63, 84, 108, 112, 123, 125–6, 132, 140, 147
Islam 63, 78, 128, 144
Israel 45, 75, 128

Jenkins, Roy 72
Jews 2–3, 5–6, 14, 19, 25, 31, 45–6, 100, 119, 121
jingoism 31, 49–51, 54, 61

Johnson, Boris 16, 54, 57–9, 62, 67, 75, 80, 99–101, 103, 105–6, 108, 112–15, 117–20, 122, 124, 130, 136, 143, 145–7, 150–1, 153
journalists 99
   see also press
jury system 149

Kenya 45–7, 49, 76
Keynes, J. M. 65–6
Kipling, Rudyard x, 8, 44, 51, 61, 84

Labour party 1, 6, 14, 25, 31, 33–4, 58, 63–5, 69, 69–80, 100, 105, 119, 122, 137, 139, 145–6, 149, 151, 153
Laing, Samuel 17, 82–3, 85, 87–8
law 119, 123
leadership 60, 79–80, 100, 139
League of Empire Loyalists 12, 75
League of Nations 48, 131–2
Lenin, VI 116
Leopold II, King 41, 52
Lever, Charles 81, 90
Leveson Inquiry 74
Liberal Democrats 73
Liberal party 14, 22, 24–5, 30–31, 33–4, 58, 65
liberalism 13–14, 17–18, 25, 29, 39, 52–3, 65–7, 89, 105, 121, 129–31, 144
Liberal Imperialism 67
lifeboats 104, 120, 123
Livingstone, David 41
Lloyd-George, David 60, 79
Lloyd, Marie 83
Loach, Ken 74
local government 58
London 31, 35, 85, 111, 134
Lords, House of 55–6, 58, 64, 119
lying in Parliament 57, 119, 122–3, 132

Maastricht Treaty 94
Macaulay, T. B. 48–9
MacDonald, J. R. 34, 73
Macmillan, Harold 59, 77, 103
Macron Emanuel 147, 152

Major, John 6
Manchester 21, 85
Marx, Karl, and Marxism 9, 16, 28, 53, 63, 75, 108, 113, 116–17, 121, 124, 131, 139, 144, 153
May, Theresa 105–6, 110, 120, 125, 132, 134
MI5, MI6, *see* Secret Services
middle classes 22–3, 72, 84, 90, 118
military and militarism 16, 32, 47, 50, 64, 66, 92, 130
Mill, John Stuart 14, 26, 30, 87
miners' strikes 79–80
'mob' 56, 62, 66, 101, 120–1, 123, 137
Mosley, Oswald 33–4, 60, 66
multiculturalism 3, 13, 48, 130
Murdoch, Rupert 74, 122
music 82–6, 88
'Musical Renaissance' 85
Muslims 5

National Health Service 18, 70, 71, 74–5, 95, 98, 106, 110–12, 125, 131, 133
national (British) identity 1–19, 63, 83, 101, 105, 115, 125, 130, 137, 143, 153
nationalization 70
nationalism 72, 124
Navy 16, 21, 93, 132
'neo-Cons' 78, 134
neoliberalism 11, 16, 30, 72, 101, 108, 115, 129, 153
New Liberalism 30, 65, 70
New Zealand 43, 53
Newcastle 87
Nici, Lia viii-ix, 1, 134, 152
noblesse oblige 102
Nolan Principles 58, 136
nonconformists 5–6, 14, 19, 25, 63
Normans 2–3, 124, 128
Northcote-Trevelyan Report (1854) 30, 58
Northern Ireland, *see* Ireland
Norway 106, 145

Official Secrets Acts 57, 104
Omdurman 53
opium 40

pacifism 7, 32–4, 92, 100
Palestine 45–6, 48, 100
Palmerston, Viscount 14, 28
Pandora Papers 148
Parliament 1, 22, 55–67, 98, 119
    see also Reform Acts
Patel, Priti 3, 104, 107, 120, 123, 149
patriotism vi, x, 1, 4–6, 8, 18–19, 25,
        30, 32–3, 35, 49, 52, 61, 67,
        71, 75, 78, 81–3, 88, 93, 100–1,
        104–5, 109, 115, 117, 120, 124,
        126, 127–41, 143–6, 152
Peppa Pig 147
personality politics 59–60
Peterloo (1819) 16, 66
Philistinism 9–11, 17–18, 81–3, 88,
        118, 129
philosophy 87
Poland and Poles 35
policing 15, 25, 28–9, 46, 66, 118, 131
'political correctness' 98
poor and poverty 3, 9, 17, 22–5, 117,
        132
populism 56, 66, 104, 117, 124, 127,
        129, 133, 144
Powell, J Enoch 29, 115
press 11, 60–2, 74–5, 80, 93–4,
        98–100, 103, 107, 109, 118–19,
        122–3, 132, 138, 146, 150, 152
privatization 71
progress 27, 36, 71
'Project Fear' 147
propaganda 51, 60, 67, 106, 119, 122
protest 18–19, 55, 107–8, 118
Prusso-Danish war 4
public schools 1, 4, 10–11, 22–4, 35,
        39, 41–2, 44, 51, 57–8, 61, 65,
        100, 102–3, 114, 129–30, 146–7

race and racism 5, 41, 41, 45–6, 50,
        53, 75–6, 99–100, 110, 120–1,
        123–5, 144
Rees-Mogg, Jacob 41–2, 54, 102–3,
        108, 113, 115, 124, 126, 131,
        137, 143, 145, 153–4
Referenda (1975, 2017) 7–8, 97–8,
        100, 106, 109, 118–19, 125, 148
Reform Acts 22, 33, 55, 62, 131
refugees 2–3, 9, 14, 104, 118, 120, 131

regionalism 5
religion 5, 63, 118, 121, 128, 144
revolutions (1848) 28
    generally 123
Rhodes, Cecil, and Rhodesia
        (Zimbabwe) 12, 42, 45, 53, 76–7
Roman Empire 128
romanticism 64
royalty 1, 4, 29, 51, 60, 80, 92, 100,
        119, 130, 132, 134, 140
rule of law 14, 123
Russia (and USSR) 28, 31, 33–6, 47–8,
        69, 76, 92, 107, 113, 116, 138,
        148

scandals 57, 73–4
science 87–8
science fiction 32, 62
Scott, Walter 82
secret services 15–16, 31–3, 60, 72–3,
        137
secularism 64
settlers 45
sewage 147
sex and sexism 41, 83, 144
Shakespeare, William 2, 10, 49, 88,
        114, 127, 129, 131, 133
Sherlock Holmes 15
single market 100
Sked, Alan 99
Skinner, Denis 57, 60
slavery and slave trade 13, 19, 25,
        40–1, 46, 52
    abolition of 52, 131
socialism 24–5, 29, 31, 36, 40, 53, 64,
        69–70, 101, 116–17, 143, 150
Social Darwinism 50–1, 63
Social Democratic Party (SDP) 73
social reform 66, 72
South Africa 12, 35, 45–6, 53, 76
South African ('Boer') War 12, 30–1,
        45–6, 48–51, 53, 61, 75, 99
sovereignty 113–14 , 126, 138, 150,
        152
Spads 58, 119, 123–4, 135–6
'Special Relationship' 77
Spitting Image 59
sport 23–4, 57, 64, 86, 121, 123, 129
'splendid isolation' 92, 101, 129

spying 100, 104, 131–2, 138
    see also secret services
Stanley, H. M. 40–1
Starmer, Keir 149
statues viii-ix
Sudan 42
Suez 53, 77
suffragism 6, 23, 31, 55, 64
surveillace, *see* spying
Sweden vi, 70, 73, 110, 123, 133–4,
    140, 150
'swinging sixties' 72

Taliban 78
tax havens 99
'Tebbit test' 3
terrorism 6, 28, 46, 100, 129, 131, 144
Thatcher, Margaret 1, 11, 16, 30, 60,
    65, 69–73, 76–7, 79–80, 83, 88,
    101–3, 115–18, 124–5, 130–2,
    137, 139, 143, 148, 153
'Thatcher revolution' 108, 115–17,
    139, 153
goleration 6, 14, 18, 133, 140
trade, *see* commerce
trade unions 19, 25, 71–4, 77, 131–2
travel and tourism 81, 90, 128
treaties 94–5, 114, 126
'Troubles' (Northern Ireland) 108
Trump, Donald 12, 99, 105, 117, 120,
    124, 134, 138, 143, 149
Trustee Savings Bank (TSB) 71
Turing, Alan 35
Turner, W. M. 88
TV and film 11, 42, 54, 78, 86, 88, 114
Twin Towers attack ('9/11') 28

UKIP (United Kingdom Independence
    Party) 56, 104–5, 124, 135, 151
United Nations 37
universities 1, 5, 24, 58, 87
unreason 150

USA x, 4, 12, 14, 27–8, 35–6, 43, 47–8,
    52–3, 63, 69–70, 74, 76–8, 92–5,
    101, 104–5, 113–15, 117, 122,
    124, 134, 150–1
USSR, *see* Russia

vice anglaise 11
'Vicky' 59
Victoria, Queen 4, 93
'Victorian Values' 72, 115, 117, 122,
    127, 132, 137, 143, 151, 154
Vikings 2, 128

Wales and Welsh 5, 39, 41, 58, 123
war films 7
war graves 93
Weiner, Martin 23
Welfare State 18, 31, 65, 69, 74, 131,
    139
Wells, H. G. 32, 60, 62–3
Wheeldon, Alice 7
Whigs 22, 65, 88
Whig interpretation 55, 121, 131
Wilde, Oscar 28, 64
Wilson, Harold 58, 60, 72–3, 77, 79,
    103, 124, 139, 148
'Winter of Discontent' 73
women 33
    see also gender; suffragism
Workers' Educational Association
    (WEA) 87
working classes 12, 15, 21–5, 34, 74,
    84, 86, 118, 131
World Wars 5–6, 10–13, 18, 31–7, 47,
    55, 69, 76, 78–9, 92–5, 97, 114,
    117, 121, 129, 132–3, 143, 150

xenophobia, *see* racism

youth 7

'Zinoviev Letter' 33, 60, 69